ANTHROPOLOGY AT THE DAWN OF THE COLD WAR

Anthropology, Culture and Society

Series Editor:
Dr Jon P. Mitchell, University of Sussex

RECENT TITLES

ANTHROPOLOGY AT THE DAWN OF THE COLD WAR

The Influence of Foundations,
McCarthyism, and the CIA

Edited by
DUSTIN M. WAX

Pluto Press

LONDON • ANN ARBOR, MI

First published 2008 by Pluto Press
345 Archway Road, London N6 5AA
and 839 Greene Street, Ann Arbor, MI 48106

www.plutobooks.com

British Library Cataloguing in Publication Data
A catalogue record for this book is available from the British Library

ISBN   978 0 7453 2587 3 (hardback)
ISBN   978 0 7453 2586 6 (paperback)

Library of Congress Cataloging in Publication Data applied for

This book is printed on paper suitable for recycling and made from
fully managed and sustained forest sources. Logging, pulping and
manufacturing processes are expected to conform to the
environmental regulations of the country of origin.

10   9   8   7   6   5   4   3   2   1

Designed and produced for Pluto Press by
Chase Publishing Services Ltd, Fortescue, Sidmouth, EX10 9QG, England
Typeset from disk by Stanford DTP Services
Printed and bound in the European Union by
CPI Antony Rowe Ltd, Chippenham and Eastbourne

CONTENTS

ACKNOWLEDGEMENTS

This book originated in a panel at the 2003 American Anthropological Association's annual meetings entitled "Anthropology at the Dawn of the Cold War." The panel featured Herbert Lewis, David Price, Eric Ross, Frank Salamone, George Stocking, Susan Trencher, and me, with Rob Hancock and Marc Pinkoski as discussants. Though not all of them chose to or were able to continue on this journey with me, their input, advice, and inspiration were invaluable in the production of this book.

I would also like to thank my professors at the New School for Social Research, whose insight and example showed me that critically engaging with anthropology's history was not only possible but necessary: Steven Caton, Deborah Poole, Rayna Rapp, Dina Siddiqi, the late William Roseberry, and especially Antonio Lauria-Pericelli, who put my feet on the path that led to this book.

Over the years, two online communities have proven invaluable as both a source of new ideas and a place to rehearse my own fevered anthropological imaginings. To the members of ANTHRO-L (especially Ron Kephart, John McCreery, Richard Senghas, Jacob Lee, Richard Wilsnack, Anj Petto, Ray Scupin, Robert Lawless, Wade Tarzia, Lynn Manners, Martin Cohen, Bruce Josephson, Richley Crapo, Tom Kavanagh, Scott MacEachern, Mike Pavlik, Thomas Riley, and Phil Young) and my fellow Savage Minds (Alex Golub, Kerim Friedman, Chris Kelty, Nancy LeClerc, Kathleen Lowery, Tak Watanabe, and newbies Thomas Erikson, Maia Green, and Thomas Strong) I offer both my gratitude and respect.

The staff at Pluto Press – Anne Beech, Judy Nash, and Debjani Roy – have been exceedingly patient as I've learned the mechanics of working with other academics and putting together a project like this.

My parents Sharyn and Marvin, my brother Aaron, my sister-in-law Allison, and my nephew Noah and niece Alyssa have offered their love, support, and, when needed, a place to live without reserve – I can never repay all that I owe them. And, finally, I couldn't have finished this book without the love and acceptance of Betsy and her children Chrys, Lea, and Styrling. This book is dedicated to all of them.

INTRODUCTION: ANTHROPOLOGY AT THE DAWN OF THE COLD WAR

Dustin M. Wax

It's said that if there's a book you really want to read and you can't find it, you must write it yourself. Such is the case with this book: while researching an ethnographic project conducted in the 1950s, I searched desperately for material to help me situate my subject in the history of the discipline at the time. I was surprised and a little disheartened to find that very little had been written on the history of anthropology after World War II, let alone explicitly dealing with the Cold War. Furthermore, what little was available, like Sherry Ortner's classic "Theory of Anthropology Since the Sixties" (1984), dealt mainly with the evolution and interplay of ideas and not with the actual events, practices, and institutional structures in and through which anthropological ideas are formed.

Given the paucity of the kind of material I felt I needed, I decided my only option was to create it myself – or, more properly, get other researchers to create it for me. The book you hold in your hands is the outcome of that decision, several years down the line. "Anthropology at the Dawn of the Cold War" was the title of a session I organized at the 2003 meetings of the American Anthropological Association (AAA), where the ideas and histories put forth here first started to take form. Since then, interest in anthropology's Cold War history has grown – and so has its relevance, as the United States has become further and further engulfed by another war against an implacable, global foe, with Islamist terrorism standing in for Soviet communism this time around. As before, anthropologists are being singled out for their political and theoretical entanglements, even as some in the modern security apparatus seek to co-opt the cultural insights of American anthropologists to the service of the government's military endeavors.

But it is not only in relation to such presentist concerns that the Cold War history of anthropology bears telling. Anthropologists have insisted since the early days of the profession that ideas do not exist in a vacuum; they must be understood in the context of

1

the cultures from which they arise. The period covered in this book – roughly from 1946 to 1964, or from the end of World War II to the opening years of the Vietnam War – were especially fruitful ones for anthropology. Yet traditional histories of anthropology have treated these years as a simple procession or succession of ideas from one person or academic cohort to another: Steward's and White's rejection of Boasian particularism in favor of an evolutionary approach to culture development; Wolf's and Mintz's embrace of Marxian materialism; Radcliffe-Brown's and Malinowski's functionalism ascending in the work of Fred Eggan and Lloyd Fallers; the influence of Lévi-Strauss's structuralism, which itself developed out of the study of language, being taken up by Edmund Leach and Marshall Sahlins; the incorporation of culture-and-personality models into the study of national character; and so on. Few historians in the discipline have been willing to locate the work and ideas either of individual anthropologists or of anthropology as a whole in the matrix of academic institutions, foundation support, state political and military prerogatives, social networks, and police action that supported, encouraged, channeled, and limited anthropological research during these years.

Given the concrete thoroughness with which anthropologists perform and present their own ethnographic research, the omission from our own official histories of the political, economic, and ideological context in which ethnography takes place is surprising, even astonishing. Consider, as a representative example, Regna Darnell's recent history of Americanist anthropology, *Invisible Genealogies* (2001), which traces the continued influence and importance of Boasian thought from Boas himself to the present. Darnell strongly emphasizes the importance of an ethnographic approach to anthropology's history, declaring "We [anthropologists] apply the same methods to the history of anthropology that we do to the study of ethnographic communities" (2001: 4) and a few pages later:

Theory is more sophisticated when it acknowledges the context in which ideas were and are propounded to the world. Chronology matters; ideas do not emerge in a vacuum. It is easy enough to criticize earlier work by applying contemporary standards, but at the price of eclipsing the context and continuity of ideas; this price is too high. (2001: 7)

Yet the index of *Invisible Genealogies*, a book which examines in its survey of twentieth-century American anthropology the work of several anthropologists active during the 1940s, 1950s, and 1960s, does not include any references to the main institutional currents of the early Cold War period (area studies, modernization, development theory, international studies), nor to the climate of political conformity and persecution which pervaded the post-war years (McCarthyism, anti-communism, the FBI, CIA, and House Un-American Activities Committee), nor to the foundations that supported anthropological research, often by acting as fronts for the CIA and other state agencies hoping to advance their own agendas (neither the Ford Foundation nor any of the Carnegie foundations are mentioned, the Rockefeller Foundation receives a passing reference), nor even to the Cold War itself. Surely these are important parts of "the context in which ideas were and are propounded"!

This is not to single out Darnell, but rather to point to an occlusion within the discipline as a whole. Darnell is simply one of many anthropologists hesitant to probe what Laura Nader has called anthropology's "phantom factor," the complex of "external factors in the making of anthropology" (1997: 108), ranging from the political forces that kept some actors marginal to the mainstream of anthropological thought to the funding priorities of corporate-backed foundations to the availability of military technologies for research. This hesitancy has several roots, including the difficulty in obtaining source materials that adequately document these factors (for instance, David Price and William Peace spent over five years working to obtain the scant 19 pages that make up Leslie White's FBI file; see Peace and Price 2001); the close relationships between many figures in anthropology's Cold War history and today's disciplinary historians, who are often their students or even their peers; an unwillingness to cast too critical an eye on a profession that offers many of us not just a livelihood but a life worth living; political, cultural, and personal proclivities that make certain social relations simply appear "natural" and unremarkable; or the desire for disciplinary autonomy that demands allegiance to the illusion of a clearly bounded and distinct field of study.

Whatever the reason, to borrow Darnell's words, the price for avoiding the context in which our history has taken place is too high. Can we truly claim to understand the ideas we've inherited from previous generations of researchers without understanding the exclusions and absences that were the condition for their emergence? Joan Vincent writes that "any dominant ideology or body of knowledge is shaped in part by that which it excludes or suppresses" (1990: 1); yet even the fact of exclusion and suppression is missing from most of our disciplinary history, especially for the years covered in this book, when exclusion and suppression were practically the *leitmotif* of American culture and academic life.

WHAT IS COLD WAR ANTHROPOLOGY?

Periodization in historiography is always necessarily tentative and open to contestation; whole careers have been built out of challenging

the notion of a "Middle Ages" or of "modernity." Defining the years
1946 to roughly 1970 as "the early Cold War," and further, applying
that characterization as definitive of the anthropology of the moment,
is not without the regular dangers attendant to history-making, and
is perhaps as difficult to justify, especially in light of recent efforts to
emphasize the continuities that have held across over a century of
disciplinary history (see Darnell 2001; Lewis 2001).

In the "long twentieth century" view of American history (Arrighi
1994), anthropology is, indeed, very much of a piece: liberal (in the
broadest sense of the term); progressive (again, in the broadest sense);
relativistic; intimately tied to the concerns of colonial and imperial
expansionism, nationalism, and state power; and fraught with the
perils of representation and misrepresentation. As Darnell argues
(2001), the concerns the motivated Franz Boas's work in the 1890s
are still being played out today, and Boas's ideas are still surprisingly
relevant. And yet, on a smaller scale, World War II marks a dramatic
shift in both the ideas anthropologists brought to their work and the
place of anthropology in the broader American political and social
context. The post-war decades are marked by a tremendous growth
of the discipline in sheer numbers, accompanied by a significant
decentering of the field from the hallowed ground that Boas and his
generations of students had staked out.

Along with this growth and decentralization came a restructuring
of the relationship between anthropology and the American state.
Anthropology had emerged from the Depression years and World
War II with a fully developed cohort of professional applied anthropologists holding firm notions of the role of anthropology in the
running of the post-war government. At the same time, wrapped up
in an ideological and intellectual battle with the Soviet Union, the
American government had its own, complementary notions of how
science, including the social sciences, could and should be applied
to the problems facing the nascent struggle for dominance between
First and Second Worlds.

This new relationship was embodied in new financial relations
between anthropologists and all levels of the state, often mediated by
major philanthropic organizations. GI Bill tuition funding allowed the
great expansion of academic institutions, fostering the enlargement of
existing departments and the creation of new ones at universities and
colleges across the nation. The Department of Defense (DoD) and the
newly created (in 1950) National Science Foundation (NSF) directly
funded advanced research within universities, while other agencies,
most notably the Central Intelligence Agency (CIA) – formed in 1947
out of the ashes of the wartime Office of Strategic Services – funneled
money indirectly to a whole host of intellectual endeavors through

front agencies and intermediaries including the Human Ecology Fund and the Ford Foundation (Price 1998; Saunders 1999).

As America geared up for what would become a permanent wartime economy, corporate interests also saw in anthropology and the other social sciences an opportunity to improve their relations with both their labor forces and their consumers. Depression-era applied anthropology, such as Lloyd Warner's industrial anthropology, had promised to shed light on the conflicts that created and exacerbated worker strife; in the post-war period, with corporations looking overseas to the decolonizing Third World, the insights anthropologists could bring to the table in Rhodesian copper mines, Puerto Rican sugar plantations, or Indonesian rice paddies seemed more relevant than ever. The Big Three foundations (Ford, Rockefeller, and Carnegie), along with an assortment of smaller foundations, government agencies, and international development agencies, all saw an upside in investing in often large-scale anthropological investigations overseas and funded accordingly.

This new relationship between social science on one hand and government and corporate interests on the other had two sides, however: while funding was made increasingly available for the right kinds of research, anthropologists who pursued the wrong kinds of research – or came to the wrong kinds of conclusions – found themselves not merely cut off from opportunities but, in many cases, actively persecuted for their political, ideological, and professional positions.

ANTHROPOLOGY AT THE DAWN OF THE COLD WAR

The intersection of the American state and American anthropology is at the core of the first chapters of this book. Whether as victims of persecution for their beliefs or as collaborators opportunistically embracing the anti-communist hysteria of the 1950s and 1960s to advance their own professional and political goals, anthropologists were deeply influenced by the McCarthyist purges and accusations of the early Cold War years. As David Price (2004) has written elsewhere, it was neither sufficient nor necessary to be an actual Communist for an anthropologist to attract the unwelcome attention of the House Un-American Activities Committee, McCarthy's own committee in the Senate, the Federal Bureau of Investigation (FBI), or any number of local organizations and institutions sucked into the Red-baiting atmosphere. Rather, the anthropologists who found themselves targeted – ironically, for the most part non-communists – were those whose work and public activities challenged the racial and sexual status quo of the pre-civil rights, pre-women's liberation era. Hounded from their jobs and even, as in the case of Paul Radin, from the country (Price 2004), their stories are stories of opportunities lost, of what might have been had they been allowed to teach, do fieldwork, and write in peace.

This is especially the case with one of anthropology's most significant figures of the post-war era, Ashley Montagu. As Susan Sperling notes in Chapter 1, "Ashley's Ghost: McCarthyism, Science, and Human Nature," Montagu had come to anthropology and the tutelage of anthropology's father-figure, Franz Boas, well prepared to embrace the flexibility of human nature and culture. A literally self-made man, Montagu had risen from the poverty of London's Jewish East End to take on a new name and a new identity, living proof of the triumph of culture over the idea of innate biological inferiority. His personal experiences and his anthropological training predisposed him, however, to look on the oppression of racial and ethnic minorities, as well as of women, as an aberration, and his effective activism and popular writing style made him stand out as a threat. Sperling takes on Montagu's dismissal from what would be his last academic appointment in the wake of the publication of the pro-feminist *The Natural Superiority of Women* in 1953 – a task made difficult by Montagu's own tendency to make and remake his own history to fit his personal needs.

Anthropologists were not only victims of McCarthyism, though – the development of an apparatus for identifying and punishing "un-Americans" provided a new set of institutional supports that some anthropologists chose to take advantage of. One such was Karl Wittfogel, whose own tortured relationship with the Communist Party led to his emergence as a staunch anti-communist during the Cold War years. In Chapter 2, "Materialism's Free Pass: Karl Wittfogel, McCarthyism, and the 'Bureaucratization of Guilt'," David Price examines this transition while he explores the freedom afforded Wittfogel to pursue a line of research – his "hydraulic theory" – that was *explicitly* Marxist in both inspiration and intention. What distinguishes Wittfogel from someone like Montagu, Price argues, is that Wittfogel "played along" with the McCarthyist regime, acting as an informer to secure his position as a "good American" while incidentally undermining the credibility of his detractors. As an informer from within the discipline, Wittfogel joins the ranks of other prominent anthropologists, notably George Peter Murdock (see Price 2004) and Clyde Kluckhohn (see Price 1998), anthropologists who found their interests met in service to the state.

McCarthyism was, however, only one aspect of the changing relationship between social scientists and the state. At the same time that some anthropologists were being punished for their activism and public beliefs and others were being recruited as informers, anthropologists were also being actively sought for their expertise on matters as far-ranging as land tenure, community leadership, disease immunity and susceptibility, intercultural relations, social change, and poverty. As the United States extended its cultural, political, and economic hegemony overseas, filling the vacuum left by the European colonial powers in the wake of World War II and decolonization, anthropological knowledge became very desirable in some sectors of the state. Although anthropologists were rarely called on to help make policy, their assistance was sought in the application and administration of policy within indigenous communities, both at home and abroad.

Julian Steward's effort to construct a more scientific and rationalized approach to anthropology than that of his Boasian forebears made him an especially attractive candidate for an American government struggling to accommodate the confusing and often conflicting demands of American Indian policy. As a former participant in Indian Reorganization Act and wartime anthropology projects, Steward was no stranger to working with and within the state, either. As Marc Pinkoski's "American Colonialism at the Dawn of the Cold War" (Chapter 3) shows, Steward's work was used to provide a set of standards for the evaluation of American Indians' legal claims, with Steward himself frequently testifying against Indian peoples – effectively advancing a concept of Indian assimilation that, with the emergence of Termination as the government's official response to the continued existence of Native American cultures, would affect the lives of tens of thousands of Indian people.

Anthropologists also served the interests of the state and of American corporations overseas, often unwittingly. Frank Salamone's "In the Name of Science: The Cold War and the Direction of Scientific Pursuits" (Chapter 4) presents a "behind-the-scenes" look at the establishment of the International African Institute, founded with Rockefeller money and aimed at extending the cultural and commercial reach of American capitalism into Africa. This kind of relationship held some dangers, though: as Immanuel Wallerstein (1997) has pointed out, the experiences of state- and corporate-backed anthropologists in the field often radicalized them, creating "unintended consequences" in opposition to the goals of anthropology's funders. Eventually, large numbers of anthropologists rejected these arrangements, as Salamone shows with his examination of the Thailand affair, the early 1970s crisis within the American Anthropological Association that consumed it for several years.

Eric Ross explores similar ground in Chapter 5, "Peasants on Our Minds: Anthropology, the Cold War, and the Myth of Peasant Conservativism," which examines the premises and practices of the Cornell Vicos Project, an attempt at reshaping Peruvian agriculture in accordance with American agri-business assumptions. Desperate to forestall the growing tendency for peasant unrest in the impoverished Third World, American policy-makers and funders backed a model of peasantry and rural change founded in cultural – rather than political and economic – forces, especially emphasizing the idea of over-population. Backed by the Carnegie Corporation, the anthropologists at Vicos advanced a vision of controlled change, hoping to channel energies away from agrarian revolt and into capitalist development.

Tracking the influence of funding on the development of anthropology is notoriously difficult and necessarily speculative (Turner 1999). As Nader's notion of the phantom factor suggests, its influence is more apparent in what is *not* there – Montagu's potential scholarly contributions, an overt Marxist theory of peasant reform, a competing concept of state development – than in what *is*. However, as Theresa Richardson and Donald Fisher point out (1999: 21), much of the work of foundations and state-backed research centers lies not so much in their explicit shaping of anthropological thought as in their establishment of networks of like-minded scholars. The effect of these networks is cumulative; they promote PhD candidates and grant recipients, shape editorial policy in scholarly journals, create curricula and teaching materials for the next generation of students, and so on. In short, they increase the ability of scholars to reproduce themselves in the discipline, while anthropologists outside of the "inner circles" find themselves relatively isolated in small liberal arts colleges, second-tier public universities, and community colleges, where they might exert powerful local influences but have little power to shape the direction of the field as a whole (Roseberry 1996).

Two essays in this volume deal with the institutional effects of such networks as they developed in the context of the Cold War, detailing the work of the foundations, associations, university departments, and other formal and informal networks whose actions and policies supported, shaped, and limited anthropology during the years after World War II. Dustin Wax's essay, "Organizing Anthropology: Sol Tax and the Professionalization of Anthropology" (Chapter 6), discusses the work of Sol Tax not as an anthropological theorist and ethnographer but as an institution-builder – an organizer of conferences, editor of journals, chair of committees, and president of organizations. Using Tax's early conference-organizing activities and his later role in the founding of *Current Anthropology* as his focus, Wax details Tax's efforts to coordinate and make visible the work of anthropologists around the world – with ramifications for Cold War intelligence and propaganda efforts, in addition to more directly anthropological concerns.

On a smaller scale, William Peace examines the academic careers of a network of Columbia graduate students and followers of Julian

Steward in "Columbia University and the Mundial Upheaval Society: A Study in Academic Networking" (Chapter 7). Formed around shared status as World War II veterans, an attraction to the work and teaching of Steward and opposition to the more "feminine" style of Ruth Benedict, and a certain sense of male camaraderie, the informally organized Mundial Upheaval Society included in its ever-changing membership rolls several of the anthropologists who would rise to prominence as the leading scholars of the 1970s. Though loosely structured (and, as a result, loosely remembered by its participants), the Mundial Upheaval Society provided for not only the exchange of ideas among its members but also the exchange of jobs, fieldwork advice, publication offers, and so on – eventually becoming the backbone of the "Columbia–Michigan axis" that would prove central to the discipline in later years.

These articles exist at the intersection of three broad theoretical "axes" or themes: the political, the ideological, and the institutional. These are, of course, broad characterizations and hardly exclusive of each other. Under "the political," I count the effects of McCarthyism and anti-communism, the development of Cold War liberalism and neo-conservativism, as well as the various rediscoveries and reworkings (and occultations and repressions) of Marx. We can also include the *geo*political – anthropology's involvement in and reaction against colonialism, and its involvement in implementing and resisting Cold War policies in the "new nations."

The second theme, "the institutional," refers to the structure and material underpinning of anthropology as an academic discipline. This includes the influx of new students taking advantage of opportunities afforded by the GI Bill and by general post-war prosperity, as well as the increase in size and number of anthropology departments to accommodate these new students and the professional anthropologists many of them would go on to become. The institutional also encompasses the increased availability of funding for certain kinds of research, and the rise of area studies with its attendant creation of area studies centers around the world. Lastly, we might also consider the changing demographics of the field, particularly the greater incorporation of minorities, women, and colonial and ex-colonial peoples.

Finally, under "the ideological" we have the ascendancy of structural and functional theories, as well as the emergence of inter-disciplinary approaches within area studies and the other "studies" fields (Russian Studies, Asian Studies, African Studies, etc.). The ideas about human behavior, social organization, and political economy that emerged in the early Cold War years became the core of the field for at least a generation of students, and still hold sway in major departments around the country.

These themes are far from a complete summary of anthropology's post-World War II history, but they do serve as a useful rubric for assessing the work that has already been done and, more importantly, the gaps that remain to be filled in the documenting of anthropology's material and intellectual history. As Rob Hancock shows in his "Afterword: Reconceptualizing Anthropology's Historiography," Cold War Studies is a new and fairly unestablished field in anthropology; great swathes of anthropology's Cold War history remain to be catalogued, documented, and conceptualized. What's more, the approaches that have dominated the history of anthropology so far may not be useful as we move into more recent events, and especially as we consider the moral and political implications of anthropological thought and practice. While the work in this volume shares certain thematic similarities, these are more a result of the infancy of a field that has yet to develop a robust diversity of theoretical perspectives, rather than the outcome of an established consensus about how and why to study anthropology's Cold War history.

THE SECOND TIME AS FARCE

One would have to be almost willfully ignorant of current affairs not to notice the parallels between the Cold War's paranoid battle against a pervasive communist threat and today's equally paranoid war against a pervasive terrorist threat. As during the Cold War, anthropology's foreign contacts, willingness to find reason and humanity in alien cultural practices, and endemic anti-nationalism and anti-militarism have made anthropologists targets for attacks on allegedly pro-terrorist, anti-American fifth columnists at home. And, as before, attacks on activist anthropologists have been accompanied by efforts to appropriate anthropology to the service of the state, through funding and public shaming of anthropologists for failing to "do their duty."

In the wake of the September 11, 2001 terrorist attacks on New York City and Washington, DC, American politics and culture have taken a turn similar to that taken in the early years of the Cold War. A kind of reflexive patriotism has taken root, encouraged by political leaders and the media who have both found the fear engendered by the attacks useful in advancing their own interests. Academics in general, and particularly those whose work raises uncomfortable questions about American policy overseas and at home, have come under a great deal of suspicion and scrutiny both in the press and among government figures. Anthropologists, with their relativism and commitment to protecting the rights and livelihoods of the people they study, have been especially targeted.

In the immediate wake of 9/11, the American Council of Trustees and Alumni (ACTA) released an assessment of American higher education entitled *Defending Civilization: How Our Universities Are Failing America and What Can Be Done About It* (Martin and Neal 2001, 2002). In an appendix that is significantly longer than the body of the report, ACTA included a "representative" sample of campus responses to the attacks by "professors across the country [that] typically ranged from moral equivocation to explicit condemnations of America" (2001: 1). Six of the 117 academics targeted by ACTA were anthropologists (another three were linguists, who we may or may not count as anthropologists), one apparently so offending the patriotic sensibilities of decent Americans that her name appears twice (the report was revised and expanded a few months later, with the names removed). This is over 5 percent of the academics mentioned, nearly 10 percent if we count the linguists, far outstripping anthropology's representation in the whole body of American academics. The anthropologists mentioned were Kevin Lourie, Hugh Gusterson, William Beeman, David Kertzer, Jean Jackson, and Catherine Lutz, who was cited twice; the linguists include George Lakoff, Noam Chomsky, and Wayne O'Neil, also cited twice.

Likewise, anthropologists have been targeted by right-wing activist David Horowitz's Discover the Networks website (www.discoverthenetworks.org), a directory of individuals, organizations, and corporations deemed radical and threatening to American national security. Anthropologists cited by Discover the Networks range from Donald Brenneis, former president of the American Anthropological Association, to graduate student Lori Allen, and include Gayle S. Rubin, Elizabeth Brumfiel, Lila Abu-Lughod, Nichoas De Genove, Nadia Abu El-Haj, and Rebecca Luna Stein. Anthropology, along with sociology, is paid particular notice throughout the site for its allegedly high percentage of leftist practitioners.

Both ACTA and Discover the Networks have the power to greatly damage an academic's career. David Horowitz has built up a large following, particularly through his online magazine *Front Page* and his various published books, which he has used to organize or inspire "Students' Rights" groups as well as to convince elected and appointed officials to pressure the schools under their authority. His "Academic Bill of Rights" has been the basis of bills introduced (and fortunately rejected, so far) in several states' legislatures, some with provisions that would allow students who were disappointed with their professor's political biases to sue for damages (VanLandingham 2005).

ACTA is more powerful still. Founded by Lynne Cheney, wife of the current Republican Vice-President, and Joseph Lieberman, a powerful Democratic senator and former vice-presidential candidate (opposite Dick Cheney, appropriately enough), ACTA counts on the university trustees and alumni in their membership to use their clout as potential donors to effect change – such as the removal of professors whom ACTA finds objectionable. Where Horowitz and his organizations have to rely on the power of public relations, ACTA is able to threaten a college's or university's fundraising abilities by directing its members to withhold alumni association funds, an important source of revenue for most schools.

Even as anthropologists' loyalties and value as academics are questioned, a great demand for anthropological knowledge is developing outside academia, in corporations as well as within military and intelligence agencies. Corporations, especially in the high-tech sector, have actively pursued anthropologists for their knowledge of local cultures and consumption patterns, to help in the design of better software interfaces, marketing campaigns, enterprise workflows, and so on, harking back to the industrial anthropology of the 1930s. Meanwhile, with terrorism showing little tendency to abate after several years of the "War on Terror" and with the invasion and occupation of Iraq almost universally considered a failure, there has been a renewed interest in anthropological knowledge and methods to train service members, improve intelligence-gathering, help design propaganda efforts, and assist with combat and occupation planning.

The Pat Roberts Intelligence Scholarship Program (PRISP) represents one effort to appropriate anthropological knowledge for the needs of the state. PRISP funds students studying languages and areas considered under-represented by national intelligence and security agencies, in exchange for a commitment of service within the Central Intelligence Agency, National Security Agency, or other US intelligence agency. The program has been heavily promoted by anthropologist Felix Moos, who has admonished anthropologists to set aside their political commitments and rally around the flag in this time of war (Moos 2005). But many anthropologists are nervous about the program, partly because of the fear of a backlash against all American anthropologists once it becomes clear that some intelligence agents are operating under the guise of working anthropologists – a fear with roots in Franz Boas's 1919 castigation of anthropologists who used their work as cover to provide information to the US government during World War I.

What PRISP is to American intelligence efforts, the Cultural Operations Research Human Terrain (CORHT) project is to the American military: an attempt to integrate anthropologists and anthropological knowledge into the military in order to refine US counter-insurgency efforts in Iraq and elsewhere. CORHT began with the compilation of a Human Relations Area Files-like database containing detailed anthropological data on Iraqi cultures, and has since developed into a staffing program embedding anthropologists and other social scientists directly into combat teams in Iraq and Afghanistan (Packer 2006). These researchers are intended to act as cultural advisors to their military units, helping to identify and manipulate the social networks through which insurgents communicate, recruit, and act.

Projects like PRISP and CORHT raise a number of issues, not least the concern about secret research raised by the Thailand affair and Project Camelot in the 1960s and 1970s. More important from the perspective of the intellectual development of the discipline is the effect that this re-establishment of relations between the American military and intelligence apparatus and anthropologists will have on the intellectual development of the discipline. Increased funding for the kinds of anthropology deemed useful for intelligence-gathering and counter-insurgency cannot help but shape the field in ways similar to the effect of government backing for area studies and overseas research in the Cold War years.

TODAY AND TOMORROW

Since the AAA shake-up in the early 1970s, anthropology has faced a growing crisis of self-confidence and relevance. As the American academic landscape changes, offering fewer and fewer possibilities to build careers as anthropologists in the academy, many anthropologists have turned to the private sector and to government work for employment in "applied" anthropology, widening a gap which has existed at least since the immediate post-World War II years. This split is apparent in the writing of military anthropologist Montgomery McFate:

Although anthropology is the only academic discipline that explicitly seeks to understand foreign cultures and societies, it is a marginal contributor to U.S. national-security policy at best and a punch line at worst. Over the past 30 years, as a result of anthropologists' individual career choices and the tendency toward reflexive self-criticism contained within the discipline itself, the discipline has become hermetically sealed within its Ivory Tower. (2005: 28)

McFate is the author of part of the US Army's new counter-insurgency field manual (Department of the Army 2006), which embraces a social scientific approach to military affairs. For several years, she has been one of the Army's strongest advocates for the usefulness of anthropological knowledge, urging the military to reconsider their tactics to adapt to the changing nature of the "War on Terror." For McFate (and others such as Felix Moos), anthropology has gone down the wrong path since the Vietnam War, retreating from messy entanglements with the military into the comfort and safety of the Ivory Tower.

Although McFate has focused her advocacy on her military cohorts, trying to get them to recognize the value of anthropology's insights to their efforts – her work appears mainly in journals and publications aimed at a military audience, not in the anthropological literature – her concerns have been echoed in the debate that erupted following the AAA's decision to run a CIA recruiting advertisement in the organization's monthly newsletter, *Anthropology News* (Fluehr-Lobban and Heller 2007; Gonzalez 2007; Goodman 2006; Gusterson and Price 2005; McNamara 2007; Nuti 2007; Price 2005, 2007). Many anthropologists feel that, taking government policy – good or bad – as a given, there is a moral imperative for anthropologists to work with policy-makers to lessen the negative impacts of war, occupation, and peace-keeping on the populations affected by them. Others counter that anthropological ethics necessitates keeping the continued well-being of our subjects in mind in all our decisions, and worry about the loss of control over the use of anthropological knowledge created as "work-for-hire" for military or intelligence organizations. The CIA advertisement has acted as a catalyst for a rethinking of the implications of ethics in anthropological practice, a concern that has been largely dormant since the crisis in the early 1970s.

The issues raised in the essays in this book are, 50 years and more after the Cold War, still very much alive. Whether we focus on Senator McCarthy waving a blank sheet of paper purportedly listing the names of "known communists" working for or with the State Department and singling out for special mention "a professor of anthropology, a woman" (most likely Ruth Benedict or Gene Weltfish; David Price, personal communication), or on ACTA, an organization headed by a standing senator and the wife of a vice-president, publishing a list of un-American scholars, it is important to remember that anthropology's service to the state has long been channeled through interests and goals that originate in the state, not in the theoretical concerns of anthropology itself. As we evaluate the work of our peers – and as we consider the gaps that continue to exist in our field – it is essential to keep in mind the continued influence of the "phantom factor" in shaping not only what is published but what is not. While it may be easy to overdraw the analogy between the "War on Terror" today and the Cold War of yesterday, it is vitally important that we not *underdraw* such parallels. Anthropology, like all humanity's creations, exists as part of culture, and it is crucial that anthropologists evaluate the work of our forebears and of ourselves as such.

REFERENCES

Arrighi, Giovanni. 1994. *The Long Twentieth Century: Money, Power, and the Origins of Our Times*. London: Verso.

Boas, Franz. 1919. Scientists as Spies. *The Nation* 109: 79.

Darnell, Regna. 2001. *Invisible Genealogies: A History of Americanist Anthropology*. Lincoln, NE: University of Nebraska Press.

Department of the Army. 2006. *FM 3-24: Counterinsurgency*. Washington, DC: Department of the Army.

Discover the Networks. URL: www.discoverthenetworks.org (accessed June 2007).

Fluehr-Lobban, Carolyn and Monica Heller. 2007. Ethical Challenges for Anthropological Engagement. *Anthropology News* 48(1): 4.

Gonzalez, Roberto J. 2007. Standing Up Against Torture and War. *Anthropology News* 48(3): 5.

Goodman, Alan. 2006. Engaging with National Security. *Anthropology News* 47(2): 63.

Gusterson, Hugh and David Price. 2005. Spies in Our Midst. *Anthropology News* 46(6): 39–40.

Lewis, Herbert S. 2001. Anthropology, the Cold War, and Intellectual History. In *History of Anthropology Annnual*, vol. 1, pp. 99–113. Regna Darnell and Frederic W. Gleach, eds. Lincoln, NE: University of Nebraska Press.

Martin, Jerry L. and Anne D. Neal. 2001. *Defending Civilization: How Our Universities Are Failing America and What Can Be Done About It*. Washington, DC: American Council of Trustees and Alumni.

—— 2002. *Defending Civilization: How Our Universities Are Failing America and What Can Be Done About It*. Revised and expanded edn. Washington, DC: American Council of Trustees and Alumni.

McNamara, Laura A. 2007. SAR Hosts Seminar on the Anthropology of Military and National Security Organizations. *Anthropology News* 48(5): 24–25.

McFate, Montgomery. 2005. Anthropology and Counterinsurgency: The Strange Story of their Curious Relationship. *Military Review* 85(2): 24–38.

Moos, Felix. 2005. Some Thoughts on Anthropological Ethics and Today's Conflict. *Anthropology News* 46(6): 40–42.

Nader, Laura. 1997. The Phantom Factor: Impact of the Cold War on Anthropology. In *The Cold War and the University: Toward an Intellectual History of the War Years*, pp. 107–46. André Schiffrin, ed. New York: The New Press.

Nuti, Paul J. 2007. Ad Hoc Commission Headlines at the Watson Institute. *Anthropology News* 48(5): 24.

Ortner, Sherry. 1984. Theory of Anthropology Since the Sixties. *Comparative Studies in Society and History* 126: 126–66.

Packer, George. 2006. Knowing the Enemy. *The New Yorker* 82(42): 60–69.

Peace, William and David Price. 2001. The Cold War Context of the FBI's Investigation of Leslie A. White. *American Anthropologist* 103(1): 164–67.

Price, David. 1998. Cold War Anthropology: Collaborators and Victims of the National Security State. *Identities* 4(3–4): 389–430.

——. 2004. *Threatening Anthropology*. Durham, NC: Duke University Press.

——. 2005. America the Ambivalent: Quietly Selling Anthropology to the CIA. *Anthropology Today* 21(6): 1–2.

——. 2007. Anthropology and the Wages of Secrecy. *Anthropology News* 48(3): 6–7.

Richardson, Theresa and Donald Fisher. 1999. Introduction: The Social Sciences and Their Philanthropic Mentors. In *The Development of the Social Sciences in the United States and Canada: The Role of Philanthropy*, pp. 3–22. Theresa Richardson and Donald Fisher, eds. Stamford, CT: Ablex Publishing Corporation.

Roseberry, William. 1996. The Unbearable Lightness of Anthropology. *Radical History Review* 65: 5–25.

Saunders, Frances S. 1999. *Who Paid the Piper? The CIA and the Cultural Cold War*. London: Granta Books.

Turner, Steven P. 1999. Does Funding Produce Its Effects: The Rockefeller Case. In *The Development of the Social Sciences in the United States and Canada: The Role of Philanthropy*, pp. 213–26. Theresa Richardson and Donald Fisher, eds. Stamford, CT: Ablex Publishing Corporation.

VanLandingham, James. 2005. Capitol Bill Aims to Control "Leftist" Profs. *Alligator Online* March 23, 2005: http://www.alligator.org/pt2/050323freedom.php (accessed June 2007).

Vincent, Joan. 1990. *Anthropology and Politics: Visions, Traditions, and Trends*. Tucson: University of Arizona Press.

Wallerstein, Immanuel. 1997. The Unintended Consequences of Cold War Area Studies. In *The Cold War and the University: Toward an Intellectual History of the War Years*, pp. 195–231. André Schiffrin, ed. New York: The New Press.

1 ASHLEY'S GHOST: McCARTHYISM, SCIENCE, AND HUMAN NATURE

Susan Sperling

He who controls the past controls the future; he who controls the present controls the past. (Orwell 1983 [1949]: 248)

In early January 1953, Lewis Webster Jones, President of Rutgers University received a note from Harry Derby, a Rutgers trustee and vice-president of the Hanover Bank of New Jersey:

Dear Harry,
For several weeks I have intended to mention a matter concerning Rutgers which I think would interest you. When I was in Milwaukee the weekend of November 8, my friends discussed with me in a very derogatory manner the appearance of Dr. Ashley Montagu before the Women's Club in Milwaukee on November 6. It seems that Dr. Montagu is Chairman of the Anthropology department at Rutgers University and executive officer of the United Nations Educational, Scientific and Cultural Organization.

According to the program, a copy of which is enclosed, Dr. Montagu was scheduled to speak on "On Being Human – The Nature of Human Nature." Also enclosed is a clipping from the Milwaukee Journal which states that in his talk Dr. Montagu made claims that not only the great religions but science, too, tells us that the most important thing is love.... It was quite apparent that Dr. Montagu's position coincided with the usual Communistic theme song, and you may be assured that the ladies were not in a receptive mood on November 6 just two days after the election ... (Ashley Montagu Papers 1953)[1]

On January 16, Rutgers President Lewis Webster Jones wrote back:

Dear Harry:
Thank you for sending me the information about Dr. Ashley Montagu. I very much appreciate your bringing it to my attention.

I hope that I will be seeing you at the trustees' meeting on the 23rd and 24th, when I hope I will have the chance to talk with you about the matter. (Ashley Montagu Papers 1953)

More than any other of Boas's many accomplished intellectual progeny, his student Ashley Montagu brought to anthropology a rigorous integration of knowledge about human biology and culture (Harnad 1980a, 1980b; Andrew Lyons 1996). Often referred to as an

17

anthropological "popularizer," Montagu's scholarly contributions spanned an astounding range of engagement. He may have been the only twentieth-century scientist to publish widely read texts on human physiology as well as genetics (Marks 2000a). Most significantly, his mastery of evolutionary biology and cultural anthropology led him to a truly integrative, non-reductionist biocultural science that is in scarce evidence in today's fragmented sub-disciplines comprising the study of humanity. The British-born Montagu, who died in Princeton in 1999 at the advanced age of 94, was, as Boas had been to an earlier generation, a key contestant in the struggle against long-persisting biological reductionist notions of human nature (Montagu 1952, 1957, 1968). He was a major public figure in twentieth-century America, and one of the century's most important theorists of race (Montagu 1926, 1942a, 1942b), gender, and human nature (Montagu 1952, 1953). As the eminent physical anthropologist C. Loring Brace said, "Montagu has done more than anyone except Margaret Mead to bring the findings of anthropology to the attention of the public" (in Harnad 1980a). But today many readers have never heard of him, or are only vaguely aware of the significance of his ideas. Not only is Montagu largely lost to popular culture, but he is little read now by academics. When I ask my college students if they have heard of Montagu, they stare back blankly. Within anthropology itself he has been systematically disappeared. His seminal contributions are not assigned to anthropology students, who learn, if they learn anything, that he was a mere popularizer. He exists only as a ghostly presence.

At the height of Cold War McCarthyism, Montagu was pushed out of his last academic job as first Chair of Anthropology at Rutgers University in New Jersey, during a period in which the FBI kept an extensive file on him, in no small part because his vision about the nature of human nature contradicted the dominant Hobbesian paradigm of competition and nature "red in tooth and claw" (Sperling forthcoming).[2] The story of Montagu's virtual disappearance can only be told in the context of the history of his times. We often decry politicized science, but science and politics have always been intimately connected. Much has been written over the last decades about the uses and abuses of biology – about, for instance, the false assertion that there are innate racial and sexual differences in intelligence – and how scientifically flawed research projects have influenced American popular culture (Gould 1986). Less has been said about how science has been shaped by powerful political influences (Schrecker 1986). As Americans experience the resurgence of governmental attempts to manipulate scientific practice and scrutiny of the ideas presented in its universities under the new security state as codified in the Patriot Act, the McCarthyism of the past may be a prologue to new, perhaps more sophisticated, forms of political control over scientific practice. Montagu's departure from academia serves as a cautionary tale about political intrusion into the creation of science from another volatile historical period in which America responded to national crisis. Montagu's integrative biocultural research agenda – one that had produced seminal insights in the anthropological understanding of race, gender, and human development – was terminated by his expulsion from academe. He became a public intellectual, advocating for greater popular understanding of the impacts of racism, sexism, and the prospects for a more just society. This was, of course, no small accomplishment. But what might have been his continued contribution to the shaping of anthropology – particularly evolutionary anthropology – at mid-century is the subject of this chapter.

Although Montagu often referred to his departure from academia as a personal choice (Andrew Lyons 1996; Montagu, personal communication), it has become increasingly clear that he paid a price for his life-long battle against the false science underlying conservative political agendas. As Montagu's biographer, I have followed the twists and turns of his extraordinary, sometimes madly ambiguous life history.[3] I was surprised to find among his papers correspondence between, and with, Rutgers administration that shed new light on the latter half of his career. These letters, along with his FBI file, were intriguing, and added significantly to my understanding of why Montagu abandoned hopes for an ambitious research career within the academy.

For a period of 15 years, the FBI kept an extensive file on Montagu, citing, among other things, his radical ideas about human nature, about the role of cooperation in human evolution, and his contention that our concept of race is largely a myth (Federal Bureau of Investigation File HQ100-402992 1953). This file (declassified under the Freedom of Information Act), along with his correspondence from the 1950s, reveal a complicated picture. Without access to his private letters with Rutgers administrators and his FBI file, I would never have questioned Montagu's explanation for his departure from academe. University records would not have helped, because Montagu's very presence at the university between 1949 and 1955 is not apparent in records of Rutgers official history (Rutgers University Archives). The departure of one of America's leading anthropologists from the academic realm has important implications for the present. Montagu's career is instructive not only because of what he was able to accomplish as one of the preeminent public intellectuals of mid-twentieth-century America, but because of what he was not able to accomplish within ivied walls.

Yet Montagu's movement from academic to popular author resists any linear narrative. Montagu despised what he considered to be the petty politics of academe and his letters to Rutgers administrators reveal a demanding personality. Andrew Lyons (personal communication) has suggested that the stresses provoked by FBI harassment might have provoked tensions in his life during this period that might well have spilled over into his relations at Rutgers. In any case, his departure from the Rutgers program marked a decisive turning point in his life and his influence largely ceased to exist within the profession (as opposed to his public popularity in the 1960s and 1970s).

A war over radically different claims about the nature of human nature has been waged across nineteenth- and twentieth-century evolutionary science and its popularizations. Social Darwinism – the claim that competition and "survival of the fittest" are the *sine qua non* of human nature – has been one of the most persistent visions in Western culture. The grist for milling this vision of biological determinism has long been provided by the pseudo-science that describes the evolution of our species as the war of all against all – a drama of endless competition among individuals, social classes, and races (Gould 1986; Lancaster 2003; Sperling 1994, 2007). The notion that "fixed" inherited biological differences are responsible for social inequality may be one of Western civilization's most ineluctable tropes, going back at least as far as Plato. Discoveries about human developmental plasticity by modern biologists have done little to curb the persistent public passion for evolutionary "just-so" stories. It is not surprising that Social Darwinism in various forms has continued to exert a profound influence among conservatives in the United States. As the beneficiaries of the status quo, American elites have often had a strong investment in the notion that innate "fitness" trumps economic and social disenfranchisement. Conservatives have found this argument attractive for over a century because it offers a rationale for the untidy inequalities of a less than just political and economic system that is, nevertheless, predicated on the ideal of equal opportunity (Gould 1981).

Social Darwinism and other forms of biological reductionism claim the inevitability of inequality, but, as Montagu frequently asserted, there are other perspectives to be gleaned from reading Darwin (Montagu 1952). Ashley Montagu, like his mentor Franz Boas, pursued a science that meticulously dismantled these oversimplified rationalizations for the status quo – and in doing so he incurred the wrath of those within academia and politics committed to scientific rationales for indelible inequality within our species.

THE EAST END KID

For many who knew him professionally and socially, as well as for his enthusiastic public, Montagu was the quintessential upper-class British professor, with his tweed jacket, perpetual pipe, and Oxbridge accent. Nothing could have been further from the truth: Montagu grew up poor in the rough and tumble world of London's Jewish East End in the twilight of the Victorian era. Professor Higgins to his own Eliza Doolittle, he forged an identity, and perhaps most importantly, an accent, that allowed him access to elite scientific training. He educated himself brilliantly: he needed only to look in the mirror to see a living repudiation of Social Darwinism.

Montagu had been, with Margaret Mead, the public voice and face of anthropology in mid-century America. Writer of *The Elephant Man* (Montagu 1971) and more than 60 other scholarly and popular books, he was a legendary iconoclast, publicly debunking widely held social myths. On the lecture circuit, or trading witticisms with Johnny Carson during frequent guest appearances on *The Tonight Show*, he defined the post-war image of the pipe-smoking upper-crust Brit as public intellectual. Montagu the public intellectual was born out of economic necessity. Although he had passionately wanted to forge an academic career, after he left Rutgers, his income was derived almost entirely from his numerous publications, lectures, and television appearances.

For over two decades beginning in the 1960s, contesting in public forums the noxious William B. Shockley (Andrew Lyons 1996) and other notorious racists, or appearing as one of television's original scientific soothsayers, he introduced a wide audience to his progressive agendas. Montagu popularized new theories about aggression, sex, and child rearing, making the bold suggestion that other cultures could actually teach us how to do a better job at life's most important tasks (Montagu 1952, 1953, 1957, 1968, 1969, 1972, 1976, 1978). Many of Montagu's most controversial ideas about the nature of our species – as early as 1926 he was challenging the contemporary received wisdom on race – are now widely accepted (Montagu 1926). Modern studies of human DNA have proven his prescient insistence that race is more accurately viewed as a cultural category rather than a biological one. We now know from studies of population genetics that there is more genetic variation within, than between, races (Lewontin 1972; Marks 1996, 2000b). Montagu had published this assertion as early as the 1940s (Montagu 1997 [1942]).

LUMPS AND BUMPS

Montagu came of age in an era abounding in false extrapolations from anthropometry, the measurement of the human body. In 1870, Italian psychologist Cesare Lombroso had a flash of insight. He had long wondered about the physical signs that might distinguish criminals from the "normal." One dark December day, while examining the skull of an infamous brigand named Vihella, he understood that:

At the sight of that skull, I seemed to see all of a sudden, lighted up as a vast plain under a flaming sky, the problem of the nature of the criminal – an atavistic being who reproduces in his person the ferocious instincts of primitive humanity and the inferior animals. Thus were explained anatomically the enormous jaws, high cheek bones, prominent superciliary arches, solitary lines in the palms, extreme size of the orbits, handle-shaped ears found in criminals, savages and apes, insensibility to pain, extremely acute sight, tattooing, excessive idleness, love of orgies, and the irresponsible craving of evil for its own sake, the desire not only to extinguish life in the victim, but to mutilate the corpse, tear its flesh and drink its blood. (quoted in Gould 1981: 153)

According to Lombroso, criminals were nature's throwbacks to our apeish past. He went on to measure the lumps and bumps on the heads of literally thousands of people and to correlate these to traits like nymphomania and violent criminality. He labeled these criminal signs writ on the body "stigmata" and published his theory in 1877 in one of nineteenth-century behavioral science's most influential, if crackpot, books, *L'uomo criminel* (Lombroso 1887). A generation of caliper-wielding anthropologists and psychologists measured the heads of men, women and children all over the world, most often concluding that immigrants and non-whites, women, the working classes, and the poor were physically and evolutionarily under par.

Around the turn of the century, in another manifestation of the belief that biology is destiny, Darwin's cousin, Francis Galton, founded the eugenics movement. Based on the notion that marriage and family size should be regulated to encourage the social breeding of "good traits" and the breeding out of the evolutionarily "unfit," Galton's eugenics thoroughly rejected the notion that environment had any role in human development. His theories gained popularity, particularly in the United States (Gould 1981).

Franz Boas became a chief critic of these approaches. Boas, himself a Jewish immigrant, had set the progressive research agenda for American anthropology in the early decades of the century (Stocking 1974). In seminal studies of early twentieth-century immigrants to America, Boas applied classic anthropometric techniques to prove that their smaller head and body measurements were not inherited ethnic or racial genetic "traits" but were a result of stunting in their impoverished homeland environments (Boas 1912). Within one generation in America these measurements changed to match those of native-born Americans. Boas's public lectures radically challenged the eugenic movement's widely accepted disparagement of immigrants as "innately unfit." (Unfortunately, Boas's research had no effect on the restrictive immigration law of 1924, which prevented Jews fleeing the Nazis – among thousands of others – from reaching American shores [Gould 1986]).

Montagu owed much to his teacher's example. His brand of "socio-biology" (it was he who invented the term in the 1940s [Montagu 1940], ironically, considering its current usage in service of biological reductionism) reflects Boas's theme: nature and nurture are inseparable in much of human development (Montagu 1970). Like Boas, Montagu took very seriously scientists' obligation to apply the fruits of research to the social issues of the day. In 1984, when William B. Shockley sued the *Atlanta Constitution* for comparing his suggestion that the intellectually "unfit" (which according to Shockley included 85 percent of black Americans) be voluntarily sterilized to Nazi eugenics, Montagu served as an expert witness in the newspaper's defense. At the trial, his remark: "Had Mozart been born to a blacksmith, there would never have been a Mozart, just a blacksmith named Mozart," provoked a roar of laughter from the audience (in Andrew Lyons 1996: 14).

Montagu's 1942 *magnum opus, Man's Most Dangerous Myth: The Fallacy of Race*, which has gone through five editions (Montagu 1997) and is still in print, was written during the war against Nazi Germany, a nation that had taken eugenics to its nightmarish political extreme. In a brilliant feat of scholarship and polemic, Montagu took on, one by one, the racist fallacies that had been justified by a century of faulty science. The book challenged the traditional scientific concept of "races" as bounded categories, emphasizing that gene frequency studies would show the great unity of humankind confronting similar challenges as hunter-gatherers during the crucial stages of human evolution.

After the end of the war, in 1950, the United Nations Educational, Scientific and Cultural Organization (UNESCO) published the First Statement on Race (Barkan 1996; UNESCO 1952), a watershed in international race politics. Montagu was the United Nations rapporteur, the final writer of this document, which formalized at the international level his concept of race as a dangerously mythic category:

From the biological standpoint, the species *Homo sapiens* is made up of a number of populations, each one differs from the other in the frequency of one or more genes. Such genes, responsible for the hereditary differences between men, are always few when compared to the whole genetic constitution of man and to the vast number of genes common to all human beings regardless of the population to whom they belong. This means that the likenesses among men are far greater than their differences. (UNESCO First Statement on Race 1950 [UNESCO 1952])

In a move that outraged many in the scientific community, Montagu called into question the very use of the term "race":

The biological fact of race and the myth of "race" should be distinguished. For all practical social purposes "race" is not so much a biological phenomenon as a social myth. The myth "race" has created an enormous amount of human and social damage. (UNESCO First Statement on Race 1950 [UNESCO 1952])

The First Statement on Race created an uproar within evolutionary science and the controversy compelled UNESCO to issue a Second Statement in 1951, which was significantly less radical. But as we have seen, it was Montagu's first iteration that has proven to be scientifically accurate. When the impact of Nazi racialism and eugenics were widely acknowledged following World War II, most physical anthropologists were relieved to purge their discipline of any connection to these retrograde and abhorrent notions. Montagu collaborated with other progressive scientists to pass anti-racist resolutions (which had been furiously criticized by many physical anthropologists before the war) for post-war anthropological societies (Marks 2000a). The abandonment and condemnation of racialist science within anthropology has largely stuck (Reynolds and Lieberman 1996), even as many of its evolutionary practitioners cling to other forms of narrow biological reductionism, most notably in studies of human gender and behavior (Sperling 1997).

Unlike many of these latter-day practitioners, Montagu saw sexism as analogous to racism and made an explicit comparison between these socially damaging pathologies (Montagu 1952). This was pretty hot stuff for the America of the early 1950s. In 1952, the year before Simone de Beauvoir's *Second Sex* (1953) first appeared in English, and eleven years before Betty Friedan's *Feminine Mystique* (1963) became a bestseller, Montagu published a crucial early work of modern feminism, *The Natural Superiority of Women*. In 1871, Darwin, no exception to the patriarchal ideas of most prominent scholars of his period, wrote in *The Descent of Man*, "The chief distinction in the intellectual powers of the two sexes is shown by man's attaining to a higher eminence, in whatever he takes up, than can woman – whether requiring deep thought, reason, or imagination, or merely the use of the senses and hands" (Darwin 2004 [1871]: 511). *The Natural Superiority of Women* is a multi-layered argument against this Darwinian passage. Montagu cited the many ways in which women's achievements in letters, arts, and sciences have been curtailed by social constraints rather than evolutionary determinism. This argument resonated deeply for many women who were experiencing the post-war narrowing of feminine opportunities, and the book enjoyed a broad readership – including the creator of the comic icon Wonder Woman, who credits Montagu with the inception of the idea for the character (Daniels 2000).

Montagu clearly enjoyed his large and appreciative public audience (Montagu, personal communication). It might even be said that McCarthyism benefited him by thrusting him into the public realm when he could no longer make a living as an academic. But his departure from academic anthropology had, I would argue, a negative impact, both on the discipline and on Montagu himself. He was a persuasive and political scientist, which was clearly one of the reasons the FBI troubled to put him under surveillance – and one of the reasons Rutgers troubled to hire him to found a department in the first place.

RASHOMON AT RUTGERS

There are at least three different narratives of which I am aware about Montagu's departure from Rutgers: Montagu's own account; the "story" told by his FBI file and correspondence between Rutgers administrators in Montagu's private papers; and the tale told by Rutgers colleagues and administrators. Montagu came to Rutgers in 1949 to found a department that would turn anthropology decisively away from the scientistic venture of endless skull measurements and false assertions about ineluctable racial differences. He entered Rutgers during a period of political turbulence that would soon boil over onto many university campuses. In 1947, under pressure from the Republican 80th Congress, President Truman issued Executive Order 9835 establishing a loyalty-security program for federal employees. Within a fairly short time, the process of scrutinizing and eliminating progressives and radicals spread from federal workplaces to other institutions. As Ellen Schrecker, pre-eminent scholar of McCarthyism in the academy, points out in her book *No Ivory Tower* (1986), those caught in the net included not only past and present Communists, but also many belonging to a variety of other progressive causes active in the US during the Cold War period. The FBI was charged with the investigation of suspect individuals through, among other things, the use of secret informers.

Montagu was appointed Professor of Anthropology at Rutgers with the understanding that he would develop a full program in physical and cultural anthropology at the university. His contract involved an agreement that he would raise part of the funding for the development of the program through outside public and private sources, with the understanding that the university would soon fund the program itself, as well as assist in further outside fundraising. H.G. Owen, Dean of Arts and Sciences, wrote enthusiastically to Montagu, "I do not need to assure you that I am very anxious to develop the facilities of the department at the earliest possible moment. I regard the institution of work in Anthropology as of the greatest importance" (Ashley Montagu Papers, H.G. Owen to Ashley Montagu 1949).

By 1951, the McCarthy witch-hunt was in full steam. The June 1950 Communist invasion of South Korea seemed a confirmation of many of the anxieties upon which McCarthy's committee played. The Republicans claimed that America was under worldwide attack and that the Democratic Party and many of its New Deal institutions were "infiltrated by communists and their sympathizers." According to Schrecker, about one in five of those called before investigating committees were educators. Most of these who claimed the Fifth Amendment right against self-incrimination and refused to name names were fired. This created a conundrum for university administrators and trustees because of the conflict between the concept of academic freedom and the removal of faculty "dissenters." Rutgers' President Lewis Webster Jones, a Cold War liberal, was a key actor in the university purges of the 1950s. Together with a number of other high-profile university presidents, he promulgated a doctrine rationalizing this apparent contradiction. In a bold piece of sophistry, the administrators claimed that firing professors who did not cooperate with House Un-American Activities Committee (HUAC) was consistent with academic freedom because the Committee was striving to protect American freedoms (Schrecker 1986).

President Jones officiated over the firings of several high-profile tenured faculty – the most famous of whom was the British classicist Sir Moses Finley (Finley returned to England to chair a department at Cambridge University). After the Cold War, Rutgers recanted its purges and offered an apology to Finley, making public many documents related to the witch-hunt (Schrecker 1986). Montagu's departure, however, was *sub rosa*, as were the firings of many untenured professors across the nation during this period, and no mention was made of him in the official published Rutgers files on the Cold War blacklist (Rutgers University Archives).

Montagu's FBI file reveals that agents repeatedly contacted Rutgers personnel about him, though they were well aware that Montagu was not a communist and made note of this fact in his file (Montagu FBI File). The document makes clear that it was not only Montagu's participation in a variety of liberal causes, such as civil rights, that concerned the Bureau, but, significantly, the very *nature of his ideas* about human nature. A 1950 entry in the file simply quotes a passage from one of Montagu's books as evidence of "communist tendencies": "A profit-motive, economic-struggle-for-existence society is a predatory society, and class-and-caste society, a divisive society, in which each person is an isolate preying upon and preyed upon by others" (Montagu FBI File).

As Oscar Wilde said, "the truth is rarely pure and never simple." The whole story of Montagu's sojourn at Rutgers may never be known. Montagu could be a challenging colleague (Fox, personal communication), and this may well have contributed to his troubles at Rutgers. Anecdotal evidence suggests that he had a quixotic and arrogant approach at times. Early in his tenure at Rutgers, for instance, he set forth his expectation that the college would provide him with a suitably impressive building in which to house the new anthropology program (Ashley Montagu Papers 1946–56). There is little doubt that this demand provoked a surprised response from a cash-strapped administration. Reality did not always live up to his ideals, energies, and expectations and he considered a number of administrators less than worthy. Of course, some of them were. It is clear that, after a brief honeymoon, the optimistic relationship between Montagu and the Rutgers administration spiraled rapidly downhill. By January 1950, Dean Owen informed an increasingly uneasy Montagu that the university's budget could not accommodate any funds at all for the anthropology program (Montagu correspondence, American Philosophical Society). The following year the Dean was writing to Montagu to evict him from his offices on the third floor of the Sociology Building, suggesting that he use two smaller rooms in another area. The flurry of increasingly acrimonious letters (Ashley Montagu Papers 1949–55) between the two indicates a disagreement about the terms of Montagu's employment at Rutgers. Montagu was untenured, and, as Schrecker points out, the kinds of strategies used to remove such tenuously employed professors did not necessitate the public display involved in a case like Moses Finley's. Instead, funds would dry up, offices would be unavailable, and similar harassment under the radar screen would usually effect a resignation. The blacklist of the time insured that those fired would not be rehired elsewhere. Yet, like Cary Grant hanging from Mt Rushmore by his fingernails in the Hitchcock classic *North by Northwest*, with the administration trying to pry him loose, Montagu clung to his affiliation with the university because the alternative was at least as unattractive.

In January 1950, Earnest Hooton, doyen of American physical anthropology at Harvard, wrote to Montagu:

It seems to me that it would be advisable for you to cut yourself loose at Rutgers, and try to get another position. A university which flirts around with the establishing of an Anthropology Department for years and then treats you in the manner you indicate, is hardly one to which you wish to attach yourself permanently. (Ashley Montagu Papers 1950)

In a letter full of outrage and pathos, Montagu wrote to Dean Owen in 1951:

We are now entering upon the third year of an impossible and to me no longer tolerable situation. It seems to me an utterly immoral and indefensible position has been taken with regard to my situation, and I must insist that I no longer be made the victim of it. I have, in middle age, been forced into a position of insecurity which is playing havoc with my health, mind, and reputation. In order to earn a living for my wife and three children I have to pot-boil and travel-lecture, and do other things which are in no way consonant with the teaching and research I planned to do. I have been placed in a most humiliating position, and rumors through my branch of the academic world reach me in all shapes and sorts of forms. The possibility of my ever obtaining another post has been seriously impaired.... If I have not suffered a breakdown as a consequence of these experiences, it is through no fault of Rutgers. (Ashley Montagu Papers 1951)

By this time, President Jones was privately speaking of bringing the "Montagu situation" before the trustees for termination of his appointment. An undated and hand-written note from Dean Owen to Webster Jones indicates Owen's frustration and outrage that that his policy of neglect had not yet forced Montagu's departure. Other voices reached Rutgers administrators. In early January 1953 Rutgers trustee Harry Derby forwarded to President Jones the note he had received from his banker neighbor in New Jersey, which is quoted at the start of this chapter. We will never know what Jones told Derby when they met to discuss Montagu. Montagu finally resigned in 1955, but his problems with the FBI persisted into the 1960s. When he organized to protest the war in Vietnam with Benjamin Spock, the State Department confiscated his passport.[4]

Other anthropologists and administrators at Rutgers have a different narrative about the Montagu affair. Evolutionary anthropologist Robin Fox, appointed in the mid 1960s as the first official Chair of the Rutgers Anthropology Department (and a friend of Montagu's despite their very different perspectives on evolution and aggression), wrote to tell me his understanding of the events, as described to him by then-President of Rutgers Mason Gross:

Ashley had been invited to see how a department might go. From the start there had been mutual hostility, according to Mason, nothing to do with politics or anything such, but to Ashley's "inflexible intolerance and arrogance." His treatment of students and "lack of understanding of their problems" was an issue. But above all, at the end of the year, knowing that the university had limited resources – a fact Mason said had never been hidden from him and which he knew perfectly well at the time – he presented an "impossible and outrageous series of 'demands'" without which he would not continue. Now it was Mason's take on this that Ashley knew perfectly well they couldn't be met, and that he intended all the time to leave; he was just angling for an advantageous arrangement.... But, Mason continued, it was (still) clear that there was no department any longer so Ashley was not the Chairman of it. We were glad to see the back of him, he concluded. Not so easy! Ashley then began using the title (Chairman) as we know on all his publications, lectures, etc. Mason said the university protested (how I don't know) but they were unwilling to get into a lawsuit with all its possible complications. They had been burned over the Finley ... business, the old guard had gone and the new was basically a liberal establishment, which wanted to live down the reactionary past. Ashley, they felt could easily exploit the new liberal atmosphere and accuse them of anti-Semitism and McCarthyism, etc. (Fox, personal communication).

While Montagu could be a very difficult colleague (and certainly he was most impatient with the Rutgers administration), Fox's explanation for Montagu's Rutgers troubles offers a version of events that adds some layers of ambiguity to what emerged from my reading of his correspondence with Rutgers administrators and his FBI file. Rutgers solicited Montagu precisely because of his important reputation as a rising star in evolutionary science. Early written exchanges with the administration indicate no hostility, and have a most congenial tone, although as time went on this changed. I know of no evidence of Montagu's mistreating students and, in fact, interviews and letters from some former students suggest otherwise. These multiple narratives may help illuminate a complex mix of causality in his expulsion from the university. Montagu represented his departure from Rutgers retrospectively as his choice. The FBI file and administrative correspondence tell a different tale, and what we might call the collective memory of the succeeding Rutgers establishment adds a third narrative, *Rashomon*-style.

JUNGLE POLITICS

While it is impossible to know how the blackballing of one influential individual affected the landscape of a young science, it is instructive to look at the direction modern evolutionary studies took at Rutgers following Montagu's departure. However large or small the role of McCarthyite fanaticism in Montagu's exit from Rutgers, the Graduate Program in Evolution, Behavior, and Culture is today a decidedly different kind of place from Montagu's vision. Some of its faculty luminaries have produced influential popular books expounding the very kind of evolutionary "just-so" stories that Montagu decried (Tiger 1987; Tiger and Fox 1971). A decade after Montagu's denouement, Robin Fox, then at the London School of Economics, was invited to found a new anthropology department. Along with his collaborator, Lionel Tiger, he published a volley of popularly written books during the 1960s and 1970s on the themes of biological determinism, competition, and dominance, likening the roots of early human culture to the "male hierarchy" of a baboon troop. This "baboonization" of human behavior helped rationalize the social order: in the Fox and Tiger scenario, human baboons with briefcases people a contemporary world modeled on an imagined past – despite the fact we humans are only very distantly related to baboons and very different in some crucial aspects of our evolutionary trajectory as a species.

Academic programs[5] have self-replicating tendencies, as those on hiring committees frequently choose candidates whose perspectives are consistent with their own. Tiger and Fox expounded a pre-socio-biological formulation of biological reductionism as explanatory of human social behavior (Sperling 1997). In the 1990s Robert Trivers, a key theoretician of sociobiology (Trivers 1971), joined Tiger and Fox at Rutgers.[6] Trivers' human research agenda exemplifies the kind of biological determinism, the obsession with competing genetic interests, which Montagu had so strongly contested. For instance, since the mid-1990s, Trivers and a number of collaborators from other institutions have been measuring subtle asymmetries in the bodies of school children in St Elizabeth Parish, Jamaica, in order to test the sociobiological hypothesis that greater bodily symmetry indicates greater Darwinian fitness (Rutgers Jamaican Symmetry Project). Fluctuating asymmetry "refers to small deviations from perfect bilateral symmetry that fluctuate randomly left to right across a population and tend to cancel out to give perfect symmetry for the population itself" (Trivers et al. 1999). According to Trivers and his research collaborators, fluctuating asymmetry is a sensitive indicator of resistance to stress over development and an important index of adult fitness, and therefore the ability to attract potential reproductive partners.

This hypothesis was first studied in research with various species that sought to define the selective value of fluctuating asymmetry across populations. These studies of fruit flies and flowering plants, for example, are equivocal, and there are serious questions about the degree to which symmetry plays a role in fitness and selection, if any. Yet, as is so often the case with sociobiology, extrapolation from selective studies of some organism is followed by an untested proposition about humans (Gould 1986; Lancaster 2003).

Symmetry is an important evolutionary feature of all higher organisms, but the precise degree of body symmetry varies across any population. Obviously there is a genetic basis for this basic body plan, but many factors besides genes may affect an individual's proportions over the course of development, as Franz Boas showed long ago. It is unclear from research on a variety of organisms that symmetry always correlates with greater health and thus biological fitness (Santos 2001). All things being equal, bodily symmetry may turn out to be one, among many, indices of overall health of an organism during development. But all things are seldom equal in human life, and many factors in the environment, both positive and negative, interact with genes to affect the course of human development. Two simple illustrations will suffice: humans almost universally favor one hand over the other, invariably resulting in a degree of hand and arm asymmetry that varies with the degree of muscle use. The contrast is most striking in athletes and others who habitually work one arm. Environmental disorders unrelated to genes, such as Fetal Alcohol Syndrome, also skew symmetry during development, factors not easily controlled for in studies of human populations. The Jamaican Symmetry Project has assigned each child (ages 5–11) a number and is attempting to longitudinally correlate degrees of asymmetry with such factors as "dancing ability, their attractiveness to others, their number of friends and the degree to which they are rated as aggressive by their classmates" (Rutgers Jamaican Symmetry Project 2006). St Elizabeth is a poor parish on an island with a Third World economy, a depleted agricultural sector, and a population largely descended from former African slaves. It probably would have been difficult to conduct such research on American children for a variety of reasons, whereas in Jamaica, researchers can pay a small fee to each family of a child enrolled in the study.[7] One wonders if Boas and Montagu are turning over in their graves!

What would Montagu's evolutionary biology program have become had he continued as chair at Rutgers? Montagu wrote in the 1950s, " 'Heredity' isn't one thing and 'environment' another. 'Heredity' includes the environment. You 'inherit' your environment just as much as you inherit your biological endowment. In fact, there can be no biological endowment without an environment" (Montagu 1957). As he had done in his earlier studies of race and intelligence, it seems clear that Montagu would have undertaken and encouraged research in biological anthropology engaging the complex links between history, culture, and biology (in contrast to the biological reductionism of Rutgers principal evolutionary anthropologists). It is clear from his research and writing that he would have been interested in how the biological and social development of poor Jamaican children relates to the political-economic context of their lives.

There are hopeful signs that such a perspective, largely side-tracked in the post-World War II period, may be making a comeback. The "Cardboard Darwinism" (Gould 1986) that germinated at Rutgers and other American universities during the Cold War is still a very influential trend in a number of disciplines, particularly in departments of biological anthropology and psychology. But there is increasing resistance to the reductionism of sociobiology within evolutionary anthropology. A number of evolutionary anthropologists are working to build a new biocultural synthesis, one which studies the intersections of human biology and culture with the political-economic realities of human populations on a global scale (Goodman and Leatherman 1998). The integrative approaches to biocultural studies pioneered by Boas and Montagu, supported by increasingly sophisticated research and databases, are perhaps undergoing a renaissance. This may reflect, among other things, responses to the evidence emerging from modern research of the developmental plasticity of the human organism in relation to many aspects of the economic, political, and social environment in which we develop.

History, whether of individuals or research programs, is often too complex, multifactorial, and contingent to be reduced to one narrative. Among other factors, Cold War ideology resonated with, and was supported by, evolutionary hypotheses that emphasized individual competitiveness in evolutionary outcomes. Politics intersected in important ways with the operations of science in specific instances to advance that perspective. The research of anthropologist David Price (2004; see also Price in this volume) has revealed that a number of progressive anthropologists, many of them Boasians, were blackballed during the McCarthy period. We don't really know the big picture: at how many universities the blacklist influenced the hiring and firing of scientists, and thus, the practice of science across many disciplines. Ellen Schrecker notes that:

The academy did not fight McCarthyism. It contributed to it.... In its collaboration with McCarthyism, the academic community behaved just like every other major institution in American life. Such a discovery is demoralizing, for the nation's colleges and universities have traditionally encouraged higher expectations.... The academy's enforcement of McCarthyism had silenced an entire generation of radical intellectuals and snuffed out all meaningful opposition to the official version of the Cold War. When by the late fifties, the hearings and dismissals tapered off, it was not because they encountered resistance, but because they were no longer necessary. All was quiet on the academic front. (Shrecker 1986: 340)

In a political period in which those considered to be enemies of the state were ruthlessly harassed, fired, and sometimes imprisoned, Hoover, McCarthy, and their agents determined that Montagu's ideas were a danger to the social, political, and economic order. Perhaps they were correct. What Montagu and his family endured during this period is a private matter, but the loss of his insights to evolutionary science during the Cold War, a significant formative period for modern biological anthropology, should be a matter for public scrutiny. Political interference in science has escalated since September 11, 2001 under the Bush administration's national security agenda. In 2004 the Union of Concerned Scientists issued a long report, signed by many notable American scientists, detailing attempts by the administration to manipulate and interfere with American science (Union of Concerned Scientists 2004). What happened a half century ago to many university faculty, and to the research they had hoped to pursue, has pressing lessons both for those interested in academic freedom and for practitioners of science today.

NOTES

1. All material on Ashley Montagu's childhood is derived from my interviews with Montagu during 1998 and 1999, and from Montagu's unpublished correspondence and papers, to which his family generously provided me access. These papers and correspondence were subsequently archived at the American Philosophical Society in Philadelphia (Ashley Montagu Papers). Andrew P. Lyons' excellent discussion of Montagu in "The Neotenic Career of M.F. Ashley Montagu" (1996) has aided my understanding of the development and breadth of Montagu's vision, as have Stevan Harnad's writings (1980a, 1980b). This chapter is dedicated to my father, Abraham Sperling, who continues to inspire my interest in iconoclasm in general and Montagu in particular.

2. Montagu was a participant in many mid-twentieth-century progressive causes, most notably those associated with the struggle to end American race segregation, and support of the United Nations and the cause of social justice on a global scale. These involvements were of interest to the FBI. It is also evident from his FBI file that agents scrutinized his writing and speeches about human nature, cooperation and competition, noting that they seemed suspect and anti-capitalist.

3. Rutgers Dean Owen and Montagu communicated enthusiastically about the prospect of Montagu developing a full and ambitious program of study in anthropology at Rutgers, as is evident from their early correspondence about the position (Ashley Montagu Papers 1946–56).

4. Marjorie Montagu, Ashley Montagu's wife, recounted to me the events surrounding his passport. It was recalled by US Department of State in response, apparently, to his anti-Vietnam War efforts. An important Supreme Court Case on this matter concerning another activist whose passport had been taken by the government, was decided against the State Department, and Montagu's passport was subsequently returned.

5. The cultural studies program at Rutgers is today chaired by a feminist and postmodernist. As at a number of other institutions, the perspectives of biological anthropologists are at odds with those of their cultural peers.

6. Sociobiologists are not necessarily political conservatives (but political conservatives such as Newt Gingrich have made much use of pop sociobiology). Trivers' political views are decidedly critical of the status quo (he is, apparently, a "white" member of the Black Panther Party, and recently collaborated with Noam Chomsky on an article and in online discussion of deception and self-deception among humans and other organisms for *Seed Magazine*).

7. A brief description of the Jamaican Asymmetry Project may be found online at: http://anthro.rutgers.edu/faculty/trivers.shtml#jamaica

ARCHIVAL SOURCES

Ashley Montagu Papers, 1935–99, Archives of the American Philosophical Society, Philadelphia.
FBI File HQ100-402992. Ashley Montagu.
Lewis Webster Jones Papers, Rutgers University Archives, Rutgers University Library, New Brunswick, NJ.

REFERENCES

Barkan, Elazar. 1996. The Politics of the Science of Race: Ashley Montagu and UNESCO's Anti-racist Declarations. In *Race and Other Misadventures: Essays in Honor of Ashley Montagu in his Ninetieth Year*, pp. 96–105. Larry T. Reynolds and Leonard Lieberman, eds. Dix Hill, NY: General Hall.

Boas, Franz. 1912. *Changes in Bodily Form of Descendants of Immigrants* (Reprinted from the Reports of the US Immigration Commission). New York: Columbia University Press.

Daniels, Les. 2000. *Wonder Woman: The Complete History*. San Francisco: Chronicle Books.

Darwin, Charles. 2004 (1871). *The Descent of Man and Selection in Relation to Sex*. New York: Barnes and Noble.

De Beauvoir, Simone. 1953. *The Second Sex*. London: Jonathan Cape.

Friedan, Betty. 1963. *The Feminine Mystique*. New York: Norton.

Goodman, Alan H. and Thomas L. Leatherman, eds. 1998. *Building a New Biocultural Synthesis: Political-economic Perspectives on Human Biology*. Ann Arbor: University of Michigan Press.

Gould, Stephen Jay. 1981. *The Mismeasure of Man*. New York: Norton.

—— 1986. Cardboard Darwinism. *New York Review of Books* 33: 47–54.

Harnad, Stevan. 1980a. Ashley Montagu Biographical Essay. *International Encyclopedia of the Social Sciences* 18: 535–37.

—— 1980b. Biographical Entry for Ashley Montagu. OAI: cogprints.Soton. ac.uk: 1653.

Lancaster, Roger N. 2003. *The Trouble with Nature: Sex in Science and Popular Culture*. Berkeley: University of California Press.

Lewontin, Richard. 1972. The Apportionment of Human Diversity. *Evolutionary Biology* 6: 391–98.

Lombroso, Cesare. 1887. *L'Homme criminal*. Paris: F. Alcan.

Lyons, Andrew P. 1996. The Neotenic Career of M.F. Ashley Montagu. In *Race and Other Misadventures: Essays in Honor of Ashley Montagu in his Ninetieth Year*, pp. 3–22. Larry T. Reynolds and Leonard Lieberman, eds. Dix Hills, NY: General Hall.

Lyons, Harriet D. 1996. Sex, Race and Nature: Anthropology and Primitive Sexuality. In *Race and Other Misadventures: Essays in Honor of Ashley Montagu in his Ninetieth Year*, pp. 347–64. Larry T. Reynolds and Leonard Lieberman, eds. Dix Hills, NY: General Hall.

Marks, Jonathan. 1996. Science and Race. *American Behavioral Scientist* 40: 123–33.

—— 2000a. Ashley Montagu: 1905–1999. *Evolutionary Anthropology* 9(3): 111–12.

—— 2000b. Human Biodiversity as a Central Theme of Biological Anthropology: Then and Now. In *Racial Anthropology: Retrospective on Carleton Coon's The*

Origin of Races (1962), pp. 1–10. Berkeley, CA: Kroeber Anthropological Society Papers 84.

Montagu, Ashley. 1926. Intelligence Tests and the Negro in America. *WASU* (Journal of the West African Student Union of Great Britain) 1: 5–7.

—— 1940. The Socio-biology of Man. *Scientific Monthly* 50: 483–84.

—— 1942. The Genetical Theory of Race and Anthropological Method. *American Anthropologist* 44: 369–75.

—— 1952. *Darwin, Competition and Cooperation*. New York: Abelard-Schuman.

—— 1953. *The Natural Superiority of Women*. New York: Macmillan.

—— 1957. *Anthropology and Human Nature*. New York: Porter Sargent.

—— ed. 1968. *Man and Aggression*. New York: Oxford University Press.

—— 1969. *Sex, Man and Society*. New York: Putnam's.

—— 1970. *The Direction of Human Development*. New York: Hawthorne Books.

—— 1971. *The Elephant Man: A Study in Human Dignity*. London: Outerbridge and Lazard, Inc.

—— 1972. *Touching: The Human Significance of the Skin*. New York: Harper and Row.

—— 1976. *The Nature of Human Aggression*. New York: Oxford University Press.

—— 1978. *Learning Non-aggression*. New York: Oxford University Press.

—— 1997 (1942). *Man's Most Dangerous Myth: The Fallacy of Race*, 6th edn. Walnut Creek: CA: AltaMira Press.

Orwell, George 1983 (1949). *Nineteen Eighty-four*. New York: Signet.

Price, David H. 2004. *Threatening Anthropology: McCarthyism and the FBI's Surveillance of Activist Anthropologists*. Durham, NC: Duke University Press.

Reynolds, Larry T. and Leonard Lieberman, eds. 1996. *Race and Other Misadventures*. Dix Hill, NY: General Hall.

Rutgers Jamaican Symmetry Project. 2006. Official Website of Robert L. Trivers. Anthropology Department, Rutgers University. URL: http://anthro.rutgers. edu/faculty/trivers.shtml#jamaica

Santos, Mauro. 2001. Fluctuating Asymmetry is Nongenetically Related to Mating Success in *D. buzzatii*. *Evolution* 55(11): 2248–56.

Schrecker, Ellen. 1986. *No Ivory Tower: McCarthyism and the Universities*. New York: Oxford University Press.

Sperling, Susan. 1994. A Kinder, Gentler Social Darwinism: Reviews of Robert Wright's *The Moral Animal*, J. Philippe Rushton's *Race, Evolution, and Behavior*, and Patricia Shipman's *The Evolution of Racism*. *The Nation* 259: 18.

—— 1997. Baboons with Briefcases vs. Langurs with Lipstick. In *The Gender Sexuality Reader*, pp. 249–64. Roger N. Lancaster and Micaela di Leonardo, eds. New York: Routledge.

—— 1999. Introduction. In Ashley Montagu, *The Natural Superiority of Women*, 5th edn. Walnut Creek, CA: AltaMira Press.

—— 2000. Ashley Montagu. *American Anthropologist* 102(3): 583–88.

—— 2006. Tribal Secrets and Pollution Anxieties: Ashley Montagu, McCarthyism, and Postwar Anthropology. *Teaching Anthropology: SACC Notes* 13(1): 30–34.

—— 2007. The Troop Trope: Baboon Behavior as a Model System in the Postwar Period. In *Science without Laws: Model Systems, Cases, Exemplary*

Narratives, pp. 110–31. Angela N.H. Creager, Elizabeth Lunbeck, and Norton Wise, eds. Durham, NC: Duke University Press.

—— Forthcoming. *Ashley Montagu: A Biography*. New York: Oxford University Press.

Stocking, George, ed. 1974. *A Franz Boas Reader: The Shaping of American Anthropology 1883–1911*. Chicago: University of Chicago Press.

Tiger, Lionel. 1987. *Men in Groups*, 2nd edn. New York: Rizzoli.

Tiger, Lionel and Robin Fox. 1971. *The Imperial Animal*. New York: Holt, Rinehart, and Winston.

Trivers, Robert L. 1971. The Evolution of Reciprocal Altruism. *Quarterly Review of Biology* 46: 35–57.

Trivers, Robert L., J.T. Manning, R. Thornhill, and M. McGuire. 1999. The Jamaican Symmetry Project: A Long-term Study of Fluctuating Asymmetry in Rural Jamaican Children. *Human Biology* 71: 419–32.

UNESCO. 1952. *The Race Concept: The Race Question in Modern Science*. Paris: UNESCO.

Union of Concerned Scientists. 2004. Statement on Scientific Integrity (February 18, 2004). Website of the Union of Concerned Scientists. URL: http://www.ucsusa.org

2 MATERIALISM'S FREE PASS: KARL WITTFOGEL, McCARTHYISM, AND THE "BUREAUCRATIZATION OF GUILT"

David H. Price

Only Nixon can go to China. (Ancient Vulcan Proverb)

Contemporary anthropologists' reactions to the life and work of German-American sinologist Karl Wittfogel are complicated by political, epistemological, and historical factors.[1] At the time of Wittfogel's death, Ernest Gellner observed that his work "continues to exercise strong attraction and repulsion" (1988: 22). Postmodern scholars universally view Wittfogel as the mechanistic black sheep misfit of the Frankfurt School;[2] orthodox Marxists despise his counter-revolutionary critique of the Soviet state; students of McCarthyism view his appearance as a friendly witness before the McCarran committee as a betrayal of fundamental principles of academic freedom and common decency. While archaeologists and cultural evolutionarily inclined anthropologists still pursue Wittfogel's hydraulic theories, most contemporary anthropologists studying irrigation systems usually cite and then quickly dismiss Wittfogel's theory of hydraulic society.

With the 1957 publication of his *magnum opus, Oriental Despotism: A Comparative Study of Total Power*, Wittfogel drew on over three decades of research on the demographic, technological, environmental, and political similarities shared by the early hydraulic states in the Old and New Worlds. Wittfogel used Marx and Engels' undeveloped notion of an Asiatic Mode of Production to examine early state formations in regions as diverse as China, Mesopotamia, Mesoamerica, Egypt, and the Indus River Valley. Wittfogel's work examined how the world's pristine hydraulic states each shared similar circumscribed environmental features that could only be exploited beyond a regional level by developing similar technologies and bureaucracies that simultaneously increased agricultural production and the state's despotic power. While *Oriental Despotism* strayed from this central

37

explanatory task and also undertook a wandering critique of all despotic governmental systems, his vision of recurrent demographic, economic, environmental, and technological features leading to the development of similar state formations became a powerful central idea in American anthropology's ecological movements in the 1950s, 1960s and 1970s.

While Wittfogel and his work have largely faded from view, his theories played an important role in maintaining overt materialist analysis in American anthropological theory during the 1950s. This chapter explores the contradictory roles played by Wittfogel during this oppressive period of Cold War witch-hunts, when Wittfogel functioned as a propagator of materialist analysis even while abetting forces of McCarthyism that were devoted to extinguishing Marxist-based materialist analysis from American classrooms.

This chapter draws upon archival materials and correspondence as well as documents released by the FBI under the Freedom of Information Act to explore how Wittfogel, a reckless Red-baiting anti-communist became the central conduit maintaining materialist strains of theory during the McCarthy period. During the 1940s and 1950s Wittfogel operated as an FBI informer and friendly witness who settled personal academic scores with Marxists and imagined Marxists with whom he disagreed. This episode provides an important insight not only into the narrow range of ecological and materialist anthropology that began to emerge in the late 1950s, but also establishes how Wittfogel collected a tangible reward for his public and private attacks on others: his position as an FBI informer and friendly witness to the McCarran committee guaranteed him an uncontested concession to openly practice a form of Marxist-derived materialist analysis that would have brought any other practicing historian or anthropologist before the sort of congressional Red-baiting commission that he abetted. My interest in examining these issues is not to criticize anthropologists who drew upon elements of Wittfogel's theoretical analysis; in fact, I am among those who have used, as well as criticized, elements of his hydraulic theory (see Price 1994, 1995). My interest in considering anthropologists' use of Wittfogel is to explore how the political economy of the 1950s influenced both the generation and acceptance of Wittfogel's hydraulic theories.

WITTFOGEL'S EARLY CAREER AND THE DEVELOPMENT OF THE HYDRAULIC THEORY

Karl August Wittfogel was born in Woltersdorf, Germany, in 1896. He joined the Communist Party in 1921, wrote communist essays and fiction and studied at the University of Frankfurt's Institute for Social

Research during the 1920s. He studied Marxist economics during the heyday of the Frankfurt School, receiving his PhD in 1928. Wittfogel's ties to the University of Frankfurt were formed by his association with the economic historian Carl Grünberg. Though Wittfogel remained at the institute after Max Horkheimer assumed the directorship, Wittfogel's more mechanical approaches to historical materialist analysis left him out of synch with the new, dominant "critical" direction of the Frankfurt School.

Wittfogel's early interest in Marxist economics and his knowledge of Chinese agrarian history led to the publication of *Wirtschaft und Gessellschaft Chinas* (Economy and Society in China) in 1931. *Wirtschaft* was a revolutionary work that presented many of the key ideas that would occupy Wittfogel throughout his career – but the tone, tact, and velocity of specific arguments would later be differentially stressed as Wittfogel's work became overbearingly saturated with Cold War anti-communism. In *Wirtschaft* Wittfogel used a Marxist materialist analysis to examine the role of centralized governmental systems in building and operating large irrigation projects.

As formulated by Marx and Engels, socialism was to develop through a unilinear path leading from feudalism through industrial capitalism to socialism. Marx and Engels' scant writings on the Asiatic Mode of Production presented problems for the Soviet state because, according to them, such political structures could evolve into a bureaucratic ruling class that controlled the means of production – instead of the egalitarian political structures which were the professed goal of the Soviet state. This problem led to the 1931 Leningrad conference's denunciation of the Asiatic Mode of Production. This denunciation launched Wittfogel on an epistemological and political quest that found him at odds with the Soviet stance and eventually communism as a whole, yet Wittfogel remained a self-styled, pseudo-Marxist, materialist scholar as he developed his hydraulic hypothesis (see Price 1994).

Wittfogel's analysis of China's historic economic and social formations led him to clash with Soviet theorists, and the resulting criticism led to his own rejection of communism after clashing with Soviet interpretations of Marx and the Asiatic Mode of Production (Lewin 1981; Peet 1985). Another significant factor influencing the nature of Wittfogel's anti-communism came from his frustrating experiences in the Party as the Nazi rise to power found German Communists battling Social Democrats instead of making common cause against Nazi Fascists (Ulmen 1978: 134–46). Wittfogel's departure from the Party left him a bitter anti-Leninist, anti-Stalinist, and anti-communist, and while he soon dumped his political Marxist orientation he retained a strong mechanical materialist analysis.

G.L. Ulmen claims that in 1931 Wittfogel was the *only* member of the Frankfurt Institute to "abandon his scholarly work in order to fight Hitler," a cause he undertook with relentless journalistic attacks on Hitler and his followers; and while Wittfogel was certainly an active anti-Nazi Ulmen's hagiographic tendencies appear to underestimate the anti-Nazi commitments of other Frankfurt scholars (Ulmen 1978: 146). For this work Wittfogel was arrested and imprisoned by the Nazis in March 1933. He was held in several concentration camps, including the Esterwegen camp. After nine months of imprisonment he was set free after his wife Olga Wittfogel rallied famous British, German, and American scholars, including Harold Laski, R.H. Tawney, Sidney Webb, and Karl Haushofer, to write letters to German officials pleading for Wittfogel's release.[3] Upon his release from the concentration camp, Wittfogel traveled to England, where he began writing a novel based on his concentration camp experiences. The novel, *Staatliches Konzentrationslager VII, Eine "Erziehungsanstalt" im Dritten Reich* was later published under the pseudonym Klaus Hinrichs (Wittfogel 1936).

Wittfogel immigrated to the US in late 1934. He soon traveled to China, and later accepted teaching positions at both Columbia University and then the University of Washington. In 1938 Wittfogel published an article on "The Theory of Oriental Society," analyzing trends in Chinese economic history. Working on the Chinese History Project with generous funding provided by the Rockefeller Foundation, Wittfogel began work on an ambitious project examining Marx's theory of the Asiatic Mode of Production as manifest not only in China, but also in pre-Columbian America and the pristine states of the Old World. With time (and in ways similar to his propensity to find communist influences in those scholars he had disagreements with) he began to see despotic "hydraulic" state formations in *any* political systems not to his liking. Wittfogel came to see all oppressive states as expressions of the same forces that gave rise to hydraulic states. His hydraulic model for understanding the peculiarities of a particular mode of production became his litmus test for interpreting all of cultural life. Wittfogel's examinations of pristine hydraulic states began on solid terraqueous ground, but he soon lost his way as he confused hydraulic despotism with all centralized state managerial formations. While his work on pristine state formations remains of interest to archaeologists and cultural evolutionary anthropologists, his classification of disparate political systems as "hydraulic societies" has been widely rejected.[4] As Donald Worster observed, "What had begun in the twenties as a search for scientific truth and positive laws of society had by the fifties become an elaborate web of inconsistencies, demonology and ethnocentrism" (1985: 28).

The FBI first became interested in Wittfogel in the early 1940s. In November 1940 the FBI reported that a Chilean political group attacked Wittfogel for opposing the entry of Otto Strasser to the United States (FBI HQ 100-381178, p. 44).[5] A July 22, 1942, "Censorship Report" given to the FBI noted that Wittfogel was then the director of the Institute of Social Research. The report noted Wittfogel's past communist and radical affiliations (FBI HQ 100 381178, p. 48)

A July 10, 1947, FBI interview with Wittfogel probed his early personal history and focused on his interactions with his former friend, the German communist Gerhard Eisler. Eisler was then under investigation as a Soviet spy and Wittfogel provided the FBI with a thorough account of his interactions with Eisler in the 1920s and early 1930s, including an account of Eisler's mandated "reeducation" by the Comintern in Moscow in the 1930s after Eisler had broken with party doctrine (FBI HQ 100-381178, p. 74). Wittfogel summarized his own political and professional development for the FBI:

... by 1928 he had a well established reputation as a researcher in economics and had taken his doctorate at Frankfort University. He stated that he had become greatly interested in the agrarian history of China and when not teaching classes was engaged in research for a book on the "History of the Chinese Agrarian Economy". He stated that one of his chief interests was the "theory of Asiatic despotism" which he explained in brief as a study of the various economies organized by the long series of despots who successfully conquered and ruled the Asiatic masses from Genghis Khan. In 1931 he published his volume, "Wirtschaft und Gessellschaft Chinas" (Economic Society of China) which he frankly stated was a study of Chinese economic history written along Marxist lines.

He stated that the beginning of the split with the Communist Party occurred when his book was reviewed unfavorably by a number of Russian economic writers because of what they apparently considered unfavorable comparisons between the margin of freedom allowed the ancient Chinese peasant as opposed to the completely regimented lives of all sections of the Soviet system. Wittfogel stated that he had not pointed this material out as a matter of comparison, but that the Russian economists criticized his inclusion of material relating that under the Asiatic despotism theories of Wittfogel the Oriental peasant had certain military and economic duties to the war lord which once served, permitted him to farm or otherwise function in the economic structure of China for his own personal profit. (FBI HQ 100-381178, pp. 74–75)

Wittfogel later clarified the importance of the Soviet's rejection of his work in his decision to leave the Party, telling the FBI that:

... the period of 1931–1933 resulted in this breaking away from the Communist Party, explaining that no single factor was responsible but that the unfavorable reviews of his book on China, the coolness of the Russian press with respect to his anti-Hitler writings, and the increased contact with persons of other political parties in the anti-Hitler fight had contributed to his estrangement from the Party. (FBI HQ 100-381178, p. 78)

The FBI did not know what to make of Wittfogel – this Marxist, former Communist, anti-Soviet historian who seemed driven by some measure of spiteful political and personal payback. In May 1947 George Taylor told the FBI that Wittfogel had been "a renegade of the Party" (FBI HQ 100-381178, p. 12).

Wittfogel had married anthropologist Esther Goldfrank in 1940. His life with Goldfrank fostered financial security and would later help connect Wittfogel with an anthropological audience receptive to elements of the hydraulic hypothesis he was developing. Goldfrank had studied under and worked with Franz Boas at Columbia University, where she became a specialist in the cultures of Pueblo and Blackfoot Indians (Goldfrank 1978). In Esther Goldfrank, Wittfogel found a like-minded anti-communist who shared his hatred of communist academics.

After the American Anthropological Association began to feel the impact of anti-communism – first with anthropologist Melville Jacobs' appearance before the Canwell Commission and the University of Washington's Faculty Committee on Tenure and Academic Freedom in late 1948, and later when archaeologist Richard Morgan experienced similar troubles at the Ohio State Museum – Esther Goldfrank shared confidences with Yale anthropologist George Murdock concerning her suspicions of the communist inclinations of some anthropologists. Goldfrank appeared unaware that Murdock had already become an FBI informer, sending J. Edgar Hoover a detailed report in January 1949 listing a dozen anthropologists he believed to be either communists or commie dupes (see Price 2004: 71–75). In September 1949, Goldfrank wrote Murdock of her concerns that anthropologist Edward Haskell was spreading communist ideologies amongst anthropologists. She wrote:

As I mentioned at the meeting I am concerned with Haskell's role in Applied Anthropology and [the] AAAS [American Association for the Advancement of Science] as set forth in Human Organization, spring 1949, page 28.[6]

You will see that not only is he Chairman of the Organizing Committee of what [Conrad] Arensberg calls the "nascent" Council for United Research – he is also our representative on this body. Since I know that he will unify research exactly one way – to coincide with the Stalin line – I feel that we should do something about this. Moreover, as Arensberg further happily announces, he will convene another three day symposium in December in N.Y. under the AAAS on Integration and Disintegration. We should certainly attend this one.

If you want to know his views they are on record in a open letter to Pearl Buck in China Today in the 'thirties, and in 1947 in a paper that he read at the N.Y. Academy of Sciences, in which he gave Marxian societal categories "according to Stalin" – and you know what that means. This is printed in their Transactions. It is dreadful to think that such persons are still being placed in positions where they can manipulate politically unaware social scientists. Jacobs and Stern have done it neatly in their popular Outline of Anthropology and apparently the Linguists are now also doing their bit. Even if [Jacobs'] paper was not too well organized, he is certainly correct when he points out that linguistics, like biology and social science, [is] now being pressed into Stalin's developmental scheme. This means an emphasis on Slavery as an early form everywhere and the elimination of the concept of Oriental society which is characterized by the bureaucracy as the ruling class – and this concept as you know does not stem from Marx, but was developed by Adam Smith and John Stewart Mill as well as others in their times.

Haskell, Lloyd Warner told me, was considered a fanatic and somewhat crazy in Chicago, and his brother's camp for children, he used to seek every means to indoctrinate them with Stalinist ideology – one of his cute little ways was to tell them stories about "Trotsky, the Rat." I hold no [grief] for Trotsky, but this sort of thing gives some [gauge] of his orthodoxy. Haskell has also played an important role as "informant" to Arensberg on Eastern European cultures in the Benedict-Mead project. (He worked [with] Georg Dimitrov, who recently died in Moscow conveniently is in State). Arensberg['s] role in all this is far from clear. He got Haskell into Brooklyn College and has been backing him ever since. When I asked him one day on the street corner whether Haskell was still at Brooklyn he said no and when I asked what he was doing, Arensberg said he was working with the peace movement, and when I said "Oh with Hiss," Arensberg blushed violently, which was unusual, and stammered which was not, and said, "Oh I really don't know the name of it." Now it would be interesting to know why Arensberg was so eager to cover Haskell, especially on a point which could be readily established. All I can think of is that I took him off guard. Sometimes I think he may be another of those Harvard boys who wants to pull the strings, – another, but this time, a Republican Hiss. He is too sophisticated not to know what is going on.

Arensberg is also very interested in Integration and Disintegration and he seemed somewhat surprised to discover that I did not share his enthusiasm for the former where the ghetto Jews were concerned. You know he is the "convener" on Eastern Europe for the Benedict-Mead project. He said, "But it fits so beautifully into Benedict's category of integration," and that obviously endowed it with all kinds of positive values. And Benedict isn't alone on this. Collier, Thompson, even Cora Du Bois and Gillin, and there are many other [who] feel that there is something sacred about integration. The question is integration for what? But what could be more comforting to a Stalinist than to cite well-known authorities whose political affiliations are clearly non-Stalinist to bolster a theory that attaches positive [value] to integration, and thus by implication raises Stalinist Russia to the peak of societal ordering. Some of us may feel with Orwell that at many levels integration has devastating drawbacks? (EG Box 1, EG to GPM, Sept. 14, 1949)

While Haskell, Jacobs, and Stern did have Marxist orientations, Goldfrank's broad speculations about others were dangerous and wrong. Goldfrank's claim that Conrad Arensberg was somehow a Marxist or involved in some lurking communist conspiracy not only mischaracterized Arensberg and his work, but also revealed the depths and dangers of Goldfrank's anti-communist paranoia. Arensberg was no communist, but neither were the other mainstream anthropologists who Goldfrank drew into her imagined web of complicity.

The notion that Ruth Benedict, Cora Du Bois, John Gillin, Laura Thompson, John Collier, and Margaret Mead were part of a larger communist conspiracy would be funny if Goldfrank had not been recklessly writing these suspicions to Murdock, himself an FBI informer. Under such circumstances, these speculations could have serious consequences.[7]

IPR, WITTFOGEL, AND THE McCARRAN HEARINGS

Senator Joseph McCarthy, Senator Pat McCarran, and other isolationist conservatives coordinated attacks on the Institute of Pacific Relations (IPR) in the late 1940s and early 1950s, claiming that the IPR had become a domestic front for the international communist conspiracy. Though the IPR had been studying Chinese history and culture since 1925, after the rise of communism in the post-war era, the progressive politics of many of the scholars at IPR brought public attacks from McCarran, McCarthy, and American business leaders like Alfred Kohlberg, who suffered financial losses after Chinese communists nationalized the textile mills he held in China. IPR scholars like Philip Jessup, Frederick Field, and Owen Lattimore were attacked as suspected communist agents, abusing their academic positions to further the interests of the Red Chinese.

Beginning in 1950, the Senate's International Security Subcommittee's (SISS) chair, Senator Pat McCarran, investigated the IPR and its journal, *Pacific Affairs*. McCarran declared that his goal was to discover:

... to what extent the IPR was infiltrated and influenced by agents of the communist world conspiracy [and] to what extent these agents and their dupes worked through the Institute into the United States Government to the point where they exerted an influence on United States far eastern policy. (in Schrecker 1986: 164)

Owen Lattimore was accused of abusing his position as editor of *Pacific Affairs* to push Soviet communist views in IPR publications and editorials, and Wittfogel was used with great effect by the SISS to support such arguments. McCarran's hearings led to charges of perjury against Owen Lattimore, charges that were not sustained though two separate trials. During such a witch-hunt it mattered little that the IPR had long been funded by such status quo maintaining foundations as the Carnegie Endowment for International Peace and the Laura Spellman Rockefeller Memorial Foundation. McCarran and McCarthy accused IPR scholars of maintaining pro-communist biases, and the resulting purges of IPR associated scholars in academia and the Department of State left a significant scar on American foreign policy. Indeed, some have argued that this loss of America's China hands at the Department of State led to the future American tragedy in Southeast Asia, as the resulting "Foreign Service purge of dissenters from our China policy left no one around to dissent from our Vietnam policy" (Navasky 1989: xvii).

In a private interview with the FBI on April 2, 1950, Wittfogel told agents that he had traveled throughout rural western China with Owen Lattimore in 1934. He reported that while traveling they:

> ... had some political discussions. At this time, Wittfogel stated that Lattimore's attitude toward the Soviet System was tolerant although Lattimore committed criticism. According to Wittfogel, in the ensuing years, of his acquaintance with Lattimore, it was his impression that Lattimore moved increasingly toward a pro-Soviet attitude and also in favor of Chinese Reds. (FBI HQ 100-381178, p. 9)

Wittfogel criticized Lattimore's uncritical acceptance of the Nazi–Soviet Pact, and he provided detailed accounts of several lunchtime conversations he had had in which Lattimore refused to criticize friends who held what Wittfogel characterized as pro-Soviet views (FBI HQ 100-381178, pp. 9–10). That Wittfogel obsessed on such disagreements for so long indicates more about his own personality that it does about Lattimore's political orientation. Wittfogel told the FBI that he had saved some of his correspondence with Lattimore that clarified why he was suspicious of his pro-Soviet views. When the FBI asked Wittfogel to turn these letters over to the FBI for inspection, Wittfogel was reportedly "extremely reluctant," but he promised to give the request "serious consideration" (FBI HQ 100-381178, p. 11).

The FBI reviewed several of Lattimore's published and unpublished letters, including some letters apparently provided by Wittfogel (FBI HQ 100-381178, p. 25); other records indicate that some other individual with access to IPR records was also providing the FBI with documents (FBI HQ 100-381178, p. 33). On April 3, 1950 Wittfogel gave the FBI access to letters he had exchanged with Lattimore between January and March 1947, including letters in which Wittfogel told Lattimore that he no longer wanted him to write an introduction to his forthcoming book on China (FBI HQ 100-381178, p. 119). The FBI noted that Lattimore had expressed friendship and gratitude to Wittfogel in various publications, feelings of friendship that apparently were not shared by Wittfogel (e.g. FBI HQ 100-381178, p. 37).

BEHIND CLOSED DOORS

In December 1950, Wittfogel testified as a friendly witness before a closed door session of Senator Patrick McCarran's International

Security Subcommittee. Wittfogel agreed to name names and to condemn his fellow scholars on condition that all he said would be withheld from public scrutiny. The committee agreed to these terms, though they acted with duplicity and no sooner had Wittfogel pointed his finger of blame than his testimony was splashed across the pages of the news. On December 8, 1950, the *Washington Times Herald* reported that Wittfogel's testimony had suggested that Owen Lattimore was a communist agent. The transcripts of these closed-door sessions remain sealed, and while they have not been released by the FBI, an 85-page report titled "Congressional Information from Executive Session" appears in Wittfogel's FBI file (FBI HQ 100-381178-Section 2). Portions of the hearing's transcripts leaked to the *Times Herald* establish Wittfogel's enthusiastic cooperation with the committee. The paper reported that Wittfogel testified:

... he first became acquainted with Lattimore in 1935 in China. They were good friends, he testified, until late in 1944, when Lattimore defended the Russian purge trials as "democratic" and voiced his contempt for "ex-Communists." Asked directly if Lattimore was a Communist, Wittfogel said it was "a very serious" question which he could not answer. He had no definite knowledge, he confessed, of any "ties or associations" held by Lattimore with the Communist Party.

"Owen Lattimore is a very complicated man and the American Communists were a bunch of suckers to him," he testified. "He was never interested in the little man. He would be interested in the big shots in Moscow. I think he despised American Communists because they were little people and had no success. I don't see in Lattimore's disposition anything that would attract him to a very unsuccessful movement like the American Communist party at that time."

Lattimore was only mildly interested in Chinese Communists in 1935, when they were a minority, but he became more interested later on, Wittfogel said, as they increased in power.

"He was sympathetic to a number of things Russia did, no doubt about it," Wittfogel testified. "The sum total of his writings makes a friendly case for Chinese Communists."

"I talked with him in 1944 about the future of Korea. He thought it was not a bad thing if Korea would be turned over to the Russians. Then both of us blew up."

Committee investigators had subpoenaed Wittfogel for questioning after obtaining a translation of an article printed in Chinese in the Central Daily News of Formosa last April 21. This article stated that Lattimore was under the influence of Wittfogel, a "first rate Marxist writer!" (FBI HQ 100-381178, pp. 142–43)

Wittfogel had expected that his attacks on Lattimore would remain out of the public's view and he was outraged when these apparently verbatim reports of his testimony appeared in the press.

But Wittfogel's disappointment at being publicly exposed fingering his friends and colleagues did not diminish his willingness to cooperate with the FBI. In June 1951 Wittfogel told the FBI that he was convinced that Philleo Nash was an agent of communism. Wittfogel reported that:

... he and his wife have always been suspicious of the political leanings of Nash and have drawn the opinion that he has Communist leaning and sympathies. [Wittfogel and Goldfrank] advised that their opinion comes from their associations in the educational field together and from the limited personal and social associations they had while [redacted] was associated with the University of Wisconsin. He advised that he has no other information to substantiate his own personal opinion. (FBI HQ 121-12261-40)

On another occasion Wittfogel reported that, while socializing with Nash, Wittfogel had "told Nash and his wife of his analysis of Marx and Lenin, which was highly critical. On this occasion Nash evinced a sullen reaction and refused to discuss the analysis, although he had previously indicated some knowledge of the subject" (FBI HQ 121-12261-47).

Even more suspicious, Wittfogel reported to the FBI, was Nash's friendliness combined with his reluctance to open up to Wittfogel. Wittfogel told the FBI that, "Nash had always tried to be very friendly, but that both he and his wife felt that Nash was concealing his inner feelings" (FBI HQ 121-12261-47). But Nash was no communist. He was a Roosevelt Democrat pressing for racial integration and moderate international relations – political work that intensified Wittfogel's suspicions (Price 2004). Wittfogel's egotism and insecurity were apparent in the FBI reports, as any individual or group that did not side with his critical analysis was seen as linked to the communist conspiracy. In the FBI's records, Wittfogel appeared confident and comfortable informing on those who disagreed with him, either politically, personally, or professionally.

In response to a subpoena, Wittfogel testified before an open session of McCarran's Senate International Security Subcommittee on August 7, 1951. Among those in attendance were George Taylor, who testified later that same afternoon, and Senator Joseph McCarthy (see Cumings 2002; Ulmen 1978: 287). Forty-five years later, when I interviewed Taylor about Wittfogel and his own testimony to the SISS, Taylor claimed that both he and Wittfogel had been put under an extraordinary amount of pressure and that they had both been reluctant witnesses (Price 1996). But there is nothing in the transcripts of these hearings supporting such a view. Taylor's claims of pressure appear to be the machinations of latter-day regret-tinged recollections: the transcripts of the hearings find Taylor and Wittfogel treated with respect and patience as they attacked former friends and colleagues.

Wittfogel testified to the committee that, after coming to Columbia University in the 1930s, he had met regularly with a group of graduate students who were reading and discussing Marxist materials. The students identified by Wittfogel in his testimony included Lawrence Rosinger, Herbert Norman, Moses Finkelstein (Finkelstein had been one of Boas's favorite assistants, who later left the United States for Britain where he became the great classical historian Sir M.I. Finley), and Daniel Thorner, all of whom refused to testify under Fifth Amendment protections after being named by Wittfogel (Tompkins 2006).

In this 1951 testimony, Wittfogel said that, as a student, Herbert Norman had not simply been interested in Marxism, he had been a Communist (FBI HQ 100-381178-599-603; Ybarra 2004). Years later, in 1957, the McCarran committee released Herbert Norman's name as a person of interest to the committee. When news of this renewed investigation reached Norman, then the Canadian Ambassador to Egypt, he became distraught and committed suicide by jumping off the rooftop of an eight-story building along Cairo's Corniche. Wittfogel later claimed that he had been bullied into stating that Norman was a communist, when all Wittfogel really knew was that Norman had been interested in discussing Marx, but such claims mattered little after Norman killed himself (Ulmen 1978: 325–34). The hearing's transcript recorded no such coercion of Wittfogel, who was a friendly and cooperative witness. To get some feeling of the warmth with which Wittfogel was welcomed by the committee, consider the welcome speech with which Chairman McCarran greeted Wittfogel as he prepared to swear him in for his testimony:

The committee, at the outset wants to express its gratitude to you for the information that you have given and that you will give us here. The United States of America is fighting for its life, is fighting for its existence, and those who, like yourself, occupy important places, are to be commended for the courage and the forthrightness that you display in coming to this committee and giving us facts.

You are here under subpoena. The country will owe you a debt of gratitude for truth regardless of what may be the result. The nation owes a debt of gratitude to all who tell the truth in these matters regardless of who may be affected.

Will you kindly stand and be sworn? (FBI HQ 100-381178, p. 511)

Most of Wittfogel's testimony concerned his former friend and colleague Owen Lattimore. During World War II, Lattimore had been an advisor to Chiang Kai-shek, but Lattimore grew increasingly critical of him during the war. After the war, Lattimore's criticisms, and claims made by Soviet defector Alexander Barmine that Lattimore was a Soviet agent (claims that were later independently discredited) brought on an FBI investigation of Lattimore. In 1950, Senator McCarthy had accused Lattimore of being "the top Soviet espionage agent in the United States" (Kahin 2002: 129).

Lattimore and Wittfogel had been friends for decades, having traveled together in China in the 1930s and become members of a small, tight network of American-based sinologists living in China. As Wittfogel's anti-communism intensified, he mixed his political, personal, and professional views with his overriding anti-communist paradigm, and Lattimore's progressive and internationalist tendencies suggested to Wittfogel that he was a communist agent. During his testimony, Wittfogel focused on Lattimore's silence and facial expression some years earlier, when asked point-blank if he were a communist. Under Wittfogel's paradigm such an expression had only one interpretation. Silence did not mean silence, it meant yes. As Ellen Schrecker wrote:

The absence of any trace of Marxism in Lattimore's writing was a ruse, for Wittfogel an obvious sign that Lattimore was one of [as Wittfogel claimed,] "those elements of the periphery who are really closely coordinated and integrated in to the movement, but who try to promote the advantages of the movement without exposing themselves." (Schrecker 1986: 165–66)

Wittfogel's claims against Lattimore were based on innuendo and impressions; and for all the damage done to Lattimore's career and reputation, Wittfogel was only a four-flusher.

Wittfogel's attacks on Owen Lattimore and other scholars also threatened the careers of several anthropologists. During his testimony, Wittfogel identified anthropologist David Aberle as one of Owen Lattimore's research associates, and Morton Fried and other anthropologists with *any* links to the Institute for Pacific Relations soon became subject to FBI inquiries after Wittfogel claimed that the IPR was a communist front influencing American foreign policy.[8]

By connecting an assortment of supposed communists and communist dupes, including Alger Hiss and Owen Lattimore, with the IPR and US policy-makers who were even distantly affiliated with IPR, McCarran connected a chain of names with his imagined communist plot. Wittfogel's lengthy testimony before McCarran's committee concluded with the submission of statements supporting Wittfogel's scholarship from numerous scholars, including the anthropologists C. Martin Wilbur, George Murdock, Clyde Kluckhohn, and Fred Eggan (FBI HQ 100-381178).

Wittfogel's cooperation with the McCarran committee demonstrates how easily the flow of the National Security State could be harnessed by witnesses to further political or personal agendas. A few words laced with innuendo to McCarran did more to derail an intellectual opponent than any number of footnotes or well-constructed volleys of logic.

SHAMING WITTFOGEL

After his testimony, Wittfogel came under private and public attack for identifying former friends and acquaintances as communists. Among those expressing their disappointment in the weeks after his testimony was Arthur Schlesinger Jr, who wrote Wittfogel to chastise him for betraying former friends. On September 6, 1951, Wittfogel angrily replied to Schlesinger, claiming that he had long given Lattimore the "benefit of the doubt," until 1947 when he came to believe he was under communist control. Wittfogel claimed that he had not wanted to testify against Lattimore and others, but that he had no choice but to name John Service, John Fairbanks, and Lattimore as holding identical views on China as communists. Wittfogel wrote that his anger was fueled by how long it had taken Lattimore to acknowledge mistaken beliefs about the Soviets. Wittfogel's thinking fused fascism with communism, as he asked Schlesinger to:

Imagine someone who, after a Nazi coup in a country bordering on Germany visited this "liberated" land with his family and permitted his son to live in one of their controlled youth camps, because they provided "cheap dormitory facilities." Imagine someone who, when the relations between his own country and those of the Hitler regime were becoming increasingly tense, considered himself so much a *persona grata* that he applied for admittance to a territory under Nazi control which was open to almost no outsiders, even including foreign Party members. Imagine someone who at such a time felt close enough to the Nazi government to be allowed to use its diplomatic pouch – and who got permission to do so. Imagine someone who, without much if any special knowledge assured his readers that the workers enjoyed a better position under Hitler than at any time previously although information from practically all independent sources sharply contradicted him. Substitute the USSR for Hitler's Germany and the Russian peasants for the German workers and you will see the Lattimore analogy. And what would you or I have done under such circumstances? Would we have touched such an individual with a ten-foot pole? (GT, KAW to AS, Sept. 6, 1951)

Schlesinger's reply was direct and harsh (Sept. 20, 1951). Schlesinger did not accept Wittfogel's rationalizations, and he used his own anti-communist credentials to attack Wittfogel for behaving dishonorably and opportunistically. His reply is reproduced below in its entirety to illustrate the tone and argument of one anti-communist American reaction to Wittfogel's attacks. Schlesinger wrote:

My Dear Karl:
I must confess myself baffled by the arguments in your letters to Jim Loeb and to me. I did not ask you to underwrite John Fairbanks' political views or his historical theories, or to "identify" yourself with them. I simply assumed that you did not regard him as a member of the Communist Party – or else you would not have broken bread with him or stayed in his house as you have

done in recent years. I had supposed that you might be prepared to come to the support of a friend who had been unjustly accused. I was clearly wrong.

I take it from your letter that you feel that, even if this specific charge against Fairbanks (CP membership is unjust), some other and more general charge is true, and that therefore the Budenz lie is justified. I find this argument to be extraordinary. I do not see what your excuses about Owen Lattimore has to do with the case. I happen to have regarded Lattimore as a politically unhealthy character for a good long time. I refused to have anything to do with him at a time when you were playing footsie with him and writing favorable reviews of his books. Yet that does not make me feel that you are therefore a suspect character. I simply do not understand your apparent belief that this error was permissible so long as you committed it, but became unforgivable one minute after you yourself woke up from it. Certainly Fairbanks was naïve, as I repeatedly told him at the time; but so were you for a longer time and with far greater consequences in terms of commitment. Can you not exercise toward others some of the same charity which you must expect others to exercise toward you? Many of us were fighting Communism at a time when you were its devoted servant.

I really despair of making this point to you, since I fear we are operating in different realms of discourse. I imagine you have no sympathy with the motives that have led Joe Alsop, for example to go to the defense of people with whom he sharply disagreed on China policy when they have been falsely charged with disloyalty; I suppose you would say that [you were] "on the right side" and Alsop "on the wrong side," and that Budenz should be supported and Alsop attacked. This is surely the old Communist doctrine of the "objective" consequences of a position – a doctrine which enables any prosecutor to convict anybody of anything. You do not seem to know the United States very well; nor are you apparently very familiar with Anglo-Saxon legal traditions or traditions of personal decency. We condemn people in this country for what they have done, not for what McCarthy or Budenz or Wittfogel or Schlesinger conceive to be the "objective" consequences of what they have done.

I urge you not to underestimate the power of decency as a political motive in this country. This doubtless sounds like sentimental nonsense to you; but you are wrong. The only ultimate hope for civilization lies in cherishing and developing the instinct for decency, humility and magnanimity in human relations. The worst enemy is what I have called the bureaucratization of guilt – the condemnation of human beings in categories and not as individuals. When this is combined with a readiness to associate with and exploit people when the going is good and then to turn against them when it becomes popular to do so, there arises, at least it seems to me, a moral miasma which poisons the whole notion of human decency.

I fought Communism before you did. I feel that this gives me some right to express myself this frankly on the issue of anti-Communism.

Sincerely yours,
Arthur Schlesinger, Jr (GT 12/25, AS to KAW, Sept. 20, 1951)

To Schlesinger and many other American academics, Wittfogel had behaved too selfishly and monstrously to be easily forgiven. Wittfogel soon found himself working and teaching in almost total isolation except for the company he kept with George Taylor, Nikolai Poppe (whose past Nazi collaboration does not appear to have bothered Wittfogel), and others in an odd group of "national security scholars" Taylor had collected and helped come to the United States during and after the war.

There was immediate and severe fallout for Wittfogel after his testimony. At Columbia University he became a pariah in most circles as the "liberal academic community rejected him" (Ulmen 1978: 295). The stigma and distrust resulting from his cooperation with McCarran did not soon dissipate. In 1952, a year after his testimony, only two students enrolled in Wittfogel's courses at the University of Washington and George Taylor advised him that he'd best stay in New York and work on the manuscript that would become *Oriental Despotism* (Ulmen 1978: 303).

Only a few years later, it would be American anthropologists who would make the most significant overtures to Wittfogel, overlooking his political actions to glean his theoretical contributions. While most historians and China scholars kept their distance from Wittfogel, this small group of American anthropologists, many of whom would later identify more with the New Left than the Old Left, embraced Wittfogel's analysis of pristine hydraulic states while politely ignoring his McCarthyistic attacks.

WITTFOGEL AND ECOLOGICAL ANTHROPOLOGY

American anthropologists' interest in Wittfogel's writings on hydraulic society during the 1950s were instrumental in the formation of what would become the ecological anthropology movement in the 1960s, but Wittfogel did more than direct anthropologists' attention to material and ecological features as causal elements in cultures, he also significantly disarticulated materialist analysis from more traditional Marxist political endeavors.

In 1953, Julian Steward invited Wittfogel to join a session he had organized at the annual meetings of the American Anthropological Association, held in Tucson, Arizona, to examine the role of irrigation in society. Wittfogel's paper, outlining his theories of hydraulic societies, was well received. In this session Pedro Armillas presented a paper on Mesoamerican irrigation, Robert McC. Adams gave a paper on irrigation and ancient Mesopotamia, Donald Collier's paper examined Peruvian irrigation, and Ralph Beals was the session discussant. Steward later published these papers and remarks as the 1955 book, *Irrigation Civilizations: A Comparative Study*, a work that was instrumental in bringing the theories of Wittfogel to American anthropologists and that brought attention to the concerns of developing strains of ecological anthropology.[9] Of all the papers appearing the 1955 published volume, each drew upon or commented on Wittfogel's work, but Wittfogel's contribution was the only one that openly referenced Marx (Wittfogel 1955: 52).

Two years later, in June 1955, Julian Steward organized a small conference in Urbana, Illinois, devoted to examining irrigation and anthropological theory. Wittfogel's participation attracted a core group of anthropologists, including a group of young anthropologists who drove to the conference from New York. Among those attending were anthropologists who would be influential in the coming ecological anthropologist movement. Conference participants included: Robert McC. Adams, Pedro Carrasco, Stanley Diamond, Fred Eggan, Morton Fried, Marvin Harris, Oscar Lewis, Robert Murphy, and Eric Wolf (Harris, personal communication March 10, 1993; Kerns 2003: 271; Ulmen 1978: 321).[10]

The conference sessions with Wittfogel were rare instances of open Marx-based materialist analysis for American anthropologists, who otherwise ignored, cloaked, or suppressed open materialist analysis during the McCarthy period. This anthropological audience appeared unconcerned about Wittfogel's political baggage. Donald Worster described this dynamic, writing that:

... even as Wittfogel was wandering off into anticommunist tendentiousness, he began to acquire a following among a new groups of scholars, the cultural ecologists in anthropology. They were less interested in either his new or his old politics than in his theory of irrigation and society. (Worster 1985: 29)

These anthropologists were influenced by Wittfogel in different ways, though their theoretical reactions were uniformly unrelated to his political position. Adams (1966) would later develop his own counter-arguments to Wittfogel's hydraulic hypothesis for Mesopotamian hydraulic developments; Mort Fried (1967, 1978) integrated the rise of hydraulic states into his schema of political evolution; Robert Murphy (n.d.) developed his own schema of hydraulic societies; and, though Marvin Harris would trace his later interest in cultural materialist analysis to other influences (see Harris 1958; Sanjek 1995: 43–45), the basic features of Wittfogel's model of the hydraulic state became an important example of how Harris would explain similarities between the development of pristine states in both the old and the new world (Harris 1977; 1999: 171–72). Even decades later, Eric Wolf would count his early reading of Wittfogel as important in his intellectual formation, describing Wittfogel's *Economy and Society in China* (1931) as a "splendid" book and as influencing his interpretation of the development of Mexican and Guatemalan society (see Friedman 1987: 109; Wolf 1959). But during the 1950s, as some American anthropologists embraced Wittfogel's hydraulic theory, there remained a negotiated silence concerning the political context in which Wittfogel generated and applied his theories of hydraulic society.

It is surprising to find these young scholars, who would later become active in radical politics during the 1960s, attracted to Wittfogel's hydraulic work without any apparent concern over his role in the McCarran hearings. It was his use of materialist theory to explain the rise of pristine states that captivated their attention. But in an era where it was dangerous for most scholars openly to practice materialist analysis, Wittfogel seemed granted a unique freedom to engage in such Marx-derived materialist analysis.

Later, in 1968, Marvin Harris contextualized Wittfogel's theories and testimony within a larger personal and political context, writing that Wittfogel:

... permitted himself to serve as a government witness in the McCarran committee's investigation of the Institute of Pacific Studies. Tragedies resulting from this episode have ill-served the cause of scholarship and have contributed to the suppression of the cultural-materialist strategy in American social science. Wittfogel's crusade to prove the multilinearity of evolution has centered more and more on the alleged moral implications of closed and open models of history. (1968: 673)

While Harris argued that Wittfogel's cooperation with McCarthysim delayed an acceptance of materialist theories in anthropology, there are other (more consistently materialist) interpretations of the functional outcome Wittfogel's alignment with McCarthyism.

CONCLUSIONS: WITTFOGEL, ANTHROPOLOGY, AND COLD WAR IMPACTS

As the Red Scare spread across America, openly Marxist – or even apolitical materialist – analysis disappeared from the work of anthropologists and other social scientists. As a fanatical anti-communist, Wittfogel was afforded the rare opportunity openly to practice materialist analysis and cite Marx in his works in ways that other scholars could not. Wittfogel's Red-baiting attacks provided him with the opportunity to engage in openly materialist analysis without being subjected to McCarthyism's witch-hunts.

Wittfogel's support for McCarthyism earned him special privileges. His attacks on former friends and his cooperation with McCarran allowed him to engage freely in forms of crude, Marx-based materialist analysis that had brought others before these tribunals. It was as if Wittfogel were the village police informer who alone was allowed to keep and display the very contraband that got others arrested – and this "contraband" was displayed and used in ways that had significant impacts on a generation of anthropologists who used Wittfogel's work.

Despite his anti-communist crusades, Wittfogel grounded his hydraulic theory in Marx – directly quoting and drawing upon Marx and Engels in a supportive manner that was rare during the McCarthy period (see Wittfogel 1957: 22, 381–84, 483, etc.). Joan Vincent's research establishes that many anthropologists during this period excised specific Marxist references or Marxian analysis from manuscripts before they were published (see Vincent 1990: 238–42). There are some noted exceptions to this trend, but most social scientists who did not cloak intellectual debts to Marx, or simply employed materialist analysis, were subjected to McCarthyistic attacks.[11]

To understand how Wittfogel was able to draw upon Marx so openly, it is important to consider the two primary ends to which Wittfogel used Marx. First, he argued that the elimination of private property and the implementation of state-managed works inevitably lead to despotism – a point he used to argue that Communist states were inherently tyrannical. Second, Wittfogel used Marx and Marxist writings to establish a materialist basis for his interpretation of these historical relationships between massive public works and political-economic systems. It was the second concern that drew anthropologists to Wittfogel, but it was the first that allowed Wittfogel the political leeway to explore what had become dangerous political texts; Wittfogel was only allowed freely to explore these ideas because he was using them to battle communism.

Compartmentalizing these two aspects of Wittfogel's life and work creates the illusion that these were two independent pieces of a life, not interlocked elements that enabled the other's existence. But the economic and political realities that govern, shape, and nurture academic inquiries are not mere epiphenomena. These pressures are the manifestations of a society's economic forces exerting pressures on the production of beliefs, in this case the production of scientific knowledge. Wittfogel's roles as a Marx-reliant, anti-communist, materialist, McCarthyite lose their meanings when separated from each other; each role enabled the existence of the Wittfogelian nexus that would have been an unlikely formation outside of the space-time of 1950s America. Had Wittfogel developed a Marxist, materialist theory of the rise of the hydraulic state that was not critical of Marx and communism, he would surely have been persecuted by the very witch-hunting committees he empowered.

By positing such relationships of causality, this analysis departs from more postmodern interpretations. While postmodern explanations throw an interesting light on questions of power, their avoidance of such meta-narratives weakens analyses of the gravitational pull of the economic forces of the Cold War's military-industrial complex.

This leaves questions of relationships between social science theory production and consumption open only to ideographic interpretations. Connecting Wittfogel's theories to the larger political-economic forces bridges this production of science and the society's base. As President Eisenhower acknowledged in his farewell speech, the production of knowledge in the academy was warped by Cold War policies as "the free university, historically the fountainhead of free ideas and scientific discovery, has experienced a revolution in the conduct of research. Partly because of the huge costs involved, a government contract becomes virtually a substitute for intellectual curiosity" (Eisenhower 1961).

It is interesting that Marvin Harris did not conclude that Wittfogel's analysis was specifically shaped by the infrastructural features of the Cold War. Given cultural materialism's view of science as an element of superstructure, that is, as inherently dependent on the machinations of a society's infrastructure, it is curious that Harris would avoid such an analysis, arguing instead that Wittfogel's role as an informer damaged the acceptance of materialism in American anthropology. Perhaps Harris's own epistemological commitment to disarticulating Marx's insistence that social science be committed not only to understanding the world, but to changing it, prevented him from appreciating how Wittfogel's political actions (paradoxically) allowed him to nurture materialism in ways that would otherwise not have been possible. But such an argument about Harris's blindspots has structural parallels in Wittfogel's insistence that Marx had avoided the obvious implications of the Asiatic Mode of Production for socialism's grand design.

It is difficult to regard Wittfogel as a sympathetic character. His motivations for betraying former friends and rejecting previously held political positions appear to have been based on perceived personal slights and a tendency to extreme reactions. As T.O. Beidelman observed, Wittfogel's career demonstrated "how the far left can easily become sympathetic to the far right" (1988). Wittfogel's career also followed a path similar to others on the American shore who, like Elia Kazan, Sidney Hook, or, more recently, Christopher Hitchens, viewed decisions to turn against old friends as mandated by the need to be true to oneself – but such claims usually recast self-serving motivations as duties.

American academics had varied reactions to Wittfogel's testimony against Lattimore. Arthur Schlesinger's letter documents one sort of reaction, and the anthropologists flocking to adopt elements of his hydraulic theory represent another. Anthropology's reaction remains as an artifact documenting Cold War anthropology's conception of itself as a science existing above the pull of political motivations. In such a setting it was natural to ignore the political context in which science was created or conducted, but this context shaped science in very profound ways. The political setting in which Wittfogel produced his work was both backdrop and foreground for the theories he produced and the audience drawn to these theories.

Seriously flawed or depraved individuals can still make significant scientific or artistic contributions. Whether it is Frank Sinatra's links to organized crime, Richard Wagner's anti-Semitism, Frank Lloyd Wright's parental negligence, Paul de Man's Nazi collaborations, or Louis Althusser's murder of his wife: professional contributions can be evaluated independently of personal or political failings. But it is another issue entirely when personal or political issues have such an importance that they inform and allow the spread of one's work. In Wittfogel's case, anthropology's decision not to acknowledge Wittfogel's contributions to McCarthyism was both caused by and perpetuated a false understanding of the role of economic and political forces in the production of scientific knowledge.

McCarthyism also exposed the failings of Wittfogel's conception of coercive power. If the McCarran committee hearings were a test, Wittfogel failed it. Not only did he betray friendships and trusts, and disregard basic notions of academic freedom, but he failed to identify the proceedings as being the theatrical props of a totalitarian movement. The committee hearings provided Wittfogel with a perfect opportunity to challenge the scourge of totalitarianism he so passionately hated. But Wittfogel joined rather than challenged this totalitarian movement, an act that undermined not only his personal character, but also his professional judgments.

NOTES

1. The original kernel of this chapter came from an argument I had with my friend and mentor Marvin Harris almost two decades ago. The chapter benefited from discussions with or the comments of Alexander Cockburn, Sig Diamond, Janice Harper, Robert Lawless, Sidney Mintz, Laura Nader, Eric Ross, Daniel Tompkins, and Dustin Wax.
2. The epistemological differences between Wittfogel and the stars of the Frankfurt School were immense, though there was a shared focus on the formation of totalitarianism or authoritarianism even while they had divergent explanations for this phenomenon. While Adorno looked to micro, psychological factors determining authoritarian personality features, Wittfogel examined material, macro features in accounting for the emergence of despotic rulers. To some extent, a focus on such formations seems natural for those who lived through the crumbling of the Weimar Republic and the rise of Nazism (see Smith 1987; Wolin 2006).
3. Karl Wittfogel was married three times. He was married to Rose Schlesinger from 1921 to 1932, to Olga Lang from 1933 to 1939, and to Esther Goldfrank from 1940 until his death in 1988.

4. Wittfogel's political troubles came to distort how scholars approached his work. At the conclusion of *Lineages of the Absolute State*, Perry Anderson famously asked that Wittfogel's interpretation of the Asiatic Mode of Production "be given the decent burial that it deserves" (1974: 548). Andre Gingrich irrationally constructs Wittfogel as a "former spartakist" whose collaboration with McCarthyism was somehow a "courageous" "defense of academic pluralism" (Gingrich 2005: 105).

5. Citations beginning with the notation "FBI HQ" refer to FBI files released under the Freedom of Information Act. The numbers and letters following these designations refer to the FBI's internal cataloging system.

6. Goldfrank's reference is to *Human Organization's* "People and Projects," which recounted Haskell's role representing the SFAA (Society for Applied Anthropology) as the convening secretary at the 1948 Symposium on Cooperation and Conflict among Living Organisms, and Haskell's supportive role in an upcoming meeting on "Social Integration and Dis-integration" that would be co-sponsored by the SFAA and the American Association for the Advancement of Science (see: *Human Organization* 1949: 28). Goldfrank's later mention of Jacobs and Stern's "popular Outline of Anthropology" refers to Jacobs and Stern (1947).

7. Goldfrank's anti-communism remained strong throughout her life. In the weeks that followed the tumultuous 1971 meeting of the American Anthropological Association, she wrote Margaret Mead that she had not been surprised that the report was rejected, writing:

> The Radical Caucus in the evening, you will remember, had an attendance of about 700 and the applause for the speakers was certainly not exuberant. I had enough by 8:30 and left. I wasn't surprised to learn that the meeting ended at 1:20 A.M. The vote [was] 248 to 14 against your report. So almost 500 persons who had been at the earlier meeting that evening had melted away. There is a good old Communist tactic – you wear down your opponents with endless and not too relevant discussion and amendments, and when you are sure you can win, you call a vote. (AAA, MME12, EG to MM Jan. 3 1972).

Goldfrank then described a recent article by Marxist anthropologist John Moore, in which Moore described Marxist influences on American anthropology and argued for a more insurgent approach to anthropology. Goldfrank wrote Mead that Moore's writings "go a long way toward removing the fog that obscures so much that has been happening in the AAA" (AAA, MME12, EG to MM, Jan. 3, 1972).

8. David Aberle had met Lattimore while at Cambridge, and had worked for him for two years on Lattimore's Mongolian history project (Aberle interview Jan. 6, 2000). When inquiries began focusing on Lattimore, Aberle said he "became frantic about working on this project. I didn't want to be pursued" (DA to author Jan. 6, 2000). Morton Fried's FBI file documents that the FBI's initial investigation of him was launched because he had written an academic book review for the IPR's journal, *Far East Survey* (FBI HQ 100-64700).

9. Angel Palerm was also among those influenced by this AAA session (see Ulmen 1978: 305).

10. Robert Murphy later recounted that Steward suddenly disappeared during the first day of the conference without any explanation, and Wittfogel

had to leave after the following day to attend a Wenner-Gren conference at Princeton (Kerns 2003: 271; Ulmen 1978: 312).
11. For example, see Peace and Price (2001: 164), for a discussion of the FBI's investigation of authors contributing to the 1949 edited volume, *Philosophy for the Future* (Sellars et al. 1949), simply because it examined the methods and theories of historical materialism.

ARCHIVAL SOURCES

AAA – Papers of the American Anthropological Association, National Anthropological Archives, Smithsonian Institution, Washington, DC.
EG – Esther Goldfrank Papers, National Anthropological Archives, Smithsonian Institution, Washington, DC.
GT – George Edward Taylor Papers, University of Washington Library Manuscripts, Special Collections, University Archives.
KW – Karl August Wittfogel Papers, University of Washington Library Manuscripts, Special Collections, University Archives.

REFERENCES

Adams, Robert McC. 1966. *The Evolution of Urban Society*. Chicago: Aldine.
Anderson, Perry. 1974. *Lineages of the Absolute State*. London: Verso.
Beidelman, Thomas O. 1988. Karl Wittfogel. *Anthropology Today* 4(6): 24.
Buckley, William F. 1988. Karl A. Wittfogel, R.I.P. *National Review* 40(12): 18.
Cumings, Bruce. 2002. *Parallax Visions: Making Sense of American–East Asian Relations*. Durham, NC: Duke University Press.
Eisenhower, Dwight. 1961. Farewell Address. Eisenhower Presidential Library. URL: http://www.eisenhower.archives.gov/farewell.htm (accessed August 2006).
Fried, Morton H. 1967. *The Evolution of Political Society*. New York: Random House.
—— 1978. Reconsiderations: Oriental Despotism. *Human Nature* 1(12): 90–93.
Friedman, Jonathan. 1987. An Interview with Eric Wolf. *Current Anthropology* 28(1): 107–18.
Gellner, Ernest. 1985. "Soviets Against Wittfogel" or, the Anthropological Preconditions of Mature Marxism. *Theory and Society* 14(3): 341–70.
—— 1988. Karl Wittfogel. *Anthropology Today* 4(5): 22.
Gingrich, Andre. 2005. The German-speaking Countries. In *One Discipline, Four Ways*. Fredrik Barth, Andre Gingrich, Robert Parkin, and Sydel Sliverman, eds. Chicago: University of Chicago Press.
Goldfrank, Esther S. 1978. *Notes on an Undirected Life*. Flushing, NY: Queens College Press.
Harris, Marvin. 1958. *Portugal's African Wards*. Africa Today, Pamphlet No. 2. New York: American Committee on Africa.
—— 1968. *The Rise of Anthropological Theory*. New York: Thomas Crowell.
—— 1977. *Cannibals and Kings: The Origins of Cultures*. New York: Random House.
—— 1999. *Theories of Culture in Postmodern Times*. Walnut Creek, CA: AltaMira Press.

Human Organization. 1949. People and Projects. *Human Organization* spring: 25–28.

Jacobs, Melville and Bernhard Stern. 1947. *Outline of Anthropology.* New York: Barnes and Noble.

Kahin, George. 2002. *Southeast Asia: A Testament.* London: Routledge.

Kerns, Virginia. 2003. *Scenes from the High Desert: Julian Steward's Life and Theory.* Urbana: University of Illinois Press.

Lewin, Gunter. 1981. Wittfogel on the Asiatic Mode of Production. In *The Asiatic Mode of Production,* pp. 158–63. Anne M. Bailey and Josep R. Llobera, eds. London: Routledge and Kegan Paul.

Murphy, Robert F. n.d. Types of Irrigation and their Developmental Implications. Unpublished MS.

Navasky, Victor. 1989. Forward. In *It Did Happen Here: Recollections of Political Repression in America,* pp. xv–xx. Bud Schultz and Ruth Schultz, eds. Berkeley: University of California Press.

Peace, William J. and David Price H. 2001. The Cold War Context of the FBI's Investigation of Leslie A. White. *American Anthropologist* 103(1): 164–67.

Peet, Richard. 1985. Introduction to the Life and Thought of Karl Wittfogel. *Antipode* 17(1): 3–20.

Price, David H. 1994. Wittfogel's Neglected Hydraulic/Hydroagricultural Distinction. *Journal of Anthropological Research* 50(2): 187–204.

—— 1995. The Cultural Effects of Conveyance Loss in Gravity-Fed Irrigation Systems. *Ethnology* 34(4): 273–91.

—— 1996. Interview with George E. Taylor. Seattle, Washington. July 17.

—— 2004. *Threatening Anthropology: The FBI's Surveillance and Repression of Activist Anthropologists.* Durham, NC: Duke University Press.

Sanjek, Roger. 1995. Politics, Theory and the Nature of Cultural Things. In *Science, Materialism and the Study of Culture,* pp. 39–61. Martin F. Murphy and Maxine L. Margolis, eds. Gainesville: University Press of Florida.

Schrecker, Ellen. *No Ivory Tower.* Oxford: Oxford University Press.

Sellars, Roy Wood, V.J. McGill, and Marvin Farber. 1959. *Philosophy for the Future: The Quest of Modern Materialism.* New York: Macmillan.

Smith, Neil. 1987. Rehabilitating a Renegade: The Geography and Politics of Karl August Wittfogel. *Dialectical Anthropology* 12: 127–36.

Steward, Julian, ed. 1955. *Irrigation Civilizations: A Comparative Study.* Washington: Pan American Union.

Tompkins, Daniel P. 2006. The World of Moses Finkelstein: The Year 1939 in M. I. Finley's Development as a Historian. In *Classical Antiquity and the Politics of America: From George Washington to George W. Bush,* pp. 95–126. Michael Meckler, ed. Waco, TX: Baylor University Press.

Ulmen, Gary L. 1978. *The Science of Society: Toward an Understanding of the Life and Work of Karl August Wittfogel.* The Hague: Mouton.

Vincent, Joan. 1990. *Anthropology and Politics: Visions, Traditions, and Trends.* Tucson: University of Arizona Press.

Wittfogel, Karl. 1931. *Wirtschaft und Gesellschaft Chinas* [Economy and Society in China]. Leipzig: C.L. Hirschfeld.

—— 1936. *Staatliches Konzentrationslager VII, Eine "Erziehungsanstalt" im Dritten Reich* [State Concentration Camp VII: An "Educational Institution" of the Third Reich] (published under the pseudonym of Klaus Hinrichs). London: Malik Verlag.

—— 1955. Developmental Aspects of Hydraulic Societies. In *Irrigation Civilizations: A Comparative Study*, pp. 43–56. Julian Steward, ed. Washington, DC: Pan American Union.

—— 1957. *Oriental Despotism*. New Haven, CT: Yale University Press.

Wolf, Eric. 1959. *Sons of the Shaking Earth*. Chicago: University of Chicago Press.

Wolin, Richard. 2006. *The Frankfurt School Revisited, and other Essays on Politics and Society*. New York: Routledge.

Worster, Donald. 1985. *Rivers of Empire*. New York: Pantheon.

Ybarra, Michael. 2004. *Washington Gone Crazy: Senator Pat McCarran and the Great American Communist Hunt*. Hanover, NH: Steerforth.

3 AMERICAN COLONIALISM AT THE DAWN OF THE COLD WAR

Marc Pinkoski

In this chapter, I would like to draw the discussion of American anthropology at the dawn of the Cold War toward a consideration of the connection between the development of neo-scientific anthropology and colonial practices in the United States.[1] I argue, simply, that the theorization of American anthropology during this time-frame requires a deep consideration of the connection between the development of so-called "scientific anthropology" and colonialism. I use one specific case example, the contributions of Julian Steward, to illustrate this connection.

In her institutional history of American anthropology entitled, "The American Anthropological Association and the Values of Science, 1935–70," Trencher (2002) argues that the second major attempt to form a coherent scientific method in the discipline was raised near the end of World War II. In a rather parenthetical manner, she explains that:

> ... a group of younger anthropologists (... the "second generation") ... [were t]rained closer to World War II than World War I ...(Julian Steward, Ralph Linton, Homer Barnett, George Peter Murdock, and Alexander Spoehr, among others) [and] often had their professional start working for the government in New Deal programs in the 1930s and thus had their early work experience in applied rather than academic settings, where opportunities had grown scarce. They sought, as Boas had nearly half a century earlier, to form a scientific and professional organization. But while the vocabulary was the same, the definitions had changed. Many members of the second-generation cohort had an epistemologically more rigid (positivist) view of science and an experientially different view of what of what constitutes professional anthropology. (2002: 450–51)

Continuing, she states:

> In 1940, there had been a move primarily by second-generation anthropologists in the AAA to what they termed a professional as well as a scientific association. Led by Julian Steward, they sought the creation of a section for applied anthropology in the AAA. But the association, primarily run by Boasians working in academia rejected the new section, which led to

the creation of a separate Society for Applied Anthropology in 1941, with Steward at the helm.... [T]he second generation laid claim to new practical and intellectual power through new avenues for AAA positions and new definitions of the "professional" allied to their view of science, which in turn opened the door wider for applied work. That is, scientific knowledge assumed as objective and value free was further understood to produce fact and truth and, thus, once established was appropriately applied in any setting. (2002: 451)

Following Trencher's history, I offer a reading of Julian Steward's contributions to the discipline during this time to demonstrate the strong connection between anthropology and colonial practices at the dawn of the Cold War. This time-period is important for understanding Steward's larger *oeuvre* and his contributions to the discipline for several reasons. First, this marked his move away from the Bureau of American Ethnology (BAE) to his short-lived stint teaching and training students at Columbia University. Second, this is when Steward began to frame his work theoretically (Kerns 2003), introducing several of his foundational essays (Clemmer et al. 1999; Kerns 2003; Manners 1973; Murphy 1977; Pinkoski 2006). Finally, this time-period also marks the beginning of Steward's association with the US Department of Justice, carrying out work where he testified and strategized against "Indian" interest in their traditional territories, conflating his theoretical work and its political application, and masking it behind the veil of a purported objective science.

Within the discipline, Julian Steward (1902–72) is most often remembered as a "scientific" anthropologist – an image that Steward promoted himself, premising his distinction from his contemporaries on what he called his scientific method (Steward 1949, 1950b, 1953a, 1955). Seemingly accepting of Steward's self-identification, the discipline overwhelmingly characterizes him as a scientific, objective anthropologist, markedly different from both nineteenth-century unilinear evolutionists, the then-dominant Boasian approach (Darnell 2001), and his contemporaries (Carneiro 2003; Haenn and Wilk 2006; Harris 1968; Kerns 2003; Ortner 1984; Sponsell 2006; Trigger 1989 Turney-High 1940; Wolf 2001).

Claims of Steward's objective, scientific approach are based on an interpretation of his ethnographic and archaeological work in the American Great Basin, work that resulted in the seminal ethnography, *Basin-Plateau Aboriginal Sociopolitical Groups* (1938, hereafter *Basin-Plateau*). They also stem from his monumental, six-volume edited collection, *The Handbook of South American Indians* (1946a, 1946b, 1948a, 1948b, 1949a, 1950a), *The People of Puerto Rico* (1956), and his edited three-volume collection on modernization and development (1967a, 1967b, 1967c), as well as from many of his foundational essays written during his 44-year academic career, exemplified by his dozens of contributions to *American Anthropologist* and the collection of his essays, *Theory of Culture Change: The Methodology of Multilinear Evolution* (1955).

To date there has been much reported on Steward within the discipline. Because he published widely, generating essays and books that were well read, even foundational to the discipline, there is a wealth of commentary and review of his work and of him as a person. In this literature, Steward is reported to have exacted a value-free account of the Indigenous peoples of the American Great Basin – the Shoshoneans as he called them – distilling an evolutionary theoretical frame that was "scientific" (Kerns 2003). Many report his novelty in the discipline to be his strong method, which generated evolutionary pronouncements that had overcome the implicit racism of nineteenth-century unilinear evolutionism (Trigger 1998). Thus branding his work as "neo-evolutionary," present-day scholars have theorized his work as a significant break from that of earlier social theorists such as Tylor, Spencer, and Morgan and claim that Steward's work is the beginning of modern, scientific anthropology reifying this notion in the discipline's history, historiography, and pedagogy (Barnard 2000; Beck 1999; Bohannan and Glazer 1988; Carneiro 2003; Erickson and Nielsen 1998; Harris 1968; Johnson and Earle 1987; Layton 1997; McGee and Warms 1996; Shimkin 1964; Sidky 2005; Silverman 2005; Sponsell 2006).

From early in his career Steward's work has been acclaimed. This is illustrated in the *American Anthropologist* review of *Basin-Plateau*, where it is claimed that the monograph is "monumental," and the reviewer eagerly recommends it "without hesitation as a model for similar works which must and will follow" (Turney-High 1940: 136). Explaining Steward's project and its relative worth to the social sciences, the reviewer states:

... Steward's acumen is sharper than that of the average field ethnographer.... His sociologic data and their analysis are set down with insight based on intimate knowledge. For this region at least he has shown where and why band organization exists and where and why it does not exist, where population has agglomerated and why, what forces geographic and culture make for the cohesive social groups and which are centrifugal. He has shown in a way which might astound some determinists how and why polygyny, monogamy, and polyandry exist within the same group among these matrimonially realistic people. Indeed, there is a ring of realism to all his people. His Shoshoneans, driven by victual desperation, whose economy was "gastric," could afford to be nothing else.... This is a work which can honestly be called magnificent. I intend to refer to it again and again. The anthropologist should not only read it with profit but should refer his social science friends to it. It is a genuinely scholarly job, free from several faults which would have been excusable under the circumstances, a mine of factual information, and a sound analytic effort. (Turney-High 1940: 138)

Steward's later work, exemplified most fully by his text *Theory of Culture Change* (1955), has created a foundation for the discipline by purporting to offer a scientific method for the study of society in relation to environment (Haenn and Wilk 2006). This perception is represented uniformly across the discipline, and is demonstrated by accounts such as Ortner's (1984), who recorded Steward's influence in her period-piece, "Theory in Anthropology since the Sixties," stating that he "emphasized that specific cultures evolve their specific forms in the process of adapting to specific environmental conditions, and that the apparent uniformity of evolutionary stages is actually a matter of similar adaptations to similar natural conditions in different parts of the world" (1984: 132).

Typically, Steward's method is understood to offer an "objective" ethnographic portrayal. It is believed that his fieldwork led to strong, objective descriptions, and that extensive analysis, through the rigorous method of cultural ecology, generated "nomothetic" rules of culture change – a method that prompted Harris, for example, to observe that: "Despite subsequent critical evaluations of certain aspects of Steward's data, the strategy of Steward's explanation continues to warrant approval" (1968: 667).

The cultural laws or rules of evolution that Steward devised are regarded as foundational in the history of American anthropology because of their presumed objective, scientific method for understanding social organization and culture change. For example, Trigger identifies Steward's work as a "more empirical approach to the study of cultural evolution" (1989: 291); and Kerns describes his work as having "a propensity for the concrete," noting that "[h]e used an impressive array of ethnographic and archaeological evidence to support a range of creative, generalizing conclusions about how, in his own words, 'similar subsistence activities had produced similar social structures'" (2003: 3).

In reproducing Steward's seminal essay, "The Concept and Method of Cultural Ecology" in *High Points in Anthropology*, Bohannan and Glazer (1988) offer a similar sentiment regarding Steward's contributions, introducing the essay with the assertion that his "is a methodology concerned with regularity in social change, the goal of which is to develop cultural laws empirically" (1988: 321); and they continue, stating that "Steward's concepts of cultural adaptation are theoretically important in that they break the circular argument that only culture can explain culture, which in a sense remains true" (1988: 322). Not to be outdone, Moore effectively sums up Steward's influence on the discipline when he states that: "[t]oday Steward's ideas are accepted as basic anthropological insight" (1997: 183), and he concludes that some of Steward's concepts "are the anthropological equivalent of gospel" (1997: 188).

STEWARD'S WORK, 1947–53

Steward was hired at Columbia University in 1946 by William Duncan Strong, his fellow Berkeley chum and former BAE colleague. Strong, as chairman of the Department of Anthropology at Columbia, was charged with hiring a replacement for Ralph Linton, who was leaving to head the Department of Anthropology at Yale (Silverman 2005). Privately, Strong and Linton recruited Steward to help confront the "psychological focus" of the department, primarily promoted by Ruth Benedict. Strong and Steward shared a materialist approach to understanding culture change, with a focus on ecology, and they both worked to submerge the Boasian relativism continued by Benedict, Margaret Mead, Gene Weltfish, and Ruth Bunzel (Kerns 2003: 239–41; Murphy 1977: 10; Silverman 2005).

Thus, when Steward joined the Department of Anthropology at Columbia, he once again joined an institution that was undergoing tremendous reorganization due to political and ideological conflicts.[2] However, this time, Murphy recounts, Steward's materialist focus jibed very well with the men returning home from wartime duty, who had "learned justice at the barrel of a gun" (Murphy 1981: 177); and, with his new method, which was soon to be called "cultural ecology," Steward supervised numerous soon to be prominent scholars' PhD dissertations, sat on their graduate committees, and greatly influenced their careers. Murphy (1977) reports that Steward supervised the completion of 35 doctoral dissertations in his six years at Columbia, and that he sat on many dozens more dissertation committees. As a whole, these students were very politically active, and some of the men formed an exclusive anthropology reading group called the "Mundial Upheaval Group" (Wolf, quoted in Friedman 1987: 109; see Peace, this volume).[3]

It was during his time at Columbia that Steward began to publish his most complete theoretical pieces. In their introduction to the recent collection, *Julian Steward and the Great Basin: The Making of an Anthropologist*, Clemmer and Myers (1999) identify four published works from this time-period that demonstrate Steward's burgeoning contribution to anthropological theory, forming the basis for his later theoretical work: "Cultural Causality and Law," published in *American Anthropologist* (1949b); "Evolution and Process," published in Kroeber's edited tome, *Anthropology Today* (1953a);[4] the monograph, *Area Research: Theory and Practice* (1950b); and finally "The Levels of Sociocultural Integration," published in the *Southwest Journal of Anthropology* (1951).

Steward's "Cultural Causality and Law" has somewhat cautiously been called "*perhaps* his single most influential article" (Murphy 1981: 195), and "*possibly* his most theoretically complete piece" (Kerns

2003: 253). In the article, Steward traces what he calls the causes of the development of the state in several civilizations in human history (Murphy 1977: 29), and hypothesizes that it is control of irrigation and the subsequent social stratification that gives rise to the power structure of the state in each case in the history of human social evolution.

Steward begins with a retrospective statement about the discipline, contending that evolutionary pronouncements had given way to historically particularist ones in the beginning of the century. First distinguishing himself from nineteenth-century evolutionists by simple assertion, he labels his contemporaries as following outdated traditions. He offers, here and elsewhere (e.g. 1955), that his theory is *sui generis*, and that his is truly a unique conceptualization of human social change (evolution). He concludes, though, that "[i]n spite of a half century of scepticism concerning the possibility of forming cultural regularities, the conviction is widely held that the discovery of cultural laws is [now] an ultimate goal of anthropology" (1949b: 2).[5]

Taking aim at the Boasians, Steward says that the particularist approach cannot identify independent cause-and-effect relationships and must fall back on the supposition of single origin hypothesis, and therefore processes of diffusion (1949b: 3), a point that he believed he had already refuted (Steward 1929). As an explicit alternative to the Boasian approach, he suggests that "regularities can be found only by looking for them, and they will be valid only if a rigorous methodology underlies the framing of hypotheses" (1949b: 5). Explaining, he says:

The present statement of scientific purpose and methodology rests on a conception of culture that needs clarification. *If the more important institutions of culture can be isolated from their unique setting so as to be typed, classified, and related to recurring antecedents or functional correlates, it follows from this that it is possible to consider the institutions in question as the basic or constant ones, whereas the features that lend uniqueness are the secondary or variable ones.* (1949b: 6, emphasis his)

His method for interpreting or distinguishing core features from peripheral ones is an extremely powerful tool in anthropology and archaeology, and has come to be known as the concept of "culture core."[6]

Clemmer and Myers also identify the article "Evolution and Process" as one of Steward's most significant theoretical contributions written while he was at Columbia. The argument is crucial for Steward's emerging theoretical project, as it is in this essay that he defines "multilinear evolution," and helps to define the discipline's reinterpretation of nineteenth-century unilinear evolutionism. In this general piece, Steward wades into the contemporary anthropological debates by presenting a polemic, reacting to his contemporaries in the Boasian tradition of American anthropology, and challenging the then-dominant trend for its lack of grand, comparative theory. Specifically, he attacks Kroeber, as well as the evolutionary approach of White, setting his project up, once again, as unique. This essay is one of the major contributions to the discipline that reintroduces social evolutionism to mainstream anthropological theory, and promotes a schematic representation of the levels of human groups. It re-establishes the nineteenth-century evolutionary paradigm, but this time distinguishes the levels through a claimed "objective" methodology for evaluating differences between cultural forms. He asserts that not all forms progress and survive to go through the stages of development, and thus claims that his approach is multilinear because not all cultural forms can and will progress and survive.

Steward says that "multilinear evolution" is "essentially a methodology based on the assumption that significant regularities in cultural change occur, and it is concerned with the determination of cultural laws" (1953a: 318). He argues that its method is about gaining "concreteness and specificity" for comparison and understanding of culture change. Its concern is the generation of taxonomic features, conceptions of historic change, and cultural causality (1953a: 313). He says his method distinguishes social levels and exacts cultural laws through objective scientific means, ultimately demonstrating, he believes, that societies exist on a true evolutionary continuum. Explaining the "meaning of evolution," Steward says:

Cultural evolution, although long an unfashionable concept, has commanded renewed interest in the last two decades. This interest does not indicate any serious reconsideration of the particular historical reconstructions of the nineteenth-century evolutionists, for these were quite discredited on empirical grounds. It arises from the potential methodological importance of cultural evolution for contemporary research, from the implications of its scientific objectives, its taxonomic procedures, and its conceptualization of historical change and cultural causality ... (1953a: 313)

Clemmer and Myers note that Steward's third important piece written during this time is the Social Sciences Research Council's (SSRC) Bulletin, *Area Research: Theory and Practice* (Steward 1950b). Though relatively unknown, this small book is one of the most curiously demonstrative pieces of literature in Steward's *oeuvre*, demonstrating the intent and application of his project with specificity and clarity. Written while he was on leave for a term at the SSRC in 1949, shortly after the completion of the Puerto Rico Project, Steward wrote what was intended as a report on methodologies and practices of "area research" from the perspective of anthropology (1950b).

Defining "areas" as abstractions determined from scientific analysis, he acknowledges that they could be cultural areas, nations, groups, dependencies, tribes; or that they could be abstracted based on other arbitrary phenomena like race, language, and technology (1950b: 7). Recognizing that an "area" could be anything left to the fancy of the scientist, he says, however, that it is the purpose of area research studies that is of primary importance. Recalling the then-recent call for area studies, he notes that it is the responsibility of social scientists:

... *[t]o accumulate and make available a body of knowledge of practical utility regarding the principal areas of the world [though it] could require investigations of every conceivable kind.* (1950b: 2, emphasis his)

Continuing directly, he notes that:

During the war there was an enormous demand for hundreds of different kinds of spot information. So far as this demand is concerned, it can undoubtedly be expected that any area specialist will make available whatever miscellaneous knowledge he happens to possess when needed. (1950b: 2)

In *Area Research*, Steward is preoccupied with what he perceives as the plight of anthropology due to its traditional subject disappearing (e.g. 1950b: 151). With respect to the discipline, he offers the Puerto Rico Project as the exemplar of a relevant anthropological research project on what he calls "complex and changing societies." He holds up the Project as an example of a strong contribution to the growth of the social sciences (1950b: 154), by showing anthropology's relevance to this growth (1950b: 95). Thus, his report focuses on a project that examines the determinants of culture change in what he considers more "complex societies," such as Puerto Rico, and he offers a role for anthropology in government research initiatives. He acknowledges that the "concepts and methods" employed in the Puerto Rico Project helped "to ascertain how the influences emanating from a highly industrialized society affected the local or regional varieties of culture found in one of its agrarian dependencies" (Steward 1950b: 154). Steward claims that, in order to "understand the influences that have been changing these communities [in Puerto Rico], it was necessary to understand the insular-wide economic, political, religious, and other institutions, including changes in the latter under United States sovereignty" (1950b: 155).

Explaining this position, he says the "ultimate justification of social science is that it can predict trends in human affairs – that it can state with some precision what will take place under specifiable circumstances" (1950b: 155). He advocates for anthropology to synthesize the analyses of other social science disciplines, creating an interpretive hierarchy and structure for the social sciences with anthropology at the top liaising with the government.

For undertaking area studies Steward introduced a new concept, "the levels of sociocultural integration," that would permit anthropology to contribute more fully to a useful social science amidst what the discipline perceived as the disappearance of "primitive peoples." In explaining this approach, he says:

> In science generally, there is a good precedent for dealing with levels of integration. The distinction between the inorganic, organic, and superorganic is a very old concept and it means that the sciences dealing with each level frame their problems in terms of special aspects of phenomena ...
>
> If the basic concept of levels is valid – and this would not seem to be very debatable – types of sociocultural organization no less than the phenomena of the inorganic and organic levels must be divided into sublevels.... According to the principle of sociocultural sublevels, each higher sublevel is more complex than the lower ones not only in the qualitative [sic] sense because it has more parts but, as in biological sublevels, that it has qualitatively novel characteristics or unique properties which are not evident in or foreshadowed by the lower ones. That is, the new whole at each higher sublevel induces changes in the very nature of the parts and creates new relationships between the parts and to the whole.
>
> This point may be illustrated with a simple and basic phenomenon. The human family is found in all societies but, like the cell, its nature and its functions vary according to the whole. In a few sociocultural units, such as the Eskimo or the Great Basin Shoshoneans, the family more or less constitutes the social, economic, educational, and political whole. The family has persisted throughout world history, but its nature and role in larger sociocultural wholes have changed tremendously. The contemporary American family, for example, has lost many of the primitive functions, while others have been so modified as to give it unique meaning and relationships that are specific to the context of modern civilization.
>
> In the historical development of sociocultural systems, the individual family units amalgamated into larger groups whose nature and functions were very different from those of the family. (1950b: 108–10)

This telling description provides Steward's Spencerian rationale regarding evolutionary typologies: because he assumes Indigenous peoples to be small, simple, and homogeneous, he believed them to be naturally assimilated by more complex forms; and, as a result, the newly emergent form cannot be an aboriginal one – it is inextricably altered by contact.

Finally, Clemmer and Myers identify "The Levels of Sociocultural Integration: An Operational Concept" (Steward 1951) as the fourth important theory piece written during this time. This article was published as Steward developed his theoretical position and explored his political acumen in the academy. It is important because he further develops the concept of the levels of sociocultural integration that originated in *Area Research*; and he also applied it for the US Department of Justice in the context of the Indian Claims Commission (ICC) in an effort to deny American Indian interests in their traditional lands. In this manner, the "levels of sociocultural integration" is the nub of his praxis, what he later comes to call the "substantive application" of his theory and method (Steward 1955: 5).

In the article, Steward combines the assumption of "multilinear evolution" with his new (but still unnamed) method of cultural ecology to establish a schema for evaluating the level of a society, and, as well, proposes a method to solve problems of acculturation (1951· 383). He contends that there are "levels" of social forms, and he urges that his method of discernment and ranking be used to categorize them into a typology. In contrast to nineteenth-century cultural evolutionists, Steward claims that the evolutionary trajectory of each society is not unilinear, saying:

Similarly, this concept applied to culture is essentially heuristic and does not purport to explain the developmental sequences of particular cultural types. The cultural evolution of Morgan, Tylor, and others is a developmental taxonomy based on concrete characteristics of cultures. The concept of levels of sociocultural integration, on the other hand, is simply a *methodological tool for dealing with cultures* of different degrees of complexity. It is not a conclusion about evolution. (Steward 1951: 380, emphasis mine)

Steward states that the "family represents a level that is lower in a structural sense, and in some cases it appears to have been historically antecedent to higher forms" (1951: 381–82). As noted in the original publication of the essay,[7] Steward developed the concept of the levels of sociocultural integration first in *Area Research: Theory and Practice* (1950b: 95, 106–14, 152, 168), identifying it as an abstraction subject to the discretion of the scientist (1950b: 8). He introduced the concept by saying: "within the cultural tradition of each area, sociocultural systems have developed through a succession of levels, each higher level being not only more complex than the lower but *qualitatively* different in that it has characteristics that were not evident in antecedent patterns" (1950b: 152, emphasis mine). He confirms this point again in "The Levels of Sociocultural Integration," noting that "the levels can be used as an analytic tool in the study of changes within any particular sociocultural system" (1951: 383).

A determination of the sociocultural levels, Steward says, is representative of the "growth continuum" of increasingly complex and newly emergent forms. This schema he patterns specifically after the biological understanding of evolution (Murphy 1981; Steward 1951: 379). The bottom level of the scale of sociocultural integration is known as the "family-level"; and representative of this level, the "family was the reproductive, economic, educational, political, and religious unit" with no higher forms of social organization (1955: 54). For Steward, each higher level on the scale is marked by increasing complexity, and is evidenced by increasing inventories of cultural traits, increasing heterogeneity, and the emergence of formal political structures.

STEWARD AND THE US DEPARTMENT OF JUSTICE

Notwithstanding the enduring claims of Steward's scientific objectivity and the political neutrality of his work, in 1949 Steward began working for the US Department of Justice providing testimony to deny Indian land rights before the Indian Claims Commission (ICC; JHSP, Box 2, Steward to Vanech, April 21, 1949). The Indian Claims Commission Act was passed by US Congress in 1946, and the commission founded under the act, the ICC, was organized as a "tribunal for the hearing and determination of claims against the United States ... by any Indian tribe, band, or other identifiable group of Indians living in the United States."

Although probably unforeseen, the ICC's broad mandate to hear claims against the United States on behalf of any "Indian tribe, band, or other identifiable group of Indians," allowed for an established line of argumentation frequent in colonial litigations. In effect, the defined list opened the door for an argument that there *could* be a group of Native Americans that was not an "identifiable" group, as it could be argued that the particular claimant was not a band, tribe, or group. Following this argument, those claimants who were found to be not of an "identifiable" group had no legal standing before the ICC because of perceived "ethnological difference," based on evolutionary conjecture.[8] As it happened, in frequent and continual practice, the US Department of Justice questioned the level of social organization of the Indigenous peoples before the court, following a line of argument in the common law regarding the colonization of new territories by limiting the aboriginal interest in the land based on social evolutionism (Asch 1992, 1999, 2002; Pinkoski and Asch 2004; Reynolds 1992; cf. Wallace 2002).[9]

Reams of documents in Steward's archives demonstrate that Steward had an intimate relationship with the US government in the creation and presentation of their legal arguments before the ICC. To begin, the Department of Justice contacted Steward in April 1949, while he was on research leave from Columbia University to the Social Science Research Council SSRC (Kerns 2003: 258). At that time, A. Devitt Vanech, Assistant Attorney General for the US Department of Justice, contacted Steward by letter, stating that "The Uintah Ute Indians of Utah [claim] to have been the exclusive aboriginal occupants of a large area of the land in Utah and Nevada" (JHSP, Box 2, Vanech to Steward, April 21, 1949). In the letter, Vanech asks Steward if he "would be willing to assist the Government in this case with regard to the aboriginal occupancy of the area in question." Vanech explained the government's request to Steward because of his "authorship of Bulletin 120 of the Bureau of American Ethnology, 'Basin-Plateau Aboriginal Social Groups' [sic], and other related studies ..." (JHSP,

Box 2, Vanech to Steward, April 21, 1949). Within a week, Steward replied succinctly and with positive interest to Vanech, requesting a clarification of duties, expectations, and recompense (JHSP, Box 2, Steward to Vanech, April 26, 1949).

The initial letters between Steward and the Department of Justice demonstrate an important fact. Steward quickly outgrew his role as a simple expert, as he took on a greater role as advisor to and strategist for the government. As such, Steward, with various representatives from the Department of Justice, began laying out the legal and anthropological framework to identify characteristics of recognizable social organization in law. The distinctions created by their enquiry led to the legal argument that there were non-identifiable groups of humans in the Great Basin, and thus a jurisdictional vacuum in the area existed.[10] The letters demonstrate, overwhelmingly, that Steward played a leading role in the discipline of anthropology on this matter and acted as a liaison with the government, often vetting, editing, and changing other anthropologists' work to suit the needs of the government's legal argument.

In his first case before the ICC, Steward presented a 71-page expert report on behalf of the Department of Justice entitled, "Aboriginal and Historic Groups of the Ute Indians of Utah: An Analysis."[11] In essence, he argues that horses permitted political organization through mounted groups that hunted the bison to extinction (1953b: 9), that predatory raiding bands emerged from this new mode of production that menaced settlers, and a general change in social organization occurred rendering the Ute "qualitatively" changed. The effect of the horse was so great that the white settlers, when they arrived in the area afterwards, made a significant mistake in their signing of treaties with the Ute. He says:

The whites did not understand the nature of Ute chieftainship. They evidently assumed that the Ute had fairly powerful political leaders, like those among many of the tribes east of the Rocky Mountains, and, as their negotiations with the Indians required persons who could speak for the tribe, they tended to ascribe powers to the "chiefs" which these men did not have. They did not recognize that individuals who rose to prominence during the Indian wars had not been tribal chieftains in native times. (1953b: 6)

Not only undermining the credibility of the signatories to the historic treaties, Steward also calls into question the possibility for any present-day Indigenous knowledge of the culture history of the Great Basin. He asserts that science cannot discern anything of the culture area before 1850 because there are few trappers' and explorers' accounts of the area. He also says that early reports from the Office of Indian Affairs should be ignored because they consist mostly of the "enumeration of 'chiefs' and 'bands' which were prominent in the Indian wars ... " (1953b: 19). And, he says, the information gleaned after the arrival of white people only shows a degraded culture; and Indians from the Great Basin know nothing of their traditions or history themselves because of culture loss (1953b: 19–20). He argues by mere assertion, offering no facts or data to support his conclusions, and, as well, offers an internally inconsistent rationale by relying on processes of diffusion to explain culture contact.[12]

In August 1952, after completing his hastily organized testimony for the Ute cases, Steward left Columbia to a take a Research Professorship at the University of Illinois in Urbana-Champaign (UIUC). After training many soon-to-be prominent American materialist anthropologists at Columbia, Steward became the third anthropologist in the joint Anthropology and Sociology Department at the UIUC in 1952. Fresh upon his arrival, Steward's stature within the discipline was greatly increased: he was quickly awarded the Viking Medal from the Wenner-Gren Foundation in honor of his editorship of the *Handbook of South American Indians* and for his work on social organization and cultural evolution; shortly thereafter, he was elected to the National Academy of Sciences (Kerns 2003: 269–71; Manners 1973: 894); and in 1955, the University of Illinois published his theoretical *magnum opus, Theory of Culture Change: The Methodology of Multilinear Evolution.* If Steward's stature rose at Columbia it certainly crested while he was at UIUC.

Steward's new position offered fewer teaching and administrative duties; and his reduced workload at the university coincided with his increased role for the Department of Justice in preparation for the much larger, and certainly much better organized, cases against the Paiute (ICC Docket Nos 87, 88, 17, 100) and the combined case, *The Indians of California* v. *the United States* (Nos 31 and 37).[13] In addition to acting as an expert witness and strategist for the Paiute cases, as he did for the Ute cases earlier, with this move Steward undertook more responsibility by supervising and heavily editing the work of Erminie Wheeler-Voegelin and his several high-profile research assistants who were also working on the cases (Steward and Wheeler-Voegelin 1954).[14]

In a detailed letter to Williams, dated July 10, 1953, Steward describes the specifics of his testimony, outlining his interpretation of the aboriginal social organization of the Paiute and his strategy for the cases. Consistent with the Ute cases, he says that the aboriginal cultural "forms" of the Paiute have broken down through contact, and that what then-presently existed was a result of the influence of "Whites" (JHSP, Box 2, Steward to Williams, July 10, 1953). Though he admits that some areas of the Northern Paiute's territory had an abundance of food and a "band" could have "emerged" there, he contends, aboriginally, scarce resources determined that no chiefs, authority, or social organization beyond the biological family could develop in the area. In fact, reproducing a line from Spencer's understanding of authority in Indigenous communities (Spencer 1969 [1876]: 159, 185), Steward reports that the Paiute had a changing leadership of shamans, but no consistent form of authority or office of leadership. He asserts that the families are "free," having no residence patterns beyond those dictated by the location of foodstuffs and water. He asserts that socially unencumbered family movement indicates that there was no chief, and as a result no bands. He distances himself from the report of the Paiute's expert, Omer Stewart, commenting that Stewart's method to establish territories through the use of place names is shoddy because he did not assume that scarcity drove social organization. He asserts, as in the Ute case, that there is nothing to distinguish the Paiute from the Shoshone, and that just because they refer to themselves as *Numa* (the People), it does not mean that the Paiute are a collective.

Following this base description, the Department of Justice framed their legal defense to deny Indian Title in the Paiute cases on Steward's ethnographic account and his theory of the "levels of sociocultural integration" as a way to argue that the Paiute had no cohesion, leadership, or common identity based on an objective "science" (Steward and Wheeler-Voegelin 1954 in Steward 1955: 101–21; Steward 1974). The US Department of Justice relied entirely on reports from Steward and Wheeler-Voegelin on the Shoshone to assert that "the government was not liable for any claims because the petitioners did not hold original Indian title" (Stewart 1959: 51; see also Ronaasen et al. 1999). In fact, based on Steward's reports, the Department of Justice argued that the traditional lands of the Paiute were in a jurisdictional vacuum, alleging that the Paiute were "inherently incapable of acquiring and/or holding 'original Indian Title'" because they were not a recognized group based on the neo-evolutionary theory of the levels of sociocultural integration (Defendant's Requested Findings of Fact, Northern Paiute Nation, quoted in Ronaasen 1993: 52; cf. Ronaasen et al. 1999; see also Steward 1955: 102–3).

Steward claimed that the Paiute, a "Shoshonean" people, lived at the family level of sociocultural integration, alleging that pre-contact Shoshone families lived in isolation with no formal ties between groups of families, and few informal ones (1955: 111–16). He likened the family to a net without any social knots that could establish connections between groups; a model that, he says, ultimately permitted "liberty" for each individual biological unit (1955: 117). Explicitly, he describes "[t]he typical Shoshonean family" as "independent and self-sufficient during the greater part of the year, perhaps during 80 or 90 percent of the time," and alleges that "the family subsisted and fulfilled most cultural functions with little assistance from other families, and that it probably could have survived in complete isolation" (1955: 108). Moreover, he claims that family-level groups were rather rare in the pre-European contact period of the western hemisphere, and he suggests that "this level" is represented "in South America by the Nambicuara, Guató, Mura and perhaps other groups," and in North America by only two: "the Eskimo" and the "Shoshonean peoples" (1955: 119). In fact, he says, "[p]erhaps there have been people similar to the Shoshoneans in other parts of the world; for the present, however, the Shoshoneans must be regarded as typologically unique" (1955: 120).

Thus, in his testimony before the ICC, Steward claimed that the Shoshone represented the lowest level of his evolutionary taxonomy, and that they were "typologically unique." He described them as "gastric," motivated solely by their want of food, as atomistic biological groups, and finally used them to create a baseline reference point of social aggregates for his evolutionary taxonomy. Occupying the lowest level of human social evolution for all people, for all time, through this description the Shoshone became a metaphor for the bottom of the evolutionary typology, and necessary for the pronouncements of his entire ecological-evolutionary project. The magnitude of this imagery led Myers (2004) to conclude that the Shoshone have become a sort of cultural "barometer" used to reference social evolution within the discipline, and Ingold (2000) to identify Steward's work as the "*locus classicus*" within the discipline of anthropology for the comprehension of the social organization of Indigenous peoples.

Steward's political location is exposed when his ICC testimony is contrasted with his original statements about Shoshone political organization. In "The Economic and Social Basis of Primitive Bands" (1936), Steward states that all bands are "politically autonomous," "communally landowning," and have rules for "land inheritance," and concludes that all people live in this state of social organization, at a minimum. Axiomatically he states:

All peoples in an area of low population density have some form of politically autonomous, landowning band, which is greater than the bilateral family. The size of the band and the extent of the territory it utilizes are determined by the number of persons who, due largely to ecological factors, habitually cooperate at least during part of the annual round of economic and social activity. Band unity is expressed in a consciousness of common interest and submission to some degree of central control during community enterprises, although such control may be lacking during parts of the year. (1936: 343)

In this early paper, written directly after his fieldwork but before joining the federal government, Steward specifies that the Owens Valley Paiute, the Southern California Shoshone, and "other Paiute" are either composite or patrilineal bands and are therefore, *de facto*, politically autonomous, land owning, and are a recognizable group with a degree of central control and common interests (1936: 338). Therein, not only did he say that all peoples live in an organized, rule-based society, he notes that:

... although the family is often the seasonal independent subsistence unit, additional social and economic factors require the unity and territorial autonomy of an aggregate of several such families, that is, the band. The most important factors which produce the band are: (1) Among the apes and most other mammals, the "social" aggregate is usually greater than the biological family. Therefore, primates provide no reason to suppose that human beings ever were divided into family groups. (2) In practically all human groups several families cooperate in some economic activity and frequently share game and even vegetable foods communally. This provides a kind of subsistence insurance or greater security than individual families could achieve ... (1936: 332)

From 1949 until at least mid-1955, Steward testified, wrote reports, advised the government, and recruited others with regard to several ICC cases.[15] According to his archives, he worked on at least Docket Nos 17, 44, 45, 87, 88, and 100. And, according to the ICC Index of Cases, Steward is listed as having prepared reports and testimony for the Uintah Ute cases, the Northern Paiute cases, and the combined case, the Indians of California (Decisions of the Indian Claims Commission 1974).[16]

CONCLUSION

Steward has been historicized biographically, with examinations of his personal life and institutional heritage (Kerns 2003; Manners 1973; Murphy 1977, 1981; Shimkin 1964), and theoretically, with a greater focus on his written texts (Carneiro 2003; Clemmer 1969; Clemmer et al. 1999; Feit 1982; Harris 1968; Pinkoski 2006; Ronaasen 1993; Sidky 2005). These two approaches to theorizing him overlap, and a coherent image of him and his theory has emerged within the discipline. For example, on the occasion of his 60th birthday, his students and several colleagues presented him a *festschrift, Process and Pattern in Culture: Essays in Honor of Julian H. Steward* (Manners 1964). For the collection, Demitri Shimkin, Steward's University of Illinois colleague, wrote the biographical introduction praising Steward's fieldwork methods and documenting his incredible contributions to anthropological science (1964: 3–10).

Likewise, in Steward's extensive obituary in *American Anthropologist*, Robert Manners (1973) details aspects of Steward's life, stressing his contributions to the discipline and celebrating his inconsistencies as a sign of Steward's true scientific method. Manners's treatment codifies several important notions of Steward within the historiography of American anthropology. He situates Steward within his institutional and genealogical traditions, tracing Steward's connections to UC-Berkeley, Cornell University, the University of Michigan, the University of Utah, the Smithsonian Institute, Columbia University, and finally the University of Illinois; and he locates Steward within his relationships to his instructors, Alfred Kroeber and Robert Lowie, and his many accomplished students.

Manners also highlights Steward's theoretical contributions, noting his ethnography *Basin-Plateau* (1938), his essay "Cultural Causality and Law: A Trial Formulation" (1949), the text *Theory of Culture Change* (1955), and the Puerto Rico Project as significant contributions to anthropological theory and method. It is because of these contributions, but not only them, that Manners concludes that:

> Steward is generally credited with introducing two conceptual terms, *de novo*, into the anthropological lexicon: multilinear evolution and levels of sociocultural integration. His name is also closely associated with the popularization of a number of other terms now widely used in anthropology and related disciplines, such as cultural ecology, the search for regularities, culture type, cultural causality, and the larger context. Whether he invented the terms or not, Steward must certainly share credit for giving to the ideas expressed by them a vitality that they might not have achieved without painstaking explorations and often brilliant analyses. Thus, for example, in his efforts to replace the stultifying culture area concept with the concept of culture type; and his revolt against the restrictions of historical particularism and the perversion of cultural relativism from methodological tool to an immutable principle of identification, Steward helped to place or to keep anthropology within the "sciences." (Manners 1973: 896)

In two other personal recollections, Robert Murphy, another of Steward's prominent students, remembers that his professor was a "kindly man" but had "enormous inner tension and conflict" (1977: 15) and recognizes *Basin-Plateau* and its "meticulously detailed description of local groups" (Murphy 1981: 184).

In the most recent and certainly most complete biography to date, Kerns (2003) focuses on one of Steward's key concepts, the "patrilineal band," and prepares a descriptive analysis of his life. Beginning with his formative years, Kerns argues that Steward was heavily influenced by problems inherent in arid environments and the labor that it takes to organize irrigation work to solve them. She demonstrates that his focus on the organization of subsistence labor and its relationship to the physical environment remained a central component in Steward's *oeuvre* on development and change throughout his career.

According to Kerns, Steward's cross-cultural analysis differentiated his approach so thoroughly from the dominant Boasian tradition as to develop an entirely new method of study. "Cultural ecology," as he called it, became the method to distil the levels of multilinear evolution and effectively re-codified evolutionary theory within a scientific rhetoric. Kerns's text provides this context; and she systematically undermines Steward's claim to an objective, scientific method for his conceptual basis for the root of society, contending that the "patrilineal band" that he assumed was merely a reflection of his own social habits and only inferred into his theoretical paradigm. The effect of this assumed model ensconced a male-centered approach to anthropological method, and was replicated and promoted in his theory and practice (Kerns 2003).

There are serious historical and contextual errors in each of these biographical accounts. For example, Manners reports that Steward "was loaned to the Bureau of Indian Affairs [BIA] at the request of John Collier who was then actively involved in the creation of his programs for reform of the Bureau, usually referred to as a New Deal for the Indians" (1973: 892). The "New Deal" or Indian Reorganization Act (IRA) was Commissioner of Indian Affairs John Collier's attempt to stem federal assimilation policies by reversing the decades-old policy of the Dawes Allotment Act (1887). However, Steward was at odds with Collier's policies, as Kerns (2003: 199) notes: "[d]espite the 1934 [New Deal] legislation, Steward regarded the assimilation of American Indians as inevitable and as the path to economic improvement." And Steward himself recounted that Collier's:

... New Deal for the Indians was remarkable in that its policies were even more radical than those of the Russian Revolution. It undertook to redirect culture change toward communal, utopian societies that were presumed to have existed earlier and to establish them within the larger framework of free enterprise.... The New Indian policy was messianic, compassionate, intolerant and unrealistic. (Steward 1969: 14)

Thus, though recognizing Steward's involvement in American Indian policy, Manners misunderstands or misrepresents Steward's work in the context of that policy.

Second, Shimkin (1964) claims that Steward's expertise as a scientist is based upon an empirical reality. He cites Steward's "[a]lmost two years of arduous ethnography [sic]" that enabled his ground-breaking theoretical pronouncements (1964: 4). However, Steward's fieldwork in the Great Basin was significantly less than Shimkin alleged.

Thomas (1983) supports a strong critique of Steward's methods and of the conclusions drawn in *Basin-Plateau*. He demonstrates that Steward worked with a very limited number of Shoshone informants when doing fieldwork; and says that:

... [i]t is particularly critical to note that Steward never worked with the lakeshore adapted Northern Paiute groups, such as the Pyramid Lake or Walker River Paiute. In fact Steward's classic *Basin-Plateau Aboriginal Sociopolitical Groups* (1938) does not even include a sketch of these societies, an extremely important omission. It seems entirely likely that the microenvironments of these large inland lakes fostered a significantly different settlement pattern and probably more complex social organization than Steward's "typical" family band. (Thomas 1983: 61)

Finally, although Kerns's biography addresses the failure of Steward's work, like that of many in his time, to appreciate the role of women in his analysis, and the contribution of women surrounding him, it does nothing to soundly question the basic assumptions that he makes about Indigenous societies as a whole and the political impact of his work.

Biographical and theoretical accounts of Steward serve to reinforce a general disciplinary lacuna regarding colonialism and North America. This misrecognition of Steward's work for the US Department of Justice is codified, for example, in Kerns's 400-page biography of him, where only four scattered pages in the entire book address his work for the US Department of Justice in the ICC cases, though he performed this work for at least seven years (Kerns 2003: 247, 259, 282–83). Moreover, when Kerns mentions Steward's ICC work, she contends that his work for the Department of Justice was not to be considered political, but rather understood as "scientific," explaining that it was Steward's "commitment [to science], without regard to politics, [that] helps explain his decision ... to testify for the federal government in the Indian Claims Commission cases" (2003: 247), notwithstanding that his testimony and his "academic" work served to represent a *terra nullius* in the American Great Basin (Pinkoski 2006).

Kerns's biography reinforces the generally accepted gap that has been created through authoritative sources of Steward's life. These include the introductory essay in Steward's *festschrift*, a biographical account that neglects to mention, or fails to understand, the importance of his association with the government (Shimkin 1964); and the recent entry on "Julian Steward" in the *Encyclopedia of Anthropology* (Sponsell 2006), where space is allotted to excuse Steward's relationship to nineteenth-century evolutionary theory, but none is devoted to an examination of his work before the ICC. In fact, and tellingly, Sponsell alleges that: "Steward focussed on traditional culture and *ignored the colonial situation that oppressed indigenous societies*, assuming the inevitability of their sociocultural assimilation or even extinction" (2006: 2129, emphasis mine).

The specific topic of Steward's work for the government before the ICC is also excluded in the biographies of Steward by Robert Murphy (1977, 1981), neither of which mention the ICC. So too is the topic overlooked in Steward's obituary, written by another of his students, Robert Manners (1973). All of these omissions are significant: first, because of the significant amount of time Steward spent in his relationship with the Department of Justice, employment that reasonably should be included in any biography. Second, because of the volumes of academic material that Steward published while he was working for the Department of Justice that had a direct and sometimes *verbatim* relationship to his testimony in claims cases (Clemmer and Myers 1999; Pinkoski 2006; Pinkoski and Asch 2004; Ronaasen 1992; Ronaasen et al. 1999). Third, and incredibly, because both Robert Murphy and Robert Manners, the authors of three of the biographies, worked for and appeared on behalf of the US government in ICC proceedings at Steward's behest and under his direction.

Undoubtedly Steward's contributions to the discipline of anthropology are great; and his contributions to American anthropology at the dawn of the Cold War are foundational to his wider theoretical project. It is also apparent that there is a disconnect between the application of his theory, its historic and political context, and its representation within the discipline. I submit that we must acknowledge this connection and incorporate it into our knowledge base when theorizing this time-period. My assertion rests solely on the notion that dehumanizing entire populations is a political act that requires a level of scrutiny for our basic anthropological project. The biggest question emerging out of this disconnect becomes why this relationship has not been examined in North America when other national traditions, following Asad's (1970) critique, have already undertaken this analysis.

NOTES

I would like to acknowledge the funding that I have received in support of my research project. I have received this support through the generosity of the Social Sciences and Humanities Research Council of Canada (SSHRC) in the form of a doctoral fellowship, and am presently benefiting from the post-doctoral funding of an SSHRC Multi-Collaborative Research Initiative, entitled Peuples autoctones et gouvernance, housed at the Centre de recherché en droit public, Universié de Montréal.

1. This occurred in Canada a quarter of a century later, and thus not at the "dawn of the Cold War." The same critique can be levied against many contemporary anthropologists who testify before Canadian courts for the benefit of deriving "Aboriginal rights" (see Culhane 1992, 1998; Pinkoski and Asch 2004). This critique is also applicable to the colonization of Puerto Rico (see Velasquez 1980).
2. Steward joined the BAE in 1935, and worked as a liaison with the Bureau of Indian Affairs (BIA) just after the Indian Reorganization Act was passed by US Congress. The "New Deal" or Indian Reorganization Act (IRA) was Commissioner of Indian Affairs John Collier's attempt to stem federal assimilation policies by reversing the decades-old policy of the Dawes Allotment Act (1887). The most important piece of legislation enacted while Collier was Commissioner was the Wheeler-Howard (Indian Reorganization) Act in 1934 (Philp 1977; Dailey 2004). The Act, best known

as the "IRA" or the "New Deal," was signed by Roosevelt on June 18, 1934, and:

> ... [a]lthough it bore little resemblance to Collier's original proposal, the IRA established a turning point in Indian history by abandoning future land allotment. It extended the trust period in restricted land, allowed for the voluntary exchange of allotments to consolidate checkerboard reservations, continued existing practices of inheritance, and restored to tribal ownership remaining surplus lands created by the Dawes General Allotment Act. (Philp 1977: 159)

Collier's programme fit well with the tenets of Boasian anthropology, and Steward openly opposed Collier's approach, believing that the initiative of home rule, for example, was a form of forced segregation that ran counter to the inevitable processes of assimilation (Steward 1969). Steward's approach differed greatly from Collier's; Kerns notes that "[d]espite the 1934 [IRA] legislation, Steward regarded the assimilation of American Indians as inevitable and as the path to economic improvement" (2003: 199).

3. In counter-distinction to his students' overt political activism, Steward championed his own work as scientific and apolitical. Kerns quotes him saying explicitly that: "[m]y teaching is entirely non-political in every sense" (2003: 247); he thus promoted his own work as neutral and objective. Manners reports that Stanley Diamond, another of Steward's prominent students, hammered his professor on this point recognizing that:

    > ... although Steward's very decision for neutrality ... is itself a decisive act that could have significant social consequences, our discipline offers neither proof nor assurances that one of these strategies is either more benign, more fecund, or more "scientific" than the other. (cited in Manners 1973: 891)

    This difference from his students' belief in open political activism was also manifest in his relationship with Eric Wolf, and is evidenced in an exchange in the journal *Science,* where Steward replied to Wolf's review and critique of his penultimate book, *Contemporary Change in Traditional Societies* (Steward 1967). In the original review, Wolf critiqued Steward precisely on this point, and Steward responded to the review declaring that:

    > The moral responsibility of scientists for social change and its attendant ills has been increasingly debated in *Science* and elsewhere since the bomb was dropped on Hiroshima. I submit, however, that the issue has been improperly phrased and an unnecessary dilemma thus created.... Today, scientific research is a basic culture value, and we obviously cannot hold any particular scientists responsible for its effects. Science must above all remain free, (Steward 1968: 147)

4. In the revamped edition of Kroeber's *Anthropology Today*, reconfigured by Sol Tax (1962), Steward's article has been excised entirely. "Evolution and Culture" is reissued as chapter 1 of *Theory of Culture Change* (Steward 1955).

5. For this assertion, he finds support, he says, from the work of White, Lesser, and Lowie, and notes that his own personal attempt to formulate

regularities is with respect to the patrilineal band. It is important to remember that, although he had "no doubt that many such laws can even now be postulated, [and the present need is] to establish a genuine interest in the scientific objective and a clear conceptualization of what is meant by regularities" (Steward 1949: 2), in his fieldwork, much to his consternation, he was never able to locate the patrilineal band (Kerns 2003)

6. This notion is reified in Canadian law as the test to discern Aboriginal rights and title (see Pinkoski and Asch 2004).

7. "The Levels of Sociocultural Integration" is reprinted as Chapter 3 of *Theory of Culture Change* (Steward 1955).

8. Cf. *In Re: Southern Rhodesia* [1919] AC 210 Privy Council (see Asch 1988).

9. It should be noted, however, that in establishing its original colonial law, the US courts did not follow the doctrine of *terra nullius*, but instead relied on the doctrine of discovery (Wilkins and Lomawaima 2001). As Reynolds (1992) clearly states, the doctrine of *terra nullius* has two closely understood meanings that appropriately describe the Department of Justice's argument before the ICC. The first relates to "a country without a sovereign recognized by European authorities," and the second relates to a "territory where nobody owns any land at all, where no tenure of any sort existed" (Reynolds 1992: 14). For the ICC cases, the Department of Justice pursued the latter meaning of *terra nullius* and argued that "Indian" Peoples appealing to the Commission had no standing before it based on evolutionary criteria. The magnitude of this legal theory is explained by Slattery (1979) as one of the four means by which any state can justify the acquisition of new territories in common law, by what is called the "settlement thesis" or the "acquisition of territory that was previously unoccupied or is not recognised as belonging to another political entity" (cited in Asch 2002: 33).

10. See: JHSP, Box 2, Steward to Vanech, April 26, 1949; Williams to Steward, May 3, 1949; Steward to Vanech, June 1, 1949, Vanech to Steward, September 6, 1949; Vanech to Steward, October 21, 1949; Vanech to Steward, November 1, 1949; Vanech to Steward, November 14, 1949; Wilkinson to Steward, April 4, 1950; Wm. Amory Underhill to Steward, February 7, 1952; Steward to Yost, February 12, 1952.

11. A copy of the report with handwritten annotations appears in Steward's archive (JHSP, Box 2); a published version appears as Steward (1974).

12. The Uintah Ute cases were decided by the ICC with Opinions and Findings of Facts offered on February 21, 1957 (ICC 1974: 360). In no uncertain terms, the court rejected Steward's testimony, and his interpretation of the culture history of the Great Basin, finding his argument to be implausible and inconsistent.

13. Together, the dockets comprise much of the western United States, including what is now: Utah, Nevada, Arizona, California, Idaho, and Colorado. The *Indians of California* case pitted Steward against Kroeber.

14. Kerns suggests that, although Steward's new position freed up his time, provided several research assistants, was generously funded, and offered greater pay, the reason for his move was because he was happy to leave the cut-throat environment of Columbia academics, the confrontational departmental politics, and the responsibility of training so many raucous

students (2003: 260). She also reports that Steward was put off by the outright challenges he received from students, and that he found their lack of middle class desires unsettling (2003: 237). Ironically, however, if Steward was trying to avoid training graduate students or the demands of having students around him, according to Kerns herself, immediately upon his arrival in Illinois he arranged teaching and research positions for several of his Columbia students. These students include Robert Murphy and Paul Ducey, Columbia PhDs from 1954 and 1956 respectively, who worked for Steward beginning in the early course of the ICC research, assisting while Steward was still at Columbia. Murphy's wife, Yolanda, joined her husband and the Department of Justice research project when it was at UIUC, as did Robert Manners and Elman Service, Frederick Lehman, Ben Zimmerman, and Eric Wolf (Kerns 2003: 264–65). Though Wolf worked as Steward's research associate during this time there is no indication that he worked on any of the ICC material.

15. I do not have confirmation of the termination of Steward's relationship with the Department of Justice. The last documented letter in the archives stating his employment with them is dated August 26, 1955. There is correspondence to indicate that Steward was kept apprised of the dealings of the Department of Justice through to 1957, when the rulings were handed down in the Ute cases. And, although not working on the case due to his time in Japan with his Ford Project, the Department of Justice continued to keep him apprised of the workings of the case, as their letter indicates:

> Dear Dr. Steward,
> There is attached a copy of the petitioners' opening brief in The Northern Paiute Nation v. United States, case No. 87 before the Indian Claims Commission. This brief will undoubtedly be of interest to you, and such comments as you may care to make will be appreciated.
>
> Sincerely Perry W. Morton – Assistant Attorney General Lands Division to Ralph A. Barney (JHSP, Box 2, June 24, 1957)

16. It is important to note that, although the ICC rejected Steward's testimony and that he "lost" every case where he was an expert witness (Lewis 2002; Stewart 1985), notwithstanding his futility before the court, Steward's description of the Shoshone remains steadfast in anthropology (cf. Haenn and Wilk 2006; Johnson and Earle 1987; Myers 2004, etc.), and his approach is represented in the discipline as a scientific and objective method for the comprehension of "band-level" societies, as described by numerous representative authors above. Moreover, it is a perception that continues to have implications in Canada, as it has helped to structure the tests for determining aboriginal rights and title in Canadian law (Asch 1988, 1992, 1999, 2000, 2002; Cruickshank 1992; Culhane 1992, 1998; Pinkoski and Asch 2004).

REFERENCES

Asad, Talal, ed. 1970. *Anthropology and the Colonial Encounter*. London: Ithaca Press.

Asch, Michael. 1988. *Home and Native Land: Aboriginal Rights and the Canadian Constitution*. Scarborough, ON: Nelson.

—— 1992. Errors in Delgamuukw: An Anthropological Perspective. In *Aboriginal Title in British Columbia: Delgamuukw vs. The Queen*, pp. 221–43. Frank Cassidy, ed. Vancouver: Oolichan Books.

—— 1999. From Calder to Van der Peet: Aboriginal Rights and Canadian Law, 1973–96. In *Indigenous Peoples' Rights in Australia, Canada, and New Zealand*, pp. 428–46. Paul Havemann, ed. Melbourne: Oxford University Press.

—— 2000. The Judicial Conception of Culture after Delgamuukw. *Review of Constitutional Studies* 5(2): 119–37.

—— 2002. From Terra Nullius to Affirmation: Reconciling Aboriginal Rights with the Canadian Constitution. *Canadian Journal of Law and Society* 17(2): 23–39.

Barnard, Alan. 2000. *History and Theory in Anthropology*. Cambridge: Cambridge University Press.

Beck, Charlotte, ed. 1999. *Models for the Millennium: Great Basin Anthropology Today*. Salt Lake City: University of Utah Press.

Bohannan, Paul and Mark Glazer, eds. 1988. *High Points in Anthropology*. New York: McGraw-Hill.

Carneiro, Robert. 2003. *Evolutionism in Cultural Anthropology: A Critical History*. Boulder, CO: Westview Press.

Clemmer, Richard O. 1969. The Fed-up Hopi: Resistance of the American Indian and the Silence of Good Anthropologists. *Journal of the Steward Anthropological Society* 1: 18–40.

Clemmer, Richard O. and L. Daniel Myers. 1999. Introduction. In *Julian Steward and the Great Basin: The Making of an Anthropologist*. Richard O. Clemmer, L. Daniel Myers, and Mary Elizabeth Rudden, eds. Salt Lake City: University of Utah Press.

Clemmer, Richard O., L. Daniel Myers, and Mary Elizabeth Rudden, eds. 1999. *Julian Steward and the Great Basin: The Making of an Anthropologist*. Salt Lake City: University of Utah Press.

Cruickshank, Julie. 1992. Invention of Anthropology in British Columbia's Supreme Court: Oral Tradition as Evidence in Degamuukw v. B.C. *BC Studies* 95: 25–42.

Culhane, Dara. 1992. Adding Insult to Injury: Her Majesty's Loyal Anthropologist. *BC Studies* 95: 66–92.

—— 1998. *The Pleasure of the Crown: Anthropology, First Nations and the Law*. Burnaby, BC: Talonbooks.

Dailey, David. 2004. *Battle for the BIA: G.E.E Lindquist and the Missionary Crusade against John Collier*. Tucson: University of Arizona Press.

Darnell, Regna. 2001. *Invisible Genealogies: A History of Americanist Anthropology*. Lincoln: University of Nebraska Press.

Erickson, Paul and Liam Murphy. 1998. *A History of Anthropological Theory*. Peterborough: Broadview Press.

Feit, Harvey A. 1982. The Future of Hunters within Nation States: Anthropology and the James Bay Cree. In *Politics and History in Band Societies*, pp. 373–412. Eleanor Leacock and Richard Lee, eds. Cambridge: Cambridge University Press.

Friedman, Jonathan. 1987. An Interview with Eric Wolf. *Current Anthropology* 28(1): 107–18.

Haenn, Nora and Richard Wilk. 2006. *The Environment in Anthropology: A Reader in Ecology, Culture and Sustainable Living*. New York: New York University Press.

Harris, Marvin. 1968. *The Rise of Anthropological Theory: A History of Theories of Culture*. New York: Crowell.

Indian Claims Commission. 1974. *Ute Indians II, Commission Findings*. New York: Garland.

Ingold, Tim. 2000. On the Social Relations of the Hunter-Gatherer Band. In *The Cambridge Encyclopedia of Hunters and Gatherers*, pp. 399–410. Richard B. Lee and Richard Daly, eds. Cambridge: Cambridge University Press.

Johnson, Allen W. and Timothy Earle. 1987. *The Evolution of Human Societies: From Foraging Group to Agrarian State*. Stanford, CA: Stanford University Press.

Kerns, Virginia. 2003. *Scenes from the High Desert: Julian Steward's Life and Theory*. Urbana: University of Illinois Press.

Layton, Robert. 1997. *An Introduction to Theory in Anthropology*. Cambridge: Cambridge University Press.

Lewis, Henry T. 2002. An Anthropological Critique. In *Forgotten Fires: Native Americans and the Transient Wilderness*, pp. 17–36. Omer C. Stewart, Henry T. Lewis, and M.K. Anderson, eds. Norman: University of Oklahoma Press.

Manners, Robert, ed. 1964. *Process and Pattern in Culture: Essays in Honor of Julian H. Steward*. Chicago: Aldine.

Manners, Robert. 1973. Julian Haynes Steward, 1902–1972. *American Anthropologist* 75(3): 886–97.

McGee, R. Jon and Richard Warms, eds. 1996. *Anthropological Theory: An Introductory History*. Mountain View, CA: Mayfield.

Moore, Jerry D. 1997. *Visions of Culture: An Introduction to Anthropological Theories and Theorists*. Walnut Creek, CA: AltaMira Press.

Murphy, Robert F. 1977. Introduction. In *Evolution and Ecology: Essays on Social Transformation*, pp. 1–39. Jane C. Steward and Robert F. Murphy, eds. Urbana: University of Illinois Press.

—— 1981. Julian Steward. In *Totems and Teachers: Perspectives on the History of Anthropology*, pp. 171–208. Sydel Silverman, ed. New York: Columbia University Press.

Myers, L. Daniel. 2004. Subtle Shifts and Radical Transformations in Hunter-gatherer Research in American Anthropology: Julian Steward's Contributions and Achievements. In *Hunter-Gatherers in History, Archaeology and Anthropology*, pp. 175–86. Alan Barnard, ed. Oxford: Berg.

Ortner, Sherry. 1984. Theory in Anthropology Since the Sixties. *Comparative Studies in Society and History* 26(1): 126–66.

Philp, Kenneth R. (1977) *John Collier's Crusade for Indian Reform: 1920–1954*. Tucson: University of Arizona Press.

Pinkoski, Marc. 2006. Julian Steward and American Anthropology: The Science of Colonialism. Unpublished PhD dissertation. University of Victoria, Victoria, BC.

Pinkoski, Marc and Michael Asch. 2004. Anthropology and Indigenous Rights in Canada and the United States: Implications in Steward's Theoretical Project. In *Hunter-Gatherers in History, Archaeology and Anthropology*, pp. 187–200. Alan Barnard, ed. Oxford: Berg.

Reynolds, Henry. 1992. *The Law of the Land*. Ringwood, Vic.: Penguin.

Ronaasen, Sheree. 1993. Cultural Ecology and Functionalism: Social Theory Framed by a Colonial Political Context. Unpublished MA thesis, University of Alberta, Edmonton.

Ronaasen, Sheree, Richard O. Clemmer, and Mary Elizabeth Rudden. 1999. Rethinking Cultural Ecology, Multilinear Evolution, and Expert Witnesses: Julian Steward and the Indian Claims Commission Proceedings. In *Julian Steward and the Great Basin: The Making of an Anthropologist*, pp. 170–202. Richard O. Clemmer, L. Daniel Myers, and Mary Elizabeth Rudden, eds. Salt Lake City: University of Utah Press.

Shimkin Demitri. 1964. Julian H. Steward: A Contributor to Fact and Theory in Cultural Anthropology. In *Process and Pattern in Culture: Essays in Honor of Julian H. Steward*, pp. 1–17. Robert Manners, ed. Chicago: Aldine.

Sidky, Homayun. 2005. *Perspectives on Culture: A Critical Introduction to Theory in Cultural Anthropology*. Upper Saddle River, NJ: Pearson.

Silverman, Sydel 2005. The United States. In *One Discipline, Four Ways: British, German, French and American Anthropology*, The Halle Lectures. Chicago: University of Chicago Press.

Spencer, Herbert. 1969 [1876]. *Principles of Sociology*, Stanislav Andreski, ed. Hamdon: Archon.

Sponsell, Leslie. 2006. Steward, Julian H. (1902–1972). In *Encyclopedia of Anthropology*, vol. 5, pp. 2128–30. H. James Birx, ed. Thousand Oaks, CA: Sage Publications.

Steward, Julian H. 1929. Diffusion and Independent Invention: A Critique of Logic. *American Anthropologist* 31: 491–95.

—— 1936. The Economic and Social Basis of Primitive Bands. In *Essays on Anthropology in Honor of Alfred Louis Kroeber*, pp. 311–50. Robert Lowie, ed. Berkeley: University of California Press.

—— 1938. Basin-Plateau Aboriginal Sociopolitical Groups. *Bureau of American Ethnology Bulletin* 120. Washington, DC: United States Government Printing Office.

—— ed. 1946a. *The Marginal Tribes. Handbook of South American Indians*, vol. 1. Washington, DC: Bureau of American Ethnology Bulletin 143.

—— ed. 1946b. *The Andean Civilizations: Handbook of South American Indians*, vol. 2. Washington, DC: Bureau of American Ethnology Bulletin 143.

—— ed. 1948a. *The Circum-Carribbean Tribes: Handbook of South American Indians*, vol. 4. Washington, DC: Bureau of American Ethnology Bulletin 143.

—— ed. 1948b. *The Tropical Forest Tribes: Handbook of South American Indians*, vol. 3. Washington, DC: Bureau of American Ethnology, Bulletin 143.

—— 1949a. *The Comparative Ethnology of South America: Handbook of South American Indians*, vol. 5. Washington, DC: Bureau of American Ethnology, Bulletin 143.

—— 1949b. Cultural Causality and Law: A Trial Formulation of the Development of Early Civilizations. *American Anthropologist* 51: 1–27.

—— ed. 1950a. *Physical, Linguistics and Cultural Geography of South American Indians: Handbook of South American Indians*, vol. 6. Washington, DC: Bureau of American Ethnology, Bulletin 143.

—— 1950b. *Area Research: Theory and* Practice. New York: Social Science Research Council.

—— 1951. Levels of Sociocultural Integration: An Operational Concept. *Southwestern Journal of Anthropology* 7: 374–90.

—— 1953a. Evolution and Process. In *Anthropology Today*, pp. 313–25. Alfred Kroeber, ed. Chicago: University of Chicago Press.

—— 1953b. Aboriginal and Historic Groups of the Ute Indians of Utah: An Analysis. Washington: United States Department of Justice, JHSP Box 10.

—— 1955. *Theory of Culture Change: The Methodology of Multilinear Evolution.* Urbana: University of Illinois Press.

—— 1968. Scientific Responsibility in Modern Life. *Science* 159(3811): 147–48.

—— 1969. Limitations of Applied Anthropology: The Case of the American Indian New Deal. *Journal of the Steward Anthropological Society* 1(1): 1–17.

—— 1974. *Ute Indians I,* Indian Claims Commission. New York: Garland.

Steward, Julian H. and Erminie Wheeler-Voegelin. 1954. *The Northern Paiute Indians.* Washington, DC: United States Department of Justice.

Stewart, Omer. 1959. Anthropology and the Indian Claims. *Delphian Quarterly* 42(3): 8–13.

—— 1985. The Shoshone Claims Cases. In *Irredeemable America: The Indians' Estate and Land Claims,* pp. 187–206. Imre Sutton, ed. Albuquerque: University of New Mexico Press.

Tax, Sol, ed. 1962. *Anthropology Today: Selections.* Chicago: Aldine.

Thomas, David Hurst. 1983. On Steward's Models of Shoshonean Sociopolitical Organization: A Great Bias in the Basin? In *The Development of Political Organization in Native North America,* pp. 59–68. Elisabeth Tooker, ed. *Proceedings of the American Ethnological Society 1979.* Washington, DC: American Ethnological Society.

Trencher, Susan. 2002. The American Anthropological Association and the Values of Science, 1935–70. *American Anthropologist* 104(2): 450–62.

Trigger, Bruce. 1989. *A History of Archaeological Thought.* Cambridge: University of Cambridge Press.

—— 1998. *Sociocultural Evolution: Calculation and Contingency.* Oxford: Blackwell.

Turney-High, Harry H. 1940. Review of *Basin-Plateau Aboriginal Sociopolitical Groups,* by Julian Steward. *American Anthropologist* 42(1): 136–38.

Velazquez, Rene. 1980. Julian Steward's Perspective on Puerto Rico. In *The Anthropology of the People of Puerto Rico,* pp. 50–58. Ronald Duncan et al., eds. San German: Caribbean Institute and Study Center for Latin America and the Inter American University of Puerto Rico.

Wallace, Pamela. 2002. Indian Claims Commission: Political Complexity and Contrasting Concepts of Identity. *Ethnohistory* 49(4): 743–66.

Wilkins and Lomawaima. 2001. *Uneven Ground: American Indian Sovereignty and Federal Law.* Norman: University of Oklahoma Press.

Wolf, Eric. 2001. *Pathways of Power: Building an Anthropology of the Modern World.* Berkeley: University of California Press.

4 IN THE NAME OF SCIENCE: THE COLD WAR AND THE DIRECTION OF SCIENTIFIC PURSUITS

Frank A. Salamone

It may be an exaggeration but it has been said that until the end of World War II the Annual Meetings of the American Anthropological Association (AAA) could be held in a large room of a major hotel. Certainly, many of the papers presented at the meetings found their way into the *American Anthropologist*. In many ways, the profession resembled a club or an extended family. Arguments could be fierce and some branches of the family could be quite hostile to other family groups. However, there was a generally shared ethos and purpose regarding the profession of anthropology.

True, as Willis (1969) has indicated, there was great resistance to including women and people of color in that family, even when Papa Franz Boas sought to include them. On the whole, however, it is hard to deny that until the United States reached the brink of World War II American anthropology was like a big family. The war changed the structure and culture of anthropology in numerous ways. The change had begun, in fact, a bit earlier, during the Great Depression. An often-overlooked fact is that many American anthropologists worked for the federal and state governments in what we would today called applied work. That work, by and large, seemed to pose few if any ethical problems for anthropologists and anthropology. It was concentrated on finding anthropological solutions for problems stemming from the Depression or otherwise helping people, such as Native Americans, to assert their cultural rights. The general attitude in anthropology was: "If the government is willing to pay money for these endeavors, so much the better."

This attitude continued with the entry of the United States into World War II. The fact that most Americans, anthropologists among them, supported the war and viewed it as a struggle for survival against fascism led many anthropologists to work with the United States government to find ways to defeat the enemy. Margaret Mead estimated that more than 95 percent of American anthropologists found themselves working in projects that supported the American war effort (Worsley 1992). So great was American support for the war effort that, in 1941, the American Anthropological Association passed a resolution which stated that it supported placing the "specialized skill and knowledge of its members, at the disposal of the country for the successful prosecution of the war" (AAA 1942: 42).

Between the end of World War II and the immersion of the United States in the Vietnam War a change came about in anthropology. In many ways it was a return to some earlier ideas, which Boas had expressed most eloquently in opposition to World War I, as well as a response to changes in American society. These changes, urging greater extension of democracy, such as the Civil Rights Movement and the Women's Movement, had great impact within anthropology and helped fuel calls for reinventing anthropology.

The response of the anthropological profession to these changes is one of the main concerns of this work. Addressing that response and setting it in its appropriate context requires an excursion into other areas, such as government funding, ethical issues, and the direction of anthropological research under the influence of secret funding. Using the example of the Rockefeller-funded International African Institute (IAI), we will explore the contours of the relationship between anthropologists and their funders. Anthropologists' post-World War II experience with the International African Institute and similar organizations set the stage for both the secret research proposed and carried out in the 1960s and 1970s, and the growing skepticism that led to the backlash against such work, culminating in the early 1970s Thailand Controversy in the American Anthropological Association.

THE EXPANSION OF GOVERNMENT INVOLVEMENT IN ANTHROPOLOGY

After World War II the academic job market exploded so that the available jobs exceeded the number of people qualified to fill them. Many anthropologists chose the university setting over that of government work. Although this trend was exacerbated by objections in the 1960s to the Vietnam War, it had begun as soon as there were academic openings. These openings were often the direct result of government policy. After World War II there was tremendous government investment in education. The GI Bill of Rights is an obvious example. Frequently, however, the money went into programs that aided government objectives. Obviously the sciences, especially physics, had proved their worth to the war effort. The Manhattan Project provided a model for government–science cooperation, even if Albert Einstein and J. Robert Oppenheimer became opponents of such endeavors. Anthropology profited from cooperation with the government and a good deal of significant work was done quite happily under government auspices so long as old attitudes prevailed and this cooperation did not appear to threaten them.

For example, many anthropologists carried out projects involving land rights, indigenous political organizations, health care, land tenure, urban life, migrant workers, water resources, race relations and discrimination, and numerous others. There was great involvement of anthropologists with political units and major funding agencies with government ties, not all of them open ties. Generally, anthropologists saw themselves as advocates for the rights of oppressed or disadvantaged people. They became expert witnesses, evaluators for projects, planners, and even diplomats. Members of the profession became deeply involved in development efforts. As long as the funding was open and publication not prohibited by terms of the contract, there was little concern over the implications of the work.

There were, to be sure, guides to research and apprehension about administrators' understanding of culture within the context of change. There was amazingly little worry, however, about the need for change in the first place. Certainly, there were those, such as Margaret Mead, who expressed regret that conditions were forcing people into change, but the spirit of the times viewed change as inevitable. Therefore, anthropologists involved in development sought to ameliorate the effects of change and to find ways to give those indigenous people involved in change some measure of control over their fates. The guides anthropologists wrote at the time give a clear picture of professional worries: *Human Problems in Technological Change* (Spicer 1952), *Cultural Patterns and Technical Change* (Mead 1953, see also 1956), *Health, Culture and Community: Case Studies of Public Reactions to Health Programs* (Paul 1955), *Traditional Cultures and the Impact of Technological Change* (Foster 1962), *Cooperation in Change: An Anthropological Approach to Community Development* (Goodenough 1963), and *Applied Anthropology* (Foster 1969). I am not implying that there was a lack of concern for ethics. Certainly, there was such concern. This concern developed slowly, though, with the professionalization of anthropology in the post-war years. In 1949, the Society for Applied Anthropology produced the first statement of ethics within the anthropological profession, followed soon after by the National Association for the Practice of Anthropology. These guidelines were written specifically to address the concerns of applied and practicing anthropologists. These efforts represented the first reactions of post-war anthropologists to the changing conditions in which their work was produced and consumed with the rise of the Cold War.

GUIDES TO ETHICAL PROFESSIONAL PRACTICE

The emergence of indigenous anthropologists who questioned the dominant, if unconscious, model of anthropological power relationships, added to the demands for professional ethical statements. Magubane, for example, drawing on the philosophical works of Mills and Lukacs, used a then-new vocabulary in anthropology – "colonial" and "colonized" – to describe the field relationship (see Frantz 1968; Wolf 1972). He argued that the questions asked by investigators and their:

... intellectual problems were irrelevant to the public issues of their time and to the private troubles of individual men and women. Instead, they are clear indications of the inability of observers to transcend the primacy of facts which are falsely reified in the capitalist tradition. (Magubane 1973: 1712)

The "facts" observers took into account were "as much if not more, the products of political considerations as of their scientific utility" (1973: 1714; see also Kuhn 1962).

In an effort to clarify some of these issues, in 1968 Charles Frantz, Stephen Boggs's successor as executive secretary of the Association and editor of the *AAA Newsletter*, produced a special statement in the *Newsletter* – "The Cultural Milieu of the Immediate Future of Anthropology" – which situated anthropology in its political roots. This interest in the relationship between anthropology's roots and its current problems had been part of its disciplinary history (see Rowe 1965). However, it was by 1968 being pursued simultaneously as an issue in intellectual history. Frantz wrote:

Anthropology is not the result of centered systematic development, but ... always ... shaped by historical expansion westward across the continent; influenced and in some cases constrained by opportunities and financial support ... it is no accident that the aborigines of the U.S. and its possessions, the Philippines and neighboring areas were the first populations to be studied in depth. (1968: 2)

Frantz further asserted that his own research indicated that up until the last two decades, US anthropologists had relatively easy access to other peoples for fieldwork.

In the meantime, new Foreign Area Research Guidelines issued by the government acknowledged responsibility for avoiding actions that would interfere with the integrity of American academic institutions. But, in Frantz's view, government guidelines that "where possible" research "should" (1) advance knowledge; (2) not be secret; and (3) be made available to the host country and support local scholars, were not strong enough. He asserted that if anthropologists in particular and American research in general were to be trusted, the sponsor must always publicly state their sponsorship of both the research and the researcher(s) involved. Further, anything that could not be made available to host country scholars and governments should not be undertaken. This view, stressing the significance of anthropology's own surroundings for anthropological work, became a subject for discussion and research and AAA resolutions (see e.g. the Anti-Warfare Resolution). These views were explored in the early 1960s, and by 1970 were asserted as part of professional statements, including the formal statement on ethics passed by the AAA ("Principles of Professional Responsibility" 1971).

The press of events outside the AAA impacted on internal discussion and events in the Association and was then reframed as part of anthropology's public professional position. In particular, issues central to the perception of the United States and American researchers as "neo-colonialist" pressed the AAA to make anthropology's professional boundaries public, and similarly pressured anthropologists to define their professional boundaries in the public sphere. However, as Boggs's study in the mid 1960s had already made clear, American anthropologists had been described as neocolonialist long before issues of funding and government influence on and use of research emerged as a significant issue for discussion. As shown in Boggs's study, others perceived American anthropologists as having a "neo-colonialist attitude" propelled by their own (professional wrapped up with personal) interests, in which they often abrogated or ignored the interests of indigenous scholars, peoples, and governments. The charge of "neocolonialism," as interpreted by Boggs, was not directed toward the American government or culture, but was more personally directed to American researchers, as those among whom research was conducted detected an individual rather than national agenda. Boggs's report (1965) noted that the first time that the term "neocolonialism" was used in reference to American anthropologists and their research was in 1947. In 1965, "neocolonialist" referred to "treating the world as your oyster, exploiting the world on your own terms rather than with an eye to the needs of the people." Further, according to Boggs, the accusation that American anthropologists were abusing their position in the world as Americans was "not well-known," even among anthropologists (1965: 1).

But definitions and public knowledge were shifting in 1965. The uncovering of previously covert relationships between governments, researchers, agencies, and universities, plus the escalation of the war in Vietnam and public reaction to it abroad and at home, impacted on American and anthropological self-definition and boundaries of practice. By 1968, Frantz's description of cultural milieu and the development of anthropology revealed and embodied this shift, as anthropology was described as the result of "westward expansion," "opportunity," and economics ("financial support") – the language of political, not personal, neocolonialism. People now had come to define neocolonialism as the political and economic exploitation of the resources of others.

Although we have no evidence that Frantz interpreted his own language in this way, nor that he intended to situate American anthropology as colonialist (a specific rather than inevitable inter- pretation), this view of anthropology as exploitative was accepted by many anthropologists (generally those who had received degrees after World War II) as applying to both public and professional realms.[1] Frantz and others such as Walter Goldschmidt (1973) argued that an anthropology funded by, and responsible to, government agencies necessarily promoted political agendas. These agendas, however, were markedly different from those taken for granted as "good" during World War II. Now the United States, as an entity viewed from abroad, was accused of carrying out a program of exploitative political domination.

Many Americans perceived the government of the United States as engaging in the same kind of exploitation at home. Massive public protests and student demonstrations took place, and myriad disenfranchised and newly enfranchised voices were raised against government activities at home and abroad. The concept of anthro- pologist as citizen returned. But the terms of the debate shifted again. Anthropologists struggling to define boundaries between citizen and scientist had previously accepted the fact that there was such a separation; what was argued were its terms and where and how one could appropriately apply them. The new argument challenged the existence of any such possible separation. Those holding this view did not argue the position of "scientists as citizens," they argued that "scientists were citizens," merging public and professional realms in civic action.

The saving grace for anthropology is, and should be the request that observations of human beings interacting are the primary subject matter … this means being able to achieve acceptance as a viewer and a listener. (*Newsletter* 1979: 21–22)

In response to concerns about "the recent proliferation of special- izations in anthropology and the resulting loss of common direction among anthropologists" (*Newsletter* 1979: 21), the AAA appointed the Committee on Anthropology as a Profession. The Committee sought to re-establish the connections among anthropologists by reminding anthropologists of their common experience as fieldworkers. The Committee's definition of an anthropologist as a "product" of the field experience was also articulated in fieldworker ethnographies.

General characteristics of the fieldwork experience were described and institutionalized within professional publications, but even as these terms were generalized they were particularized; that is, they expounded features of fieldwork experience as common to the group, and were described as individually experienced. The focus was often on the cost to the anthropologist as an individual in ways similar to the depiction of fieldwork offered in fieldworker ethnographies. For example, *Human Organization*, which published a long-running exchange on the subject of fieldwork, featured an editorial which was reprinted in the *Newsletter* (1979: 3–4). It said in part:

> He ... [the fieldworker] does not have the aura of a medical degree and a need on the part of the person to whom he is talking to be helped. He is an interloper; he has no place or function in the community. He is intensely vulnerable to the emotional current about which at first, he can have little knowledge.

But the effort to reconstitute the discipline using this "common denominator" experience as a ritual image for the profession's straits was unsuccessful. Moreover, there has been a steady retreat from the tougher ethical standards that emerged from the bloody battles at AAA meetings in the 1960s and early 1970s. The stronger ethical codes have been watered down and ignored as the recent scandal over Chagnon's research has demonstrated (Tierney 2000). Let us step back a bit and look at some history to get a better idea of the present situation.

A BRIEF LOOK AT AFRICAN STUDIES AND THE ROCKEFELLER FOUNDATION

> Malinowski assured the foundation that its funds would be put to constructive use, supporting the application of anthropology as social engineering in areas into which western capitalism was pressing. (Henrika Kuklick)

John D. Rockefeller established the Rockefeller Foundation (RF) in 1913 as a philanthropic institution "to promote the well-being of mankind throughout the world." The Foundation has distributed over $1.8 billion and has been deeply involved in operations as well as grant-giving. Almost from its inception, it has divided its work into five areas of administration: agricultural and natural sciences, arts, humanities, social sciences, and international relations. In 1929 the Rockefeller Foundation and the Laura Spelman Memorial Fund merged. The merger added the Spelman Fund's $58 million endowment to the RF's own endowment funds. Moreover, the merger led the RF into fresh areas of research and augmented the support of natural and social sciences, humanities, and agriculture. It soon became clear that a few grants in strategic areas would strengthen the influence of the RF in developing research along desired lines; that is, lines profitable to more commercial Rockefeller interests.

The Laura Spelman Rockefeller Memorial had been founded to support the social sciences, missionary work, and the welfare of women and children. In May 1922, the Memorial decided to systematize its charitable activities. It appointed Beardsley Ruml as director. It was Ruml who moved the Memorial deeply into the social sciences, including economics, sociology, political science, psychology, anthropology, and history. Under Ruml the Memorial focused on three major programs: social science and science technology; child study and parent education; and interracial relations. It was interested in both research and the dissemination of scientific knowledge and slanted its grants accordingly. The Memorial sought the practical outcome of improving people's lives through the application of scientific knowledge – in other words, through social engineering.

Moreover, the Memorial aimed at fostering cooperative research among social scientists. It did so by actively promoting the work of universities and research organizations, such as professional societies. As part of its work it supported the Social Science Research Council, which was organized in 1923 to correlate and stimulate research in the social sciences. The Memorial funded other agencies that spread knowledge and carried out research. A list of its projects provides an example of its influence: Social Science Abstracts, the Brookings Institution, the Institute of Pacific Relations, the National Bureau of Economic Research, the Child Study Association of America, Teachers College of Columbia, the State University of Iowa, the Association for the Study of Negro Life and History, and the International African Institute under its original name of the International Institute for African Language and Culture (Laura Spelman Rockefeller Memorial Foundation Archives).

The Memorial, moreover, was interested in exploring the issue of race relations. It was that interest that led it to fund the International African Institute. A memorandum written in 1925 makes it clear that the Memorial had decided to go into African studies to keep control of Africa in European hands and was pursuing an appropriate agency to aid it in carrying out these objectives (Laura Spelman Rockefeller Box 55 Series 3, Folder 587; International Institute for African Language and Culture 1925–29).

The role of the Rockefeller Foundation in developing its interests in Latin America has been admirably documented and discussed (e.g. Colby 1995). However, its interests in Africa have not received similar attention. Understanding the involvement of the RF in promoting the development of the International African Institute, and British social anthropology and its functionalist paradigm, is instructional in understanding American post-war cooperation with various funding agencies, especially governmental ones.

The International African Institute (IAI) was founded in 1926 shortly before the merger of the Rockefeller Foundation and the Spelman Fund. The IAI notes that the founding of the International Institute of African Languages and Cultures in 1926 was made possible by a grant from the Laura Spelman Rockefeller Foundation Memorial (IAI Report, 1939 RF475S). The RF had in fact played an even greater role in shaping the IAI. Its work on education in America for black Americans led members of the Advisory Committee on Education in the Colonies to approach the RF for help in establishing an international organization that would deal with practical problems in Africa and would use language as a means for solving these problems and understanding the people. The committee determined that anthropology was essential to this undertaking.

They turned to Bronislaw Malinowski, a noted British anthropologist, for advice and leadership in establishing such a group. They were led to Malinowski through advice from Rockefeller agents who assured them that the work of the London School of Economics anthropology department was good. J.H. Oldham, one of the IAI's founders, who became the IAI's director from 1931 to 1936, considered Malinowski a genius. For his part, Malinowski assured Lord Lugard, the IAI's first director and the former Governor of Nigeria, that their ideas on colonial rule and the development of the subject peoples were in complete accord.

From these auspicious beginnings, the IAI began with a strong interest in promoting practical fieldwork problems. In addition to its pioneering fieldwork studies, the IAI fostered the publication of research on Africa. In 1927, it began the publication of the premier journal in African studies, *Africa*. The IAI also generated a number of specialized monograph series on African language and culture, and was in the forefront of training researchers from all over the world who wished to conduct anthropological and other research in Africa. Forging links with African universities was also part of its applied agenda. As a result of all these initiatives it is difficult to envision the field of Africanist anthropological studies without reference to the IAI and its work. The scholars associated with it form a veritable who's who of anthropology, including Bronislaw Malinowski, Meyer Fortes, and E.E. Evans-Pritchard, to name a few. Their work continues to form the core foundation of the anthropological canon. And yet, without the support of the Rockefeller Foundation in its early days and into the post-war period, the IAI might have collapsed, changing completely the direction of British social anthropology in Africa. The deepening effects of the Depression on Africa enhanced the strong influence of the RF on the development of African Studies.

As a result, Rockefeller money became increasingly important. Moreover, it was the expressed aim of the IAI to continue to prepare those people who would be responsible for the governance of Africa and the solutions to its problems. It was this aspect – the preparation of a phalanx of trained workers who would understand Africa thoroughly and govern it for the colonial powers – that the IAI used in its successful bid to gain RF support for its work. The IAI planned to concentrate on how to facilitate the Westernization of African societies, as a means to control them. In this direction, it believed, lay the means to aid the colonial governments in solving basic problems in changed situations. It sincerely believed that there was no contradiction in using Western maturity to guide young Africa's development. The approach was unashamedly paternalistic.

Oldham pledged the IAI's cooperation with the RF in solving the problems of administration and governance by putting the abilities of scholars at the disposal of administrators. Chief among these problems was indirect rule. Too often, administrators had used it as an excuse for not giving any sort of aid. In the IAI's opinion it had been used to excuse non-interference. The IAI argued that, rather than an excuse for non-interference, indirect rule should be a means for guiding people to adapt to the exigencies of the modern world through following an evolutionary path of development. The IAI further argued that indirect rule must be based on a thorough understanding of the precolonial situation in traditional societies. As Oldham put it:

… it must be based on an intimate knowledge of native life and institutions. It requires an understanding of the tribal organisation before the coming of the white man, of the forces which held the group together, of the ways in which the chief social institutions function and of the forces of change and disruption to which they are at present subject.

Such views captured the functionalist perspective on the colonial situation.

The IAI offered a number of examples of how anthropology could be a resource for colonial officials. For example, it aided Margery Perham's comparative study of indirect rule, helping her get anthropological training with Malinowski at the London School of Economics. Audrey Richards's work on local chiefs in Rhodesia provided another example of the type of work the IAI supported, while S.F. Nadel's work in Nigeria and Isaac Schapera's in South Africa also provided clear examples of acceding to the IAI's judgment.

In this research tradition, the IAI proposed carrying out a study of the economic changes that occurred in African societies as a result of changes produced by contact with the Western world through colonialism. These included the introduction of Western crops, dependence on cash crops, induction into the Western labor system, family disruption, and changes in the traditional social order. The

IAI reasoned that the functional approach was the most effective way to investigate these problems because the first requirement in solving colonial administrative issues is a thorough knowledge of the traditional system. Functionalist anthropologists concurred, arguing that only through understanding the traditional system and where it was breaking down could the colonial government successfully replace it through introducing new values and providing incentives for Africans to work in European enterprises.

Malinowski debunked descriptions of colonial societies as stable, integrated cultures even as his students wrote functionalist studies in this tradition. He argued that anthropologists' understanding of the colonial situation compelled them to use their knowledge on behalf of subject peoples – those residents of the Empire most likely to be exploited by colonialists. Social unrest was inevitable unless colonialists were taught to respect the values and rights of subject peoples (Kucklick 1991: 188).

Interestingly, once functionalist anthropologists found a means of support independent of colonial government, they spoke out clearly against the colonial status quo and dropped the flattering fiction that colonial officers were like functional anthropologists who gained understanding through a type of mystical union with their subjects. Indeed, it is important to reiterate that Malinowski not only saw no conflict in working with colonial governments, it was his active participation that ensured the IAI received RF money. The foundation regarded Malinowski as the leading figure in British scientific anthropology and his methods as conducive to their objectives (Interview between Malinowski and John van Sickle of the RF in 1926, Memorandum re: the International Institute of African Language and Culture, RF).

The partnership between Malinowski and the RF, mediated through the IAI, proved profitable for both partners. Malinowski found grant support for his students, an outlet for his own and his students' publications in Africa, a new audience for anthropology in the colonial world and those interested in its doings, and influence over the colonial administration. In turn, the RF found a means to implement its own policies peacefully in the colonial world. The RF managed to avoid the political entanglements it feared would impede its various programs and to promote those causes in which it believed. Many of those anthropologists who later criticized applied anthropology so vigorously were perfectly willing to praise the RF, colonial administrators, and missionaries for their help in producing work that aided the furtherance of colonial objectives.

Jack Goody (1995) argues strongly against this view of the relationship of social anthropology to colonialism and the RF. He maintains that neither of these agencies influenced the strong empirical foundations of the discipline nor its theoretical position. However, Goody tends to ignore influence outside of social anthropology on its development, as if it developed in a vacuum. His work is itself a rather functionalist analysis in the classic tradition. However, social anthropology not only has a history but one tied into the movements of its milieu, as Asad (1971) asserted some time ago.

Certainly anthropology, like other disciplines, can and does transcend its environment. However, it cannot wholly deny the influence of the environment on anthropology's concerns, as Goody seeks to do. Combating the social and cultural forces of one's circumstances, after all, is just another way of affirming their existence and influence. Certainly, anthropology must take into account its own social conditions and the cultures of its own natives if it is to understand its history.

Moore (1991: 21–21) discusses the context in which British social anthropology found itself. Basically, it was one in which funding was scarce and Malinowski and others turned to foundations, such as the RF, to provide help. In order to get funding, anthropologists had to go along to get along. Specifically, they had to accept the constraints of working with colonial governments and remaining politically non-controversial. They also had to provide a practical or applied aspect to their research and subordinate theory to this practical application. All these social and cultural processes came together in the IAI. As Moore (1994: 22) indicates, anthropologists increasingly involved themselves in African social research and development work as a form of applied anthropology, both in rural and in urban areas. She somewhat cavalierly dismisses the controversies that have surrounded British social anthropology's involvement with colonialism and the effect that such involvement has had on its subsequent development. She discards criticism of the connection as merely politically correct responses, or the result of territorial skirmishes, noting that both of these observations may be true without lessening the importance of critiques of the impact of social anthropology's connection with British colonialism. Furthermore, prominent anthropologists criticized the British connection of social anthropology with colonialism at the time it occurred.

Herskovits, for example, took Malinowski's applied anthropology to task because he believed that the systematic use of anthropology to aid the British government in administering its African colonies jeopardized the independence of the discipline and threatened to distort the anthropologist's understanding of the cultures under investigation. In his article "Acculturation and the American Negro" (1927: 221), Herskovits observed that a basic justification of ethnological research is that it gives a broad background against which to judge our own rules of behavior, and a more inclusive view of human cultures than can be attained by any other social discipline.

This view suggests that there were contemporary critics who were not simply being politically expedient in their criticism of Malinowski and the IAI and its connection with British colonialism. Clearly, Herskovits perceived the danger of applying ahistorical functional solutions to contemporary problems. Melville Herskovits, Franz Boas, and others feared the model of German anthropology's ties with Nazi Germany (Jackson 2003: 115); a difference of degree, not of kind, from what Herskovits saw existing in British anthropology. This hidden history of the IAI leaves little doubt that during the pre-war period, when the RF kept it afloat, the IAI was a coordinator between private and government interest, with the work in its early period of development clearly connected with colonial and Rockefeller interests. However innocent or even necessary such liaisons may have been at the time, in retrospect they cast suspicion on the purpose of the work. Moreover, it appeared to many at the time, including Herskovits, that the research supported by the IAI was part of a functionalist agenda aimed at facilitating the work of the colonial government and enhancing the wealth of the Rockefeller empire.

Cooperation with missionaries, government officials, and the wealthy and aristocratic elite laid the IAI and social anthropology open to charges from even so sympathetic a critic as James Coleman (RF 401 1966), who was at the time a member of the IAI executive council. Coleman's confidential agency report to the Ford Foundation is ironic in retrospect, since he was in the employ of both the Ford and Rockefeller Foundations when he warned of the dangers of funding and its possible biasing of research.

It is hard to escape the conclusion that much of the IAI's work was motivated by racist assumptions, often unconsciously. Additionally, the RF clearly set out to benefit from the research through governmental contacts, information, and ties with rising African leaders. The IAI followed the adage that knowledge and power and cultural knowledge can be used to gain access to a group's innermost symbols and meanings. For, after all, wasn't that the claim of functionalism itself? The RF was interested in resources, as its records make clear, but also in the groups that controlled those resources and the keys to their most intimate social and cultural secrets. Functionalism has long been criticized, sometimes incorrectly, for its conservative bias. Consciously or not, the IAI, with Malinowski's eager aid, allowed its need for funding to prevail, and permitted the Rockefeller Foundation to direct its research agenda as well as the course of social anthropology's development in Africa. Malinowski clearly used his ties with the RF to gain control of British social anthropology. The IAI's relationship to the RF and to colonialism has obvious lessons for American anthropology as I discuss in the next section.

THE 1960s, RESOLUTIONS, AND THE VIETNAM WAR

The debate over ethics is not limited to the recent past, but rather has substantial time depth. As early as 1919, Franz Boas raised concerns in a letter to *The Nation*, in which he accused four anthropologists of serving as spies under the guise of their researcher role. Boas wrote:

A person, who uses science as a cover for political spying, who demeans himself to pose before a foreign government as an investigator and asks for assistance in his alleged researches in order to carry on, under this cloak, his political machinations, prostitutes science in an unpardonable way and forfeits the right to be classed as a scientist. (Boas 1919)

David Price (2000) follows up on Boas's famous letter, noting that the American Anthropological Association did not censure the four anthropologists Boas singled out (though he refrained from naming them). Rather three of the four of them – Samuel Lothrop, Sylvanus Morley, and Herbert Spinden – voted on the executive council ten days later to censure Boas and pressure him to resign from the National Research Council. The fourth, John Mason, was also a member of the Council but did not vote for censure. In fact, he wrote Boas a very apologetic letter, asking his pardon for his actions and excusing himself by pleading patriotism during wartime. Lothrop, on the other hand, was not only unapologetic but continued his spying, according to Freedom of Information records David Price (2000) has obtained.

In actions too often repeated in the history of the American Anthropological Association, the AAA accused Boas of endangering fieldworkers and using the occasion for his own political ends. The AAA dared to cite Boas for abuse of his professional position. It is an argument made by established institutions whenever they are caught covering up unethical deeds: the Nixon White House, the Vatican, and other institutional cover-ups come readily to mind. Whistle-blowers are rarely popular. It is interesting that Lothrop's spying was aided through the Rockefeller Foundation's grant for research in Peru. The FBI considered Lothrop a good agent. However, it later realized that his main informant was providing fabricated information, and Lothrop quit his spy work over the controversy.

However, the damage had been done to anthropology. The failure of the AAA to condemn secret research and spying under the cover of conducting fieldwork set a precedent that unfortunately lasts to this day. Boas was clear in being particularly concerned with the damage that hiding one's spying under the guise of fieldwork would do to the credibility of anthropology and the security of anthropologists. Interestingly, those who caused the danger tried to blame Boas for it. The tactics remain the same for much of the twentieth century.

It is important to note that those who worked openly for the federal government did not earn Boas's censure, although he may not have approved of using anthropological knowledge for war efforts. Margaret Mead, Ruth Benedict, Gregory Bateson, Clyde Kluckhohn, and others worked in the study of culture from a distance project – a World War II project to "know our enemy" through the use of secondary sources, where direct access would have been impossible and dangerous – but did not use fieldwork to hide spy activity. However, according to Price (2000), many anthropologists *were* spies during World War II. They worked for the Office of Special Services, Army and Naval Intelligence, and the Department of War. After the war some worked for the CIA, created in 1947. Others received funding from CIA fronts, usually without knowing that these granting institutions, like the Human Ecology Fund, were fronts.

Even more outrageous than individual violations of ethics and the ideals of anthropology were the violations on the part of the AAA itself. As Price notes, the AAA itself collaborated with the CIA, supplying it with a cross-listed database of members and their interests. The secret agreement between the executive board and the CIA gave the agency the right to use CIA computers and personnel to produce and use these lists. These lists summarized the field research of AAA members, giving their language skills, geographic interests, and theoretical positions. Anthropologists, such as the anonymous one who reported to the CIA in Guatemala on the affiliations of prisoners taken in the 1954 coup, collaborated in morally reprehensible actions carried out by the agency. Later, as government officials realized that policy-makers had little information with which to develop a plan for dealing with the northern people in Vietnam, they began to employ social scientists, including anthropologists (Belshaw 1976: 264). The significance of the region increased dramatically as the Vietnam War expanded. These factors encouraged a prodigious increase in the amount of research. In the early 1960s, Western social scientists "flooded" the area, including Thailand (Jones 1971: 347), and the Hill Tribes Research Centre was established to exploit long-standing rivalries and prejudices between the lowlanders and the marginalized hill people (Belshaw 1976: 265). Jones raises the most basic question:

Did the anthropologists who rushed into the area to do basic descriptive studies consider these political facts? It is safe to say that most of us did not. Was it an accident that the strategic and political concerns about the hill areas and the questionable loyalty of the hill people to Thailand coincided with the growing anthropological concern about the lack of knowledge of the area? Was it also an accident that, about that same time, a considerable amount of money became available for basic research on this "little known area"? The situation which developed led to a decade of concentrated research on hill people to the almost total neglect of valley culture and society. (1971: 348)

As the apparent strategic significance of the region increased, the amount of research fund sources increased. Scholars could make use of funds from agencies of the American government such as the Advanced Research Projects Agency (ARPA) of the Department of Defense.

The presence of anthropologists doing counter-insurgency research in Thailand was exposed in 1970 by the Student Mobilization Committee to End the War in Vietnam. This resulted in a major crisis in the discipline, which seems to have intensified interest in various ethical concerns. It is clear that the conflicts concerning ethics, generated during the Vietnam era, contributed a great deal to the understanding of our responsibilities. The process that these discussions developed was very painful and disturbing. In retrospect, many respected scholars were unfairly accused, yet the increase in understanding may have been worth it.

Eric Wakin (1992) notes that the 1971 AAA conference saw the rising up of younger anthropologists against their elders. The members rejected Margaret Mead's report exonerating the accused anthropologists involved in Project Camelot and in Vietnam War-related activities. The 1971 Principles of Professional Responsibility explicitly stated that no secret research, no secret reports or debriefings of any kind should be agreed to or given by members of the AAA.

Unfortunately, subsequent revisions of the Principles of Professional Responsibility have watered down this clear and strong language, essentially saying that only those anthropologists who want to be spies should be spies. That is like saying that only those citizens who want to be criminals can be such, and that we trust citizens to keep the law without a police force. The naivety is simply too much to believe; indeed one must question whether naivety is the only relevant accusation here.

The primary issue in anthropological ethical debates is the potential negative results that may stem from the research. This goes to the core of anthropology's ethical concerns and of anthropology itself. If anthropologists don't understand this fact then the profession has indeed lost its soul. Without the community we study, we have nothing worth studying. To injure that community is to do ineradicable harm to us as well as to the community. It is masochistic as well as sadistic.

Cora Du Bois (1961) relates an incident that exemplifies the potential for harm of "normal fieldwork" in a frightening way. Du

Bois had carried out her well-known study of the Alor in an area of what is now Indonesia which came to be occupied by the Japanese during World War II. It was reported to Du Bois after the war that many of the people she had worked with in the field had innocently mentioned that they wished the Americans would win the war, because they were good people. The Alorese in question had never heard of America prior to Du Bois's fieldwork. She reports that the Japanese heard that certain Alorese were stating that America would win the conflict. The Japanese military government rounded up the persons in question and publicly executed them.

CONCLUSION

Mythologies are found in every profession. Anthropology is no exception. Lemke (1990: 129) says that there is a mystique of science, one which has myths that favor a small elite. The myths of objectivity and certainty privilege those in power and promote an authoritarian culture that justifies anything done in the name of science. Justification is lent to many practices that common sense would oppose. In the name of science, terrible things are done that reasonable people would otherwise oppose. "Science is presented as authoritative, and from there it is a small step to its becoming authoritarian" (Lemke 1990: 31). It is an even smaller step to justify any policy in its name.

Lakoff and Johnson (1980) describe a myth of objectivity that pervades science writing and fails to explain human thoughts and experiences. This positivism argues for an objective world that is complete in itself without reference to the humans who occupy it. It fails to take into account the role of metaphors. It fails to examine or even recognize the metaphor of the objectivity of science. Failing to do so gives it a privileged position and allows for the justification of research that allows the bombing of innocent civilians, secret research, lack of accountability for one's actions in the field, and so on.

It is time now for the AAA to find the courage to make it clear, once again, that secret research under the guise of fieldwork is just wrong. It is not those who seek to bring the truth into clear and sharp focus who are wrong. It is not those who hate the darkness who endanger anthropologists. It is those who seek to excuse violators of the code of a self-correcting science who must be confronted. They endanger both anthropologists and the humanistic goals of the profession. And yes, they seriously endanger the very people common decency enjoins us to protect, or, at the very least, not harm.

NOTES

1. I am dedicating this work to Charles Frantz, who was my dissertation director. I have maintained a more than 30-year friendship with Chuck and have met few people of Chuck's high ethical integrity. We have discussed these issues at length from time to time, and I believe that I understand his position. However, I do not claim to be speaking for him. Chuck is perfectly capable of speaking for himself and has done so on many occasions. Any misinterpretations are my own.

ARCHIVAL SOURCES

Laura Spelman Memorial Foundation Archives
RF 401 1966 Coleman Report on IAI.
RF Box 55, Series 3, Folder 587.
Institute for African Language and Culture 1925–29.
IAI Report 1939 RF475S.
Interview between Malinowski and John van Sickle of the RF 1926.
Memorandum re: the International Institute of African Language and Culture, RF.

REFERENCES

American Anthropological Association. 1942. Report. *American Anthropologist.* 44(2): 281–98.

American Anthropological Association. 1971. Principles of Professional Responsibility. Washington, DC: AAA. URL: http://www.aaanet.org/stmts/ethstmnt.htm

Asad, Talal, ed. 1971. *Anthropology and the Colonial Encounter.* London: Ithaca Press.

Belshaw, Cyril. 1976. *The Sorceror's Apprentice: An Anthropology of Public Policy.* New York: Pergamon Press.

Boas, Franz. 1919. Scientists as Spies. *The Nation* 109: 79.

Boggs, S.T. 1965. Anthropologists and the Sponsorship of Anthropological Research. Fellow Newsletter. *American Anthropological Association* 6(10): 1.

Colby, Gerald. 1995. *Thy Will Be Done.* New York: HarperCollins.

Du Bois, Cora. 1961. *The People of Alor.* New York: Harper and Row.

Foster, George M. 1962. *Traditional Cultures and the Impact of Technological Change.* New York: Harper and Row.

—— 1969. *Applied Anthropology.* Boston, MA: Little, Brown, and Co.

Frantz, Charles. 1968. The Current Milieu and the Immediate Future of U.S. Anthropology. *Anthropology Newsletter* 9(5): 7–12.

Goldschmidt, Walter. 1973. Anthropology and the Coming Crisis: An Auto-ethnographic Appraisal. *American Anthropologist* 79(2): 293–308.

Goodenough, Ward Hunt. 1963. *Cooperation in Change.* New York: Russell Sage Foundation.

Goody, Jack. 1995. *The Expansive Moment.* Cambridge: Cambridge University Press.

Herskovits, Melville J. 1927. Acculturation and the American Negro. *Southwest Political and Social Science* 55a: 104–16.

Jackson, Walter. 2003. Herskovits and the Search for Afro-American Culture. In *Malinowski, Rivers, Benedict, and Others*, pp. 95–126. George W. Stocking Jr, ed. Madison: University of Wisconsin Press.

Jones, D.J. 1971. Contribution to "Anthropology on the Warpath: An Exchange." *New York Review of Books* 22 June: 54.

Kucklick, Henrika. 1991. *The Savage Within: The Social History of British Anthropology, 1885–1945*. Cambridge: Cambridge University Press.

Kuhn, Thomas. 1962. *The Structure of Scientific Revolutions*. Chicago: University of Chicago Press.

Lakoff, George and Mark Johnson. 1980. *Metaphors We Live By*. Chicago: University of Chicago Press.

Lemke, Jay. 1990. *Talking Science: Language, Learning, and Values*. Norwood, NJ: Ablex.

Magubane, Bernard. 1973. The "Xhosa" in Town Revisited: Urban Social Anthropology – A Failure of Method and Theory. *American Anthropologist* n.s. 75(5): 1701–15.

Mead, Margaret. 1956. *New Lives for Old: Cultural Transformation – Manus, 1928–1953*. New York: William Morrow and Co.

Moore, Henrietta L. 1994. *A Passion for Difference: Essays in Anthropology and Gender*. Cambridge: Polity Press.

Paul, Benjamin D. 1955. *Health, Culture, and Community: Case Studies of Public Reactions to Health Programs*. New York: Russell Sage Foundation.

Price, David. 2000. Anthropologists as Spies. *The Nation* 271(16): 24–27.

Rowe, John H. 1965. The Renaissance Foundations of Anthropology. *American Anthropologist* 67(1): 1–20.

Spicer, Edward. 1952. *Human Problems in Technological Change: A Casebook*. New York: Russell Sage Foundation.

Tierney, Patrick. 2000. *Darkness in El Dorado: How Scientists and Journalists Devastated the Amazon*. New York: W.W. Norton.

Wakin, Eric. 1992. *Anthropology Goes to War: Professional Ethics and Counterinsurgency in Thailand*. Madison: University of Wisconsin Press.

Willis, William S. 1969. Why North American Anthropology has Ignored North American Negroes. SMU Graduate Anthropology Club, March.

—— 1972. Skeletons in the Anthropological Closet. In *Reinventing Anthropology*, pp. 121–52. Dell Hymes, ed. New York: Random House.

Wolf, Eric. 1972. *The Human Condition in Latin America*. New York: Oxford University Press.

Worsley, Peter. 1992. Foreword. In *Confronting the Margaret Mead Legacy: Scholarship, Empire and the South Pacific*, pp. ix–xviii. Lenora Foerstel and Angela Gilliam, eds. Philadelphia, PA: Temple University Press.

5   PEASANTS ON OUR MINDS: ANTHROPOLOGY, THE COLD WAR, AND THE MYTH OF PEASANT CONSERVATISM

Eric B. Ross

When peasants became an explicit subject of modern anthropological study after World War II (Foster 1967: 4), it did not happen because its conventional subjects had disappeared nor because anthropologists were conceptually ready to make such a transition. On the contrary, most of their writing on peasants through the 1950s suggests quite the opposite; through the early 1950s, the few articles on peasants that appeared in anthropological journals still typically referred to them largely in terms of "folk culture" (Lewis 1955: 145). But the new demands of the Cold War, which would profoundly influence so many US academic disciplines (see Latham 2000; Nader 1997; Price 2004), pushed anthropologists to consider the world of peasants. As this occurred, their work tended to reflect, directly or indirectly, the premises of "modernization theory," a highly influential body of writing – largely articulated at the Center for International Studies (CENIS) at MIT – through which Western academics and policy-makers during the post-war years described certain goals – and the way to achieve them – as desirable for the developing world in general (cf. Latham 2000) and for peasants in particular.

Such thinking was perhaps nowhere better reflected than in the Cornell-Peru Project at the Andean hacienda community of Vicos, an "intervention" that, in the conventional Cornell view, became "a paradigm for international development in the third world in the decade of the 1960–70s" (Isbell and Zapata 2005–2006). But, to the extent that Vicos was a model for rural change, it was because it grew out of and along with the West's strategic and ideological response to a post-war world of insurgent peasantries whose aspirations filled its political elite with profound apprehension. In the end, it is in that context that the Vicos Project, despite its reputation as a classic case of benign "applied anthropology," must be understood.

THE PERILS OF MODERNIZATION

As World War II was drawing to a close, one of the main preoccupations of Western policy-makers was how to deal with the rising tide of rural mobilization and insurgency that seemed to have become a dominant and persistent feature of the global political landscape, and which was linked in the minds of Western policy-makers with the advance of communism. As peasants thus came to be viewed as a perilous factor in the development process, the implications were summed up by the renowned agricultural economist, Wolf Ladejinsky, when he observed:

We must realize how serious a threat an agrarian revolution could be at this point of history.... The only way to thwart Communist designs on Asia is to preclude such revolutionary outbursts through timely reforms, peacefully before the peasants take the law into their own hands and set the countryside ablaze. (in Walinsky 1977: 132)

At the heart of such reforms was an emphasis on technical change rather than agrarian transformation. With this came a necessary conviction that peasants were too conservative to be the actual instruments of such change. Hence, Frank Notestein, perhaps the most eminent demographer of his generation and a leading academic member of the Rockefeller institutional network, observed in a paper to the Eighth International Conference of Agricultural Economists in 1952 that peasant social organization did not have the capacity for high technological achievement (Notestein 1953). This view was consistent with the main tenets of emergent modernization theory (see Hagen 1962; Lerner 1958) which sought to place innovation in the hands of market-oriented large landowners – or outside agents – to whom the task could be safely entrusted. This view was consistent with the Rockefeller interest in the package of agricultural innovations that became known as the Green Revolution, but it was not necessarily the only option. Anthropology, however, would play an important role in this crucial aspect of post-war development policy by helping to create the myth that peasants – regarded as a threatening source of radical political change throughout the Third World – were nevertheless too conservative in their cultural values to be autonomous agents of rural change, let alone of agricultural innovation. Culminating in such constructions as Foster's "Image of Limited Good" (Foster 1965), anthropologists elaborated an argument that peasants were more constrained by "tradition" than by agrarian structures and, therefore, could not really be expected "to improve their living standards at their own initiative" (cited in Huizer 1972: 53).

Agrarian change was therefore argued by policy-makers to be something that had to be guided by outsiders – as long as they were not "agitators" – many of whom would work within the new framework of "community development," with its emphasis on changing (i.e. Westernizing) "traditional" attitudes and values. The Cornell anthropologists who worked at Vicos would use the somewhat more telling phrase: "controlled change."

INDIA AND COMMUNITY DEVELOPMENT

It was in India that these ideas were first put to the test, in the aftermath of the Chinese communist victory in 1949, when it was "The subcontinent of India," according to Notestein again, that "comes most forcibly to mind as the next possible location for a serious outbreak of communism" (quoted in Ryder 1984: 676). Thus Max Millikan, the ex-CIA economist who became the first director of CENIS, wrote that, when the Center:

... was starting its programme of research into the problems of the newly emerging nations, we concluded that it was wise to pick a few underdeveloped countries for intensive study and to seek funds to carry on a variety of kinds of field work on the spot in these countries. We arrived very early at the conclusion that one country which merited a good share of our attention was India. (Millikan 1962: 9)

By the late 1950s, India had become a focal point of major foundation attention. The Ford Foundation – then closely associated with US intelligence agencies – rapidly expanded its programs in India to the point where its activities there overshadowed all its other efforts outside the United States (Caldwell and Caldwell 1986: 4), reflecting the view of Paul Hoffman, new head of Ford, that "India ... is today what China was in 1945" (quoted in Rosen 1985: 11).

Uttar Pradesh (then United Provinces) – home of a long succession of peasant uprisings and setting for the founding of the Communist Party of India (*Taraqqi* 2000) – was considered the most appropriate site for India's first experiments in what was called community development. In 1947, a pilot project was initiated there, in Etawah district (Mayer and Associates 1958), with the idea, as economist George Rosen observed, that:

If it was successful it would serve as a model for meeting the revolutionary threats from left-wing and communist peasant movements demanding basic social reforms in agriculture. (1985: 49)

By the early 1950s, the potential of the so-called Etawah Project seemed so alluring that Ford's president, Paul Hoffman, proclaimed that: "There is no reason why all 500,000 of India's villages could not make a similar advance" (quoted in Rosen 1985: 11). The Ford and Rockefeller foundations offered to sponsor a nation-wide community development program modeled on Etawah (Rosen 1985: 50).

Eventually, the US government and Ford would provide more than $100 million for such programs during the course of India's First and Second Plans in the 1950s (Brown 1971: 4) and US anthropologists played an important role, with Cornell's India Project under Morris Opler being a major framework for many of them (Cohen 1955: 53; Davies 2001: 339; Rosen 1985: 35).

CORNELL ANTHROPOLOGISTS AND THE STUDY OF CHANGE

Opler's India Project was one of a number of interconnected activities that eventually came together to form "an ambitious worldwide anthropological undertaking" by Cornell's anthropologists to study "an accelerated process of global change" (Doughty 1977: 144) in India, Thailand, on a Navajo reservation in the US, and, ultimately, in Peru (Keyes 1994), in the form of the Vicos Project. But the background to this emergent, cross-cultural project was necessarily broader than just India and reflects the convergent interests and backgrounds of the individuals who devised it.

In 1936, Lauriston Sharp had joined the Cornell Economics Department (Bowen 2003: 4). He soon became chair of the new Sociology and Anthropology Department and, at the end of World War II, during which he had worked (in 1945) for the State Department's Division of Southeast Asian Affairs (Bowen 2003: 4), hired the psychiatrist Alexander Leighton, who had not only worked for the Office of Strategic Services (OSS) and the Office of War Information (OWI) during the conflict (Simpson 1994: 26), but – as Chief of the Morale Analysis Division for the US Navy Medical Corps – had conducted research on Japanese Americans in the internment camp run by the War Relocation Authority (WRA) at Poston, Arizona (Davies 2001: 321–22; Tremblay 2004: 7–8). (As it happened, his Cornell colleague Morris Opler had *also* worked for the WRA at the Manzanar camp and for the OWI as well [Price 2002: 18; Unrau 1996; Webster and Rushforth 2000: 328].) Out of such wartime backgrounds, Leighton and Sharp (with support from Opler):

... developed a grand scheme to study and direct culture change in the postwar world. According to Leighton, the new program "addressed the question of facilitating the introduction of modern agriculture, industry, and medicine to areas that are deficient in those technologies." The program attempted to do so without evoking "hostility towards the innovator." (Davies 2001: 323)

Very much in keeping with the lessons learned through Cornell's prior association with agricultural missionaries, such a project, with its rather uncritical confidence in the benefits of Western technological innovation (Davies 2001: 327), would ensure that Cornell in general, and its anthropologists in particular, would be credible allies of

Washington policy-makers and major US foundations through the Cold War years, with their common ideological and tactical commitment to modernization through directed change at the community level. Needless to say, the view that outside innovators should encounter little hostility from rural communities appealed to Washington.

Part of the Cornell program involved a field seminar in applied anthropology, centered among the Navajo and run by Leighton into the early 1950s. It was meant to "provide applied anthropology training for specialists and administrators actively involved in the introduction of new technology to under-developed regions of the world" (Davies 2001: 317). But it was particularly in the Peruvian side of the program that the idea of community development would find unprecedented expression. It was there that Carnegie Corporation finances, already supporting the university's other anthropological programs, helped to create the Cornell-Peru Vicos Project, which leading figures in anthropology would extol over the next few decades out of all proportion to its substantive achievements.

THE CARNEGIE CORPORATION AND POST-WAR GEO-POLITICS

It is important, at this point, to understand the role of the Carnegie Corporation. As one of the principal funders of the Social Science Research Council (SSRC), it had already established an important influence in the development of US social science with regard to national foreign policy objectives, a role that reflected its long-standing and intimate associations with the US power elite.[1] During World War II, it had helped to develop what became the Human Relations Area File (HRAF; Carnegie Corporation 1955), which had important intelligence-gathering functions, chiefly in the Pacific. And, as the HRAF continued to serve the intelligence community after the war, so Carnegie generally played an ongoing role in the early years of the Cold War, when, among other things, it was a major supporter of such US government intelligence-oriented projects as the Russian Research Center at Harvard (Diamond 1992: 65–80), in the creation of which John Gardner, former OSS operative and Vice-President of Carnegie, was intimately involved.

The Russian Studies Center was just one of the more conspicuous examples of the Carnegie Corporation's role as a source of funding of projects of interest to the US ruling class (Trumpbour 1989: 66). That particular affinity had long been reflected in the fact that it was a major sponsor of the Council on Foreign Relations (CFR), with which its presidents and trustees had been associated since the 1920s (Feldman 2002; Oppenheimer 1997).[2] In the same way, when the RAND Corporation – created initially as a think-tank for the US Army Airforce – was established in 1948, the president of Carnegie, psychologist Charles Dollard, was on its first board of trustees (Simpson 1994: 58).

So, as Oppenheimer (1997) notes, Carnegie "was not entirely a dispassionate funder of educational and scientific projects." Simpson goes further and writes of how the programs of Carnegie and the Defense Department:

... were in reality coordinated and complementary to one another, at least insofar as the two organizations shared similar conceptions concerning the role of the social sciences in national security research. (Simpson 1994: 59–60)

Carnegie was the major source of funding for the comparative culture change studies of Cornell anthropologists and, above all, for the Vicos Project.

THE CARNEGIE–CORNELL CONNECTION

The connection between Carnegie and Washington depended on universities such as Cornell, and the war not only did much to enhance these ties, it also blurred the conventional boundaries between public, private, and philanthropic institutions. But the Cold War interests of the US elite brought about a strategic convergence. No one exemplified this more than James Perkins, a leading figure at the Carnegie Corporation during most of the first decade of the Vicos Project, who became president of Cornell in 1963 (Grace-Kobas 1998). Perkins exemplifies the diverse interconnections that increasingly pervaded the governmental, academic, and foundation sectors as a reflection of the imperatives of the Cold War. In 1951–52, he took a brief leave to serve as the deputy chair of the Research and Development Board of the Department of Defense (Grace-Kobas 1998) and, in 1957, served as a member of the Gaither Committee (Domhoff 1970: 135; Snead 1999: 47), which helped to define the Eisenhower administration's views on the arms race. He would later become a director of Chase Manhattan, the Rockefeller bank, and of Nelson Rockefeller's International Basic Economy Corporation (IBEC), the family's highly diversified vehicle for investment in Latin America, promoting Green Revolution-style seeds and inputs (Colby and Dennett 1995: 474, 784–86). Perkins was also on the Board of Trustees of the RAND Corporation and was, for many years (1953–72), a director of the Council of Foreign Relations (Council on Foreign Relations 2005). If his ascendancy to the presidency of Cornell consolidated that university's historic role as a key player in foundation-sponsored research on rural change in the developing world, the emergence of the university's anthropology program in cultural change, around

Leighton, Sharp, and Opler, epitomized it. By 1963, Carnegie's John Gardner, having moved on to become Kennedy's Secretary of Health, Education, and Welfare (Social Security Online 2005), would write that "anything that Cornell University wants to study is within our charter" (Gardner 1963). Vicos certainly was.

The steps toward Vicos are not entirely clear. But in 1948, despite the fact that Latin America had emerged as a vital area of concern for US policy-makers and for politically influential private investors such as the Rockefeller family, the Cornell anthropology research project in technology and culture change, largely financed by Carnegie, still lacked a Latin American dimension. It was here that Holmberg found his niche.

In 1943, the Institute of Social Anthropology (ISA), under the direction, first, of Julian Steward and then of George Foster (Laurenzo 2005; Manners 1996: 327), had been established within the Smithsonian (along with the Ethnogeographical Board, with which it shared many key figures).[3] It had, as one of its principal aims, "to keep Latin America within the U.S. political orbit" (Adams 1964: 2). That objective did not cease with the war's end and, when the ISA was eventually disbanded in 1952, most of the anthropologists working there moved to the International Cooperation Agency (ICA) – the predecessor of USAID[4] – which was closely connected with US government intelligence interests. Adams observed that:

Within the ICA, anthropologists in Bolivia and southern Peru were, I presume, more than coincidentally, utilized in areas where there were thought to be serious problems of communist agitation. (1964: 2)

Among the anthropologists in this region who worked for the ISA during and just after the war, was Allan Holmberg. Holmberg's background was singularly appropriate for such activities. As a Yale student of George Peter Murdock in the late 1930s, he had assisted in the emergence of the Human Relations Area Files (Doughty, personal communication 2005), which began in 1937 as the Cross Cultural Survey of Yale's Institute of Human Relations and developed during World War II in collaboration with the United States government, which saw the HRAF as a means of providing cultural intelligence to help in setting up military government on Pacific islands during and immediately after the war (Carnegie Corporation 1955; Nader 1997: 123).[5] He was also a student of psychologist John Dollard, whose brother, Charles, happened to be the president of the Carnegie Foundation (Holmberg 1950a: 1; RAND Corporation 2005; Simpson 1994: 58–59).

Holmberg himself spent part of World War II – before the entry of the United States – in the Bolivian tropical lowlands, studying the indigenous Sirionó (Holmberg 1950a: 1–3). But by 1942 he was employed by the US State Department, before going to work for the US Army's Rubber Development Corporation (Holmberg 1946),[6] for whom "he spent the next three years organizing the production of wild rubber in eastern Bolivia" (Steward 1946).[7] He returned to Yale in 1945 to finish his doctoral dissertation (Steward 1946) and then went back to Peru the following year for the ISA. Here he served, among other things, as the cultural anthropologist on the Viru Valley Project, an archaeological survey on Peru's north coast that had been developed by a group of Smithsonian anthropologists, including Gordon Willey[8] (ISA), William Duncan Strong and Wendell Bennett (both Ethnogeographical Board) and Steward (ISA), and which was officially sponsored by the Institute of Andean Research in New York – of which Strong was the Chair – and the newly established Viking Fund (Wenner-Gren Foundation) (Gorenstein 2002: 1255).[9]

The Viru Project was an important step in Holmberg's shift of focus to the Peruvian highlands. While he was still completing his dissertation, his Yale connections had brought him to the attention of an influential circle of senior anthropologists who, in the last years of the war, had acquired considerable influence in determining the professional future of the discipline. It was sufficient that, suddenly, in 1948, Sharp wrote to Holmberg, inviting him, "sight unseen" (Sharp 1948: 3), not simply to join Cornell's emerging anthropology program, but to participate "in the further development of it practically from the ground up" (1948: 3). It was an extraordinary opportunity for someone who had really achieved so little.

Sharp described how their program of field research already included projects in Uttar Pradesh and Siam (Thailand), and that their wish was now to develop one in Latin America. There was nothing in the works yet, but "we believe," he wrote:

... we could obtain support for either or both of two possible projects, one in connection with the Rockefeller brothers' private industrialization program in Venezuela, the other in connection with the Rockefeller Foundation program in Mexico. (Sharp 1948: 2)

The latter probably referred to the Rockefeller agricultural research that helped to begin the Green Revolution. If so, then the thrust of Cornell's anthropological inquiry into culture change, which, as Sharp said, was focused on "the diffusion of modern technologies from the North Atlantic cultures to other, less industrially developed areas of the world" (Sharp 1948: 1), was clearly on such technology as an adjunct of US capital.

By the following September, Holmberg had left the ISA and moved to Ithaca.[10] In November 1948, he submitted, through Morris Opler, the Chair of the Cornell Sociology and Anthropology Department,[11] an initial proposal to the Carnegie Foundation for what would lead to the Vicos Project. Based on an ethnological survey of the Callejón de Huaylas, conducted with the Institute of Ethnology of the University of San Marcos in Lima, Holmberg suggested that:

Because of its natural resources, its labor supply, its proximity to the coast, and its industrial importance for the future of Peru, Callejón de Huaylas would seem to be an excellent place to initiate a project in the field of technology and culture change. (Holmberg 1948: 1–2)

The view of "culture change" as part of a process of integration of a large rural population into the national economy reflected one of the main thrusts of the modernization paradigm. But, if Holmberg imagined that the Callejón was destined for Tennessee Valley Authority-style development, his idea of how to study the social changes that might have followed was based on an understanding of Andean history that was even more limited than his comprehension of lowland history had been in regard to the Sirionó. Barbara Lynch would later make the point that Holmberg and his Cornell colleagues persistently regarded Vicos "as a medieval society, isolated from history, rather than a product of it" (Lynch 1982: 22). But Holmberg's characterization of Vicosinos, from the start, reached even further back than that. One of the reasons that he proposed to center his study around the village of Macará was that, about three miles way, he said, there was "an Indian farm (Vicos) where the natives can be studied *under aboriginal conditions*" (Holmberg 1948, my italics). He seemed to think he was still among the Sirionó, even though they themselves have proven to be far from "aboriginal" (Isaac 1977). There is no hint, however, that anyone in Ithaca considered Holmberg's perspective particularly faulty and so the proposed work at Vicos became a central part of the already existing Cornell study of comparative technological and social change.

The Vicos strand of that study inevitably remained embedded in and reflected its Peruvian political and institutional context. But the nature of that context has been largely obscured or misrepresented by the official Cornell view, which begins with the statement that its "intervention in the northern Andean community of Vicos, Peru [began] in 1952," and goes on, in the words of Henry Dobyns, a prominent member of the Cornell team, to assert that Vicos was simply, "throughout its history, a cooperative effort of the Peruvian Indian Institute [Instituto Indigenista Peruano]" (1971). The actual scenario was far more complex. By 1948, Holmberg had already undertaken preliminary ethnological research at Vicos

(Holmberg 1948) in collaboration with the Instituto de Etnología at the University of San Marcos in Lima (Holmberg 1948), which he proposed to Carnegie "would tie in very well with the areal research program now underway here at Cornell" (Holmberg 1948).[12] Second, the standard scenario tends to minimize the role of Carnegie and others who influenced the nature of the project.

In essence, for a project that not only achieved legendary status, but also seemed to covet it, there has always been such an aspect of ambiguity and inconsistency in the accounts by its principal participants, that, as Richard Adams noted two decades after its inception, much about the project – including its sponsorship – was still unclear from what was openly published by the anthropologists most involved in it (Adams 1973). The "fuller scholarly and research reporting" that he hoped for and anticipated over 30 years ago has never materialized, and Dwight Heath's observation in 1980 that the Cornell work at Vicos was a "tangled skein of theory and practice, individuals and institutions, progress and problems" (1980: 455) remains just as true today.

A DEEPER VIEW OF VICOS

One partial explanation may be that more interesting things were going on than suited the academic demands for analytical clarity. When Ward Goodenough characterized the project as "a very visible example" of where "cultural knowledge has been successfully used to accomplish objectives that would have been unattainable without it" (1963: 174), he was obliquely referring to the demands of the Cold War and his own view that anthropology should make itself relevant in the cause of counter-insurgency. Vicos, at the very least, was part of the West's Cold War strategy.

There are good reasons to speculate on Vicos in terms of its political value in the Peruvian region. In 1945, a coalition of liberal and leftist parties, including the Alianza Popular Revolucionaria Americana (APRA), had elected José Luis Bustamante y Rivero (1894–1989) as president. Bustamante instituted numerous liberal reforms and abolished certain dictatorial powers of the presidency. But, in October 1948, rightist revolutionary leaders, led by General Manuel Odria, unseated Bustamante, seized the government, and outlawed APRA. It was in this problematical climate that Holmberg's ostensible aim was to develop Vicos as a model whose "anticipated results," according to Mangin, could be "diffused throughout Peru and the world" (Mangin 1979: 67).

If Holmberg and his Cornell associates really imagined that this was likely, it flies in the face of reality. According to Lynch, the sublease of the hacienda (and its inhabitants) to Cornell by the Public

Benefit Society – which "represented the regional elite" (Lynch 1982: 16) – required existing relations of production to be maintained. In light of this, the stated aspirations of the Cornell anthropologists – so clearly circumscribed from the outset – would seem naïve, to say the least. Indeed, this seems a fair characterization of Doughty's observation that:

Just why the conservative Odria dictatorship would permit such a project to begin with was often conjectured by the CPP personnel, but plausible reasons or policy have never been identified. (1987a: 441)

Yet, Doughty himself actually suggested the answer when he noted that:

In 1960, Indian communities and haciendas' serf populations were increasingly pressuring the government to take action on land reform. The government response was invariably hostile to these ... (1987a: 444)

Land reform had been a political issue in Peru since the period immediately after World War I and the lack of any effective democratization of land holding in the highlands eventually gave birth to an era of peasant mobilization (Colby and Dennett 1995: 469; Lastarria-Cornhiel 1989: 136) that was met by harsh resistance from the ruling oligarchy embodied by the Odria dictatorship. There is no doubt that Holmberg, Henry Dobyns, and their Peruvian partners were aware of how Vicos fit into the increasingly tense highland landscape, since, on the one hand, the Instituto Indigenista Peruano – their principal Peruvian partner – included army generals on its executive board, while, on the other, in a 1962 paper, Dobyns and his colleagues noted that, in the departmental capital of Huaraz, there was resistance to the Vicos Project from the Communist Party: "which appears to recognize that every success of the project diminishes by that much their chances of fomenting a violent revolution" (Dobyns et al. 1971 [1964]: 112–13).

That this was perceived early on to be a major selling point of the Vicos Project is clear from the proposal that the Cornell Anthropology Department submitted through Sharp (then the department chair) to the Carnegie Corporation's John Gardner on April 19, 1951, in which it was observed that:

... the hope of the Andean countries as a whole lies in the mountain regions where their masses of hard-working Indians live, and unless these are soon given opportunities and assistance in changing and improving their lot considerably, present conditions of unrest and dissatisfaction are apt to lead to more and bloodier revolutions within the next few years.... We would like, therefore, to attempt to change these conditions in as controlled a manner as possible ... (Sharp 1951)

This certainly was in accord with the pointed advice from Gardner, who wrote back to Sharp in June that:

> If native people are to be taught to take their fate in their own hands, then they had better be educated as to the various ways in which they can be gulled by unscrupulous leaders. This means, I should think, fairly intensive indoctrination in local forms of "democratic" group action with strong emphasis upon active and realistic political participation. It seems to me that without this, the whole effort to raise the status of backward peoples may be the greatest device ever invented for playing into the hands of unscrupulous demagogues. (Gardner 1951: 2)

There is little doubt that Washington, whose power brokers Gardner knew well, was generally becoming aware of the possibilities inherent in the community development model which Vicos embodied, although, through the 1950s, policy-makers, taking their lead from John Foster Dulles, were still inclined to back a more direct and forceful approach. But, a decade later, in the period immediately following the Cuban Revolution and especially after the failure of US-backed armed intervention at the Bay of Pigs, the Vicos model grew in importance and would soon find its fullest expression in the emergence of the Peace Corps during the Kennedy and Johnson years, when Gardner was an influential member of the government and Vicos even became a Peace Corps training center.

The political advantages inherent in the Vicos approach were openly acknowledged by John Gillin in his comments to the Society of Applied Anthropology, when he observed:

> The experience of Vicos contains numerous suggestions for the "cold war." Through our foreign-aid programs, I presume that we are trying to bring the peoples of the modern world to our side. The numerous defects in our national programs can be corrected on the basis of the experience of Vicos. (Gillin in *Informaciones* 1961: 142)

Especially after the Cuban Revolution and the failure of the Bay of Pigs, there was a necessity to devise more subtle forms of intervention. The Vicos project was not only represented as offering a real hope to the *campesinos* of the Peruvian highlands, but its proponents even went so far as to imply that it was actually the real revolutionary option. Doughty, for example, has described the project, in the Peruvian context, as "nothing less than revolutionary" (1977: 144). Dobyns called Holmberg "a truly revolutionary anthropologist," putting him on a par with Jomo Kenyatta, the leader of Kenya's Mau Mau uprising (Adams 1973: 444), a claim which even Adams, a supporter of the US policy, found it hard to entertain (Adams 1973). But Vicos clearly was meant to reclaim political ground that the United States had lost in some of the potentially most volatile regions of Latin America.

The fact, however, that Doughty (1987b) and others ever seriously thought that Vicos might have become a model for land reform in that vast, complex region suggests some degree of unreality – though perhaps no more than the case of Etawah in India. Backed by Carnegie, it was nonetheless elevated to a high status in the West's Cold War strategy of "community development" and what Gardner had called for – "fairly intensive indoctrination in local forms of 'democratic' group action with strong emphasis upon active and realistic political participation" – emerged, in the jargon of the Cornell anthropologists and their collaborators as "directed value accumulation" (Lasswell and Holmberg 1969).

HAROLD LASSWELL JOINS THE VICOS TEAM

One of those collaborators was Harold Lasswell, who, in the late 1920s, along with Edward Bernays and Walter Lippmann, had been one of the undisputed pioneers of the techniques of propaganda and, as it was sometimes called, "psychological warfare" (Simpson 1994: 16, 43–44).[13] By the 1950s, he was working closely with his former students, Nathan Leites, of the RAND Corporation – where Lasswell was a "permanent consultant" for a quarter of a century (Oren 2000: 553) – and CENIS's Daniel Lerner, author of that classic of modernization theory, *The Passing of Traditional Society* (1958), and a former member of the Army's Psychological Warfare Division, who would become "a fixture at Pentagon-sponsored conferences on U.S. psychological warfare in the Third World during the 1960s and 1970s" (Simpson 1994: 84; see Lasswell and Lerner 1951, 1965; Lasswell et al. 1976, 1979). A key figure in the shaping of the modernization paradigm, Lasswell's involvement with Vicos sets the Cornell-Peru Project securely within the modernization framework. It was a framework with strategic interests, and Lasswell reflected them, as much in his activities as in his writings. As a member of the influential Council for Foreign Relations and a member of the planning committee which directed the disbursement of a substantial Ford Foundation grant for CENIS's communication studies –which, as Simpson observes, "were from their inception closely bound up with both overt and covert aspects of U.S. national security strategy of the day" (1994: 82–83) – he connected Vicos to a web of Cold War initiatives that stretched from Stanford and RAND in the West to CENIS in the East.

Just after World War II, Lasswell himself took up an appointment at Yale, in the law school (Almond 1987: 261), where he may have come into contact with Holmberg, who completed his doctoral dissertation a year later. Lasswell's official interest in Vicos, however, "dates from his contact with Allan R. Holmberg when both were Fellows of the Center for Advanced Study in the Behavioral Sciences [at Palo Alto] in 1954–55" (Dobyns et al. 1971 [1964]: 237).[14] According to Doughty:

Holmberg was much taken with Harold Lasswell's concepts of institutional human values and their inter-relationships and how that could be utilized in the context of analyzing and, to the degree possible, guiding what the project was able to do. (Doughty, personal communication 2005)

By late 1955, Holmberg and Lasswell – joined by several others– had submitted a grant proposal both to Ford and Carnegie, which offered to turn Vicos into a veritable laboratory for the behavioral sciences. Carnegie, to its credit, was unimpressed, but by then it was clearly tiring of the whole Cornell approach. A year earlier, the foundation's William Marvel (himself a member of the CFR) had written an internal memorandum which said:

I assume that our interest now is in determining what the prospects are that the comparative analysis of which the Cornell group has spoken so often, so volubly, and so unspecifically, will actually add up to anything and will provide a basis for wider generalizations. (Marvel 1955: 4)

Marvel's reaction to the Holmberg–Lasswell proposal of 1955 was even more cutting. He noted that he had "[s]pent only three days at Vicos last summer, but I am yet to be convinced that this is likely to be the scene of *the* major breakthrough in the social sciences in this decade" (1955: 1). Observing that the proposal seemed "more a playing with words than a playing with concepts or ideas," he went on to say:

This is another chapter in the history of the famed Cornell project where the principals seem ready to ask for new and larger money before they have delivered anything in the way of written or published results on the money already given them. (Marvel 1955: 1)

Nonetheless, Lasswell had begun seriously to address the implications of Vicos for his own work (Lasswell 1962); he did some research at Vicos (Dobyns et al. 1971 [1964]: 237) and collaborated with Holmberg on a "general theory of directed value accumulation and international development" (Lasswell and Holmberg 1969) – very much in the CENIS vein. By the mid-1960s he was such an intimate part of the Vicos group, linking it to his own history of psychological and policy studies, that he co-edited one of its most important products, *Peasants, Power and Applied Social Change: Vicos as a Model* (Dobyns et al. 1971 [1964]), with Henry Dobyns and Paul Doughty, two of the project's foremost anthropological members.

By the early 1950s, Lasswell – who would use Vicos to refine his notion of the "policy sciences," that is, social sciences that could meaningfully contribute to the formulation of national policy – had already developed his concept of the "continuing policy (or decision) seminar," which was "concerned with working out the implications of the contextual, problem-oriented, multi-method approach" as a means of informing and guiding the direction of an on-going project. Vicos played a major role in his elaboration of this technique and:

One of the earliest explicit seminars was installed at Stanford in 1954–55 as a means of aiding Holmberg in his reassessment of the project as a whole. Cooperating with Holmberg were a political scientist, a psychologist, and an economist. They met regularly for the academic year in the same environment and developed a chart room to provide an auxiliary to recall and to effect the concept of systematic study. (Lasswell 1971: 191)

Besides culminating in a research proposal which Marvel (1955: 2) thought reduced Vicosinos to the status of laboratory rats, the collaboration of Lasswell and Holmberg in the "chart room" at Stanford – the prototypical Cold War university – and Lasswell's centrality in the emergence of modernization theory, underscores, as much as the strategic interests of the Carnegie Corporation, that the Vicos model had come to represent an important tool in the US strategy for dealing with the nature of change in the developing world.

As such, it was not simply a model, in Lasswell's words, for "integrating communities into more inclusive systems" (1962). Its real value, in the period of the Cold War, was that it offered a way to counter ideological or practical opposition to incorporation of Third World countries into the post-war Western capitalist system. Such integration was an intrinsic part of the modernization paradigm, as Holmberg clearly understood when he wrote "that lack of integration between the Sierra and Coast meant that the enormous Sierra labour reserve could not be efficiently tapped as an industrial work force" (1982: 3).

But this was where the geo-political imperatives of modernization ran counter to historical realities. As Lynch had concluded – and as the Cornell anthropologists seemed to deny – Vicos, in fact, had never been *un*-integrated with the modern economy. On the contrary:

Prior to the project, Vicos had not been a highly stable, traditional society, but a society constantly adapting to the changing consequences of its integration into Peruvian national society on extremely unequal terms. (Lynch 1982: 75)

CONCLUSIONS

As Gunder Frank (1967) had pointed out, much of the apparent backwardness of such communities was the product of an historical process of underdevelopment which, partly as a result of the impact of World War II on the global economy, had unleashed waves of peasant mobilizations from Bolivia to the Philippines. But, as in the case of Vicos, peasant aspirations for systemic change were *not* the starting-point for most anthropological analysis. Had they been, anthropologists, as Huizer, Whyte, Alberti, and others have suggested, might have "come to help [local people] to struggle against the repressive system, rather than with minor improvement schemes" (Huizer 1972: 53). Most, however, tended to adopt the Rostow model, with its roots in the CENIS view of modernization, the prevailing development paradigm at a time when one of Washington's chief strategic goals was to produce self-sustaining economic growth in the Third World, both to ensure the productivity of the West and to help immunize developing countries against agrarian insurgency and communism (Packenham 1973: 61–65).

The Vicos Project, like so much of anthropology's contribution to community development during this period, did little to address the growing need for structural change. Indeed, according to William Stein, the emphasis on cultural values meant that researchers viewed Vicos society "in terms of pluralism and cultural dimorphism, not as a whole, which led us to justify existing conditions and, in large part, to ignore the significance of exploitation" (Stein 1985: 238). Lynch, in her comprehensive summary of the Project, went further when she drew the conclusion that, by working within the dominant framework of Peruvian institutions, the Project had actually "acted as a brake on social change" (1982: 99). The papers of the Carnegie Corporation, which she never consulted, support that interpretation.

Foster claimed that the significance of Vicos lay in the fact that "the anthropologists ... were project administrators, with authority to make and execute decisions as well as to carry out research" (1969: 30). But this rather blandly ignores some fundamental questions. What interests and aims led to those decisions, what premises and assumptions justified them, and what did anthropologists do, as individuals and/or as a discipline, to give credibility to such assumptions which reflected ideas about development that had been shaped by the broad geo-political concerns of the United States during the Cold War? More pointedly, how did anthropology give legitimacy to such a view of development by emphasizing the community as a unit of analysis or, even more, as in the case of Vicos, as the unit of change, and, in the process, help to reduce the prospects for more fundamental, systemic economic and social transformation, which might have better served the people of Vicos and the wider peasant world?

US foreign policy objectives over the decades since the end of World War II were founded on a set of assumptions about the parameters of what was called modernization and about who should properly be the agents (and beneficiaries) of change. Far from doing very much to question those assumptions – particularly with regard to the role of peasants in rural change – anthropology, certainly in the 1950s and 1960s, did a great deal to enhance them. Not only was its notion of "peasant conservatism" essential to the viability of the community development paradigm as an integral feature of modernization, and as an alternative to more radical and systemic forms of agrarian change, but its reverent treatment of Holmberg and the Vicos Project gave that approach a credibility that was far more productive for the discipline – and its need for professional status in the eyes of government – than it ever was for those whom it studied. In the process, anthropology contributed to the making of the contemporary world. But it is a world in which the fate of peasants is now highly problematical.

NOTES

This chapter grew out of a working paper, "Anthropology, the Cold War and the Myth of Peasant Conservatism," published by the Institute of Social Studies in 2005. Evolving through many forms, the chapter is indebted to a variety of friends and colleagues, among them: Haroon Akram-Lodhi, David Barkin, Helen Hintjens, William Mitchell, David Stoll, and, as always, David Price. I am especially grateful to the Columbia University Rare Book & Manuscript Library for the opportunity to look at the archives of the Carnegie Corporation of New York, to the University of Illinois Archives, Urbana, for access to letters from their collection of the Julian H. Steward Papers, and to the National Anthropology Archives in Washington. In particular, I want to express my thanks to Karen Woodard for her many hours looking through those archives on my behalf.

1. When it was founded in 1911, the Carnegie Corporation's endowment of $125 million had made it the world's largest philanthropic organization (Jackson 1994: 11)
2. According to Trumpbour:

    > A 1971 study identified fourteen out of nineteen directors of the Rockefeller Foundation and ten out of seventeen of the Carnegie Corporation's directors as belonging to the CFR ... [while] the Ford Foundation ... was run from 1966 to 1977 by CFR members ... (1989: 66)

3. The Ethnogeographical Board was created during World War II. Directed by William Duncan Strong, its offices were at the Smithsonian. The chief aim of the Board, in much the same manner as the HRAF, was to organize the collecting of data in strategic areas, for purposes of advancing the war effort – but with obvious long-term considerations in mind, as well. As such, the Board is regarded as one of the true precursors of the area studies approach that would be promoted by Carnegie and the other major foundations in the 1950s and 1960s, when it became one of the central organizing principles of Cold War academe (see Cumings 1998). But its aims were exceedingly practical. Thus, for example, in 1942 it

convened a meeting at Yale to consider the issue of labor requirements in the mines of highland Bolivia (Bennett 1942).

4. Beals (1964: 186) refers to Louis Miniclier, who served as the head of the Community Development Division of the ICA from 1954, when it was founded, to 1964, as "the nation's largest employer of anthropologists."

5. The relationship of HRAF to the intelligence needs of government did not abate with the end of World War II. According to William Lambert of Cornell:

> Since 1948, and particularly since the beginning of the Korean War, a large proportion of the energies of the Human Relations Area Files staff have been directed toward a coverage of relevant materials on selected strategic areas for use in government service. (Lambert 1955: 2)

A conference on the research program of the HRAF, held in the mid-1950s, included representatives not only from the major US foundations, but from the US Army's Office of Psychological Warfare, the National Security Training Commission and the National Security Committee. There was also someone from the Arabian-American Oil Company, and the ubiquitous Clyde Kluckhohn (Carnegie Corporation 1955: 1), a former OSS operative and director of the Russian Studies Center. According to Clellan Ford, director of HRAF in the 1970s, by this period the organization "was receiving support from the government at the level of $200,000 a year." A quarter of that came from the CIA (Ford, quoted in Tobin 1990: 476).

6. The Rubber Development Corporation, which oversaw the exploration of wild rubber sources in the Amazon to compensate for the loss of Southeast Asian rubber due to the Japanese military occupation of former Western colonies, was a venture of the US Army (Browman 1999).

7. Even at this early stage in his career, in early 1942, Holmberg was known to individuals such as Steward and his colleague at the Bureau of American Ethnology, Alfred Metraux (Metraux 1942).

8. Gordon Willey had finished his doctoral research at Columbia in 1942 and then taught for a year at the university before moving to the Bureau of American Ethnology in Washington, where he was the assistant editor on the *Handbook of South American Indians* under Steward (Gorenstein 2002: 1255).

9. Steward had made his initial contacts with Paul Fejos, the Research Director of the Viking Fund, as it was originally known, shortly after the ISA had been created and while the founder of the Fund, the Swedish industrialist Axel Wenner-Gren, was still on a US wartime blacklist because of his German sympathies (Steward 1943; cf. Ross 1999).

10. Holmberg would never submit a manuscript on his Viru Valley work. In January 1950, he wrote to Gordon Willey at the ISA that he had a heavy teaching schedule at Cornell, but hoped to complete the manuscript by the fall of that year. He went so far as to say, impressively, that: "The manuscript will run between 800 and 1000 pages, double-spaced typing.... The title of the work will be: Fiesta and Siesta in a Peruvian Town: A Cultural Study of Viru Valley" (Holmberg 1950b). In late September, however, he wrote to Foster that: "Although the Viru manuscript is not finished, I have been working every spare minute I can on it" (Holmberg

1950c). But, a year later, Foster was writing to Holmberg: "I would appreciate a note about the status of the Viru report, and whether or when you expect to let me have it" (Foster 1951). Holmberg's reply, in early January 1952, was that he was "up to my neck in work on our Callejón project and I just haven't had time to finish up the Viru paper" (Holmberg 1952). The monumental book had been downsized to a paper – but it would never be completed.

11. Although the obituary of Opler in the *American Anthropologist* says that he "moved to Cornell in 1949" (Webster and Rushforth 2000).

12. Cornell had begun to receive substantial support from Carnegie to develop a comparative program in "culture and applied science" in 1947. In 1951 Cornell received an additional five-year grant from Carnegie, which was supplemented by funding from the Wenner-Gren Foundation, the Special Science Research Council and, a few years later, the Rockefeller Foundation (Wood 1975: v).

13. Lasswell's PhD dissertation, published in 1927, was entitled "Propaganda Technique in the World War" (Almond 1987: 269).

14. The Center was, from its inception, an important node in the network of the academic/policy elite. Established in 1954 with an enormous grant from the Ford Foundation, one of its founder members was Dr Frank Stanton (who also served as one of the Center's trustees between 1953 and 1971), the president of the Columbia Broadcasting System, 1946–71 (Ford Foundation 1954: 51–53). Stanton was also the chair of the RAND Corporation, 1961–67, and one of its trustees from 1957 to 1978, in addition to serving as a trustee of the Rockefeller Foundation during part of this time (*Public Agenda* 2005). One of the Center's first fellows, in addition to Holmberg, was Clyde Kluckhohn (Parsons and Vogt 1962: 6).

REFERENCES

Adams, Richard. 1964. Politics and Social Anthropology in Spanish America. *Human Organization* 23(1): 1–4.

—— 1973. Review of *Peasants, Power and Applied Social Change: Vicos as a Model* (edited by Henry Dobyns, Paul Doughty, and Harold Lasswell). *American Anthropologist* 75: 443–44.

Almond, Gabriel. 1987. Harold Dwight Lasswell. In *National Academy of Sciences, Biographical Memoirs*, vol. 57, pp. 249–74. Washington, DC: National Academy Press.

Babb, Florence. 1985. Women and Men in Vicos, Peru: A Case of Unequal Development. In *Peruvian Contexts of Change*, pp. 163–210. William Stein, ed. New Brunswick, NJ: Transaction Books.

Beals, Ralph. 1964. Introduction [to The Uses of Anthropology in Overseas Programs]. *Human Organization* 23(3): 185–86.

Bennett, Wendell. 1942. Conference on Bolivian Indians. Yale University, September 20. Mimeo.

Bowen, John. 2003. The Development of Southeast Asian Studies in the United States. In *The Politics of Knowledge: Area Studies and the Disciplines*. David L. Szanton, ed. Berkeley: University of California Press. University of California International and Area Studies. Digital Collection, Edited Volume

No. 3: URL: http://repositories.cdlib.org/uciaspubs/editedvolumes/3/10 (accessed June 2007).

Browman, David. 1999. Hugh Carson Cutler. Bulletin. Society for American Archaeology 17(1). URL: http://www.saa.org/Publications/saabulletin/17-1/SAA23.html (accessed September 2005).

Cady, John. 1974. Oral History Interview, with Richard Mckinzie. Truman Presidential Museum & Library. URL: http://www.nps.gov/manz/hrs/hrm. htm (accessed December 2005).

Caldwell, John and Pat Caldwell. 1986. *Limiting Population Growth and the Ford Foundation's Contribution*. Dover, NH: Frances Pinter.

Carnegie Corporation of New York. 1955. Memorandum (by AP) on the Conference on the Research Program of the HRAF, New Haven, CT, October 24. Box 174 (folder 14). Columbia University Rare Book & Manuscript Library.

Colby, Gerard and Charlotte Dennett. 1995. *Thy Will Be Done: The Conquest of the Amazon – Nelson Rockefeller and Evangelism in the Age of Oil*. New York: HarperCollins.

Council on Foreign Relations. 2005. History of CFR. Appendix (Historical roster of directors and officers). URL: http://www.cfr.org/about/history/cfr/appendix.html?jsessionid=a22fda9e762aeadb7229f79d56cfe22e (accessed September 2005).

Cumings, Bruce. 1998. Boundary Displacement: Area Studies and International Studies during the Cold War. In *Universities and Empire: Money and Politics in the Social Sciences*, pp. 159–88. Christopher Simpson, ed. New York: The New Press.

Davies, Wade. 2001. Cornell's Field Seminar in Applied Anthropology: Social Scientists and American Indians in the Postwar Southwest. *Journal of the Southwest* 43(3): 318–41.

Diamond, Sigmund. 1992. *Compromised Campus: The Collaboration of Universities with the Intelligence Community, 1945–1955*. New York: Oxford University Press.

Dobyns, Henry, Paul Doughty, and Harold Lasswell. 1971 [1964]. *Peasants, Power, and Applied Social Change: Vicos as a Model*. Beverly Hills, CA: Sage Publications.

Domhoff, G. William. 1970. *The Higher Circles: The Governing Class in America*. New York: Vintage Books.

Doughty, Paul. 1966. Pitfalls and Progress in the Peruvian Sierra. In *Cultural Frontiers of the Peace Corps*, pp. 221–41. Robert Textor, ed. Cambridge, MA: MIT Press.

—— 1977. Review of *Directed Culture Change in Peru: A Guide to the Vicos Collection*, by Deborah Wood. *American Anthropologist* 79: 144–46.

—— 1987a. Vicos: Success, Rejection, and Rediscovery of a Classic Program. In *Applied Anthropology in America*. Elizabeth Eddy and William Partridge, eds. New York: Columbia University Press.

—— 1987b. Against the Odds: Collaboration and Development at Vicos. In *Collaborative Research and Social Change*, pp. 129–58. Donald Stull and Jean Schensul, eds. Boulder, CO: Westview Press.

Feldman, Bob. 2002. Time for Ford Foundation and CFR to divest? Questions, Questions … 8 October. URL: http: //www.questionsquestions.net/feldman/ff_divest.html (accessed May 2005).

Ford Foundation. 1951. Letter to Allan Holmberg. October 1. National Anthropology Archives, Smithsonian Institution, ISA Box 7.

—— 1954. *Report for 1954*. New York: The Ford Foundation.

—— 1957 *Annual Report*. New York: The Ford Foundation.

Foster, George. 1948 The Folk Economy of Rural Mexico with Special Reference to Marketing. *Journal of Marketing* 13(2): 153–62.

—— 1965. Peasant Society and the Image of Limited Good. *American Anthropologist* 67(2): 293–315.

—— 1967. Introduction: What is a Peasant? In *Peasant Society: A Reader*, pp. 2–14. Jack Potter, May Diaz, and George Fosters, eds. Boston, MA: Little, Brown and Co.

—— 1969. *Applied Anthropology*. Boston: Little, Brown and Co.

Frank, Andre Gunder. 1967. *Capitalism and Underdevelopment in Latin America*. New York: Monthly Review Press.

Furedi, Frank. 1989. *The Mau Mau War in Perspective*. London: James Currey.

Gardner, John. 1947. Letter to Clyde Kluckhohn, September 8. Carnegie Corporation of New York papers. Series III. A. 4, Box 164. Columbia University Rare Book & Manuscript Library.

—— 1951. Letter to Lauriston Sharp, June 5. Carnegie Corporation of New York papers. Series III. A.2, Box 124. Columbia University Rare Book & Manuscript Library.

—— 1963. Letter to Frederick M. Eaton, May 15. Carnegie Corporation of New York papers. Series III. B.1, Box 526. Columbia University Rare Book & Manuscript Library.

Gillin, John. 1960. Some Signposts for Policy. In *Social Change in Latin America Today: Its Implications for United States Policy*, pp. 14–62. Council on Foreign Relations. New York: Harper and Brothers.

Goodenough, Ward. 1951. *Property, Kin and Community on Truk*. New Haven, CT: Yale University Press.

—— 1963. *Cooperation in Change: An Anthropological Approach to Community Development*. New York: Russell Sage Foundation.

—— 2003. In Pursuit of Culture. *Annual Review of Anthropology* 32: 1–12.

Gorenstein, Shirley. 2002. Gordon Randolph Willey. *American Anthropologist* 104(4): 1254–56.

Grace-Kobas, Linda. 1998. James A. Perkins, President Emeritus, Dies at 86. *Cornell Chronicle* August 27. URL: http://www.news.cornell.edu/Chronicle/98/8.27.98/perkins.html (accessed September 2006).

Griffin, Keith. 1979 [1974]. *The Political Economy of Agrarian Change: An Essay on the Green Revolution*. London: Macmillan.

Hagen, Everett. 1962. *On the Theory of Social Change: How Economic Growth Begins*. Homewood, IL: Dorsey Press, for the MIT Center for International Studies.

Heath, Dwight. 1980. Review of *Long-term Field Research in Social Anthropology*, edited by George Foster et al. *American Anthropologist* 82(2): 455–57.

Hoffman, Paul. 1951. *Peace Can Be Won*. Garden City, NY: Doubleday.

Holmberg, Allan R. 1946. Letter to Julian Steward, January 17. National Anthropology Archives, Smithsonian Institution, ISA Box 7.

—— 1948. Proposed Research for Venezuela and a Proposal for Research in Peru. Submitted to Carnegie with cover letter by Morris Opler, Cornell University Department of Anthropology, 11 Nov. Carnegie Corporation of New York papers. Series III. A.2, Box 124. Columbia University Rare Book & Manuscript Library.

—— 1950a. *Nomads of the Long Bow: The Siriono of Eastern Bolivia.* Institute of Social Anthropology, Publication No. 10. Washington, DC: Smithsonian Institution.

—— 1950b. Letter to Gordon Willey, January 9. National Anthropology Archives, Smithsonian Institution, ISA Box 7.

—— 1950c. Letter to George Foster, September 27. National Anthropology Archives, Smithsonian Institution, ISA Box 7,

—— 1952. Letter to George Foster, January 2. National Anthropology Archives, Smithsonian Institution, ISA Box 7.

Huizer, Gerrit. 1972. *The Revolutionary Potential of Peasants in Latin America.* Lexington, MA: Lexington Books.

India Planning Commission. 1958. *The New India: Progress through Democracy.* New York: Macmillan.

Isbell, Billie Jean and Florencia Zapata. 2005–2006. *Vicos: A Virtual Tour from 1952 to the Present.* Cornell University. URL: http://instruct1.cit.cornell.edu/courses/vicosperu/vicos-site/credits.html (accessed August 2006).

Jackson, Walter. 1994. *Gunnar Myrdal and America's Conscience: Social Engineering and Racial Liberalism, 1938–1987.* Chapel Hill: University of North Carolina Press.

Jonas, Susanne and David Tobis (eds). 1974. *Guatemala.* New York: NACLA.

Keyes, Charles. 1994. Lauriston Sharp and the Anthropological Study of Thailand: Some Reflections. *Thai-Yunnan Project Newsletter* No. 25, June. URL: http://www.nectec.or.th/thai-yunnan/25.html (accessed June 2004).

Lambert, William. 1955. A Report on the Present Status of the Human Relations Area Files. Carnegie Corporation of New York Papers. Box 174 (folder 14). Columbia University Rare Book & Manuscript Library.

Lasswell, Harold. 1962. Integrating Communities into More Inclusive Systems. *Human Organization* 21: 116–21.

Lasswell, Harold and Daniel Lerner. 1951. *The Policy Sciences: Recent Developments in Scope and Method.* Stanford, CA: Stanford University Press.

—— and —— eds. 1965. *World Revolutionary Elites: Studies in Coercive Ideological Movements.* Cambridge, MA: MIT Press.

Lasswell, Harold and Allan Holmberg. 1969. Toward a General Theory of Directed Value Accumulation and Institutional Development. In *Political and Administrative Development*, pp. 354–99. Ralph Braibanti, ed. Durham, NC: Duke University Press.

Lasswell, Harold, Daniel Lerner, and John Montgomery. 1976. *Values and Development: Appraising Asian Experience.* Cambridge, MA: MIT Press.

Lasswell, Harold, Daniel Lerner, and Hans Speier (eds). 1979. *Propaganda and Communication in World History*, 3 vols. Honolulu: University of Hawaii Press.

Lastarria-Cornhiel, Susana, 1989, Agrarian Reform of the 1960s and 1970s in Peru. In *Searching for Agrarian Reform in Latin America*, pp. 127–55. William C. Thiesenhusen, ed. Boston, MA: Unwin Hyman.

Latham, Michael. 2000. *Modernization as Ideology: American Social Science and "Nation Building" in the Kennedy Era.* Chapel Hill: University of North Carolina Press.

Laurenzo, R. 2005. Julian Steward: An Archaeological Innovator. URL: http://www.utexas.edu/courses/wilson/ant304/biography/arybios97/laurenzobio.html (accessed May 2005).

Lerner, Daniel. 1951. *Propaganda in War and Crisis: Materials for American Policy*. New York: George W. Stewart.

—— 1958. *The Passing of Traditional Society: Modernizing the Middle East*. Glencoe, IL: The Free Press.

Lewis, O. 1955. Peasant Culture in India and Mexico: A Comparative Analysis. In *Village India: Studies in the Little Community*, pp. 145–170. McKim Marriot, ed. Chicago: University of Chicago Press.

Lynch, Barbara. 1982. *The Vicos Experiment: A Study of the Impacts of the Cornell-Peru Project in a Highland Community*. AID Evaluation Special Study No. 7. Washington, DC: USAID.

Mcnamara, Robert. 1968. *The Essence of Security: Reflections in Office*. New York: Harper and Row.

Manas. 1952. What Is Happening in India? *Manas* 5(19). URL: www.manasjournal.org/pdf_library/VolumeV_1952/V-19.pdf (accessed September 2005).

Mangin, William. 1979. Thoughts on Twenty-four Years of Work in Perú: The Vicos Project and Me. In *Long-term Field Research in Social Anthropology*, pp. 65–84. George Foster et al., eds. New York: Academic Press.

Manners, Robert. 1996. Julian Haynes Steward. *Biographical Memoirs*, vol. 69: 325–36. National Academy of Sciences. URL: http://www.nap.edu/books/0309053463/html/324.html (accessed May 2005).

Marvel, William. 1955. Memorandum on Proposal on Experimental Research in the Behavioral Sciences by Holmberg et al. Carnegie Corporation of New York papers. Series III. A.2, Box 124. Columbia University Rare Books and Manuscript Library.

Mattelart, Armand. 1979. *Multinational Corporations and the Control of Culture: The Ideological Apparatuses of Imperialism*, Michael Chanan, trans. Brighton: Harvester Press.

Mayer, Albert and Associates. 1958. *Pilot Project, India: The Story of Rural Development at Etawah, Uttar Pradesh*. In collaboration with McKim Marriott and Richard Park. Berkeley: University of California Press.

Metraux, Alfred. 1942. Letter to Julian Steward, 26 March. National Anthropological Archives, Smithsonian Institution. ISA, Box 11 (Correspondence).

Millikan, Max. 1962. Foreword in Wilfred Malenbaum, *Prospects for Indian Development*. London: Allen and Unwin.

Nader, Laura. 1997. The Phantom Factor: Impact of the Cold War on Anthropology. In *The Cold War and the University: Toward an Intellectual History of the Postwar Years*, pp. 107–46. Noam Chomsky et al., eds. New York: The New Press.

Notestein, Frank. 1953. Economic Problems of Population Change. In *Proceedings of the Eighth International Conference of Agricultural Economists*. G. Cumberlege, ed. London: Oxford University Press.

Oppenheimer, Martin. 1997. Social Scientists and War Criminals. *New Politics* 6(3) (n.s.). URL: http://www.wpunj.edu/~newpol/issue23/oppenh23.htm (accessed September 2005).

Oren, Ido. 2000. Is Culture Independent of National Security? How America's National Security Concerns Shaped "Political Culture" Research. *European Journal of International Relations* 6(4): 543–73.

Packenham, Robert. 1973. *Liberal America and the Third World*. Princeton, NJ: Princeton University Press.

Parsons, Talcott and Evon Vogt. 1962. Clyde Kay Maben Kluckhohn. *American Anthropologist* 64: 140–61.

Price, David. 1997. Anthropologists on Trial: The Lessons of McCarthyism. Paper presented at the American Anthropological Association meetings, Washington, DC.

—— 1998. Cold War Anthropology: Collaborators and Victims of the National Security State. *Identities* 4(3–4): 389–430.

—— 2000. The AAA and the CIA? *Anthropology News* November: 13–14. URL: http://www.cia-on-campus.org/social/price.html (accessed May 2005).

—— 2002. Lessons from Second World War Anthropology: Peripheral, Persuasive and Ignored Contributions. *Anthropology Today* 18(3): 14–20.

—— 2004. *Threatening Anthropology: McCarthyism and the FBI's Surveillance of Activist Anthropologists.* Durham, NC: Duke University Press.

Public Agenda. 2005. Frank Stanton, Former President, CBS. URL: http://www.publicagenda.org/aboutpa/aboutpa_whoswho_detail.cfm?list=16 (accessed September 2005).

Raffer, Kunibert and Hans Singer. 1996. *The Foreign Aid Business: Economic Assistance and Development Co-operation.* Cheltenham: Edward Elgar.

Rand Corporation. 2005. History and Mission. URL: http://www.rand.org/about/history/ (accessed September 2005).

Rosen, George. 1985. *Western Economists and Eastern Societies: Agents of Change in South Asia, 1950–1970.* Baltimore, MD: Johns Hopkins University Press.

Ross, Eric B. 1998a. *The Malthus Factor: Poverty, Politics and Population in Capitalist Development.* London: Zed Books.

—— 1998b. Cold Warriors without Weapons. *Identities* 4(3–4): 475–506.

—— 1999. Axel Wenner-Gren, the Nazi Connection and the Origins of the Viking Fund. Paper presented in the session, "Playing with Power: Anthropologists and the Cold War," at the 98th Annual Meeting of the American Anthropological Association, November 17–21, 1999, Chicago.

—— 2003. Modernisation, Clearance and the Continuum of Violence in Colombia. Working Paper Series No. 383. The Hague: Institute of Social Studies.

Ryder, Norman. 1984. Obituary: Frank Wallace Notestein (1902–1983). *Population Studies* 38(1): 5–20.

Sharp, Lauriston. 1948. Letter to Alan Holmberg, May 12. National Anthropology Archives, Smithsonian Institution. Correspondence 1948–52, ISA Box 7.

—— 1951. Letter to John Gardner, April 19, and "A Proposal for a Program of Experimental Field Research in Technological Change." Carnegie Corporation of New York papers. Series III. A.2, Box 124. Columbia University Rare Books and Manuscript Library.

Simpson, Christopher. 1994. *Science of Coercion: Communication Research and Psychological Warfare 1945–1960.* New York: Oxford University Press.

Snead, David. 1999. *The Gaither Committee, Eisenhower, and the Cold War.* Columbus: Ohio State University Press.

Social Security Online. 2005. Cabinet Officials – John Gardner. URL: http://www.ssa.gov/history/gardner.html (accessed May 2005).

Stein, William. 1985. Townspeople and Countrypeople in the Callejón de Huaylas. In *Peruvian Contexts of Change*, pp. 211–331. William W. Stein, ed. New Brunswick, NJ: Transaction Books.

Steward, Julian H. 1943. Letter to Paul Fejos, September 23. National Anthropology Archives, Smithsonian Institution, ISA Box 7.

—— 1946. Memorandum to Raymond Zwemer, 29 April, with enclosure. National Anthropology Archives, Smithsonian Institution, ISA Box 7.

—— 1954. Letter to Frederick Johnson, March 9. Julian H. Steward Papers, University of Illinois Archives.

—— ed. 1963 [1948]. *Handbook of South American Indians*, vol. 3, *Tropical Forest Tribes*. New York: Cooper Square Publishers.

Taraqqi. 2000. The Seventy-five-year-old Legacy to be Taken Forward. Association of Indian Progressive Study Groups (AIPSG). URL: http://www.geocities.com/aipsg/1200kanpur.htm (accessed June 2005).

Tobin, Joseph. 1990. The HRAF as Radical Text. *Cultural Anthropology* 5(4): 473–87.

Tremblay, Marc-Adelard. 2004. Alexander H. Leighton and Jane Murphy's Scientific Contributions in Psychiatric Epidemiology. Paper presented in the Leighton Symposium, Canadian Anthropology Society, Dalhousie University, Halifax, May 10, 2003.

Trumpbour, John. 1989. Harvard, the Cold War, and the National Security State. In *How Harvard Rules: Reason in the Service of Empire*, pp. 51–128. John Trumpbour, ed. Boston, MA: Southend Press.

Unrau, Harlan. 1996. The Evacuation and Relocation of Persons of Japanese Ancestry during World War II: A Historical Study of the Manzanar War Relocation Center. US Department of the Interior, National Park Service. URL: http://www.nps.gov/manz/hrs/hrs.htm (accessed June 2007).

Walinsky, Louis (ed.). 1977. The Selected Papers of Wolf Ladejinsky: Agrarian Reform as Unfinished Business. Washington, DC: World Bank.

Webster, Anthony and Scott Rushforth. 2000. Morris Edward Opler (1907–1996). *American Anthropologist* 102(2): 328–29.

Whyte, William Foote and Giorgio Alberti. 1976. *Power, Politics and Progress: Social Change in Rural Peru*. New York: Elsevier.

Wolf, Eric and Joseph Jorgensen. 1970. Anthropology on the Warpath in Thailand. *New York Review of Books* 15(9). URL: http://www.nybooks.com/articles/10763 (accessed June 2005).

6 ORGANIZING ANTHROPOLOGY: SOL TAX AND THE PROFESSIONALIZATION OF ANTHROPOLOGY

Dustin M. Wax

In 1958, at the beginning of his career as an activist lawyer, Ralph Nader wrote a letter to Sol Tax soliciting advice on a publication he was considering starting.

I propose starting a monthly newspaper devoted to news, feature and editorial coverage of all aspects of that amorphous area – American Indian affairs.... I anticipate contributions from those working in the legal, educational, health, economic, political and anthropological areas of Indian affairs in an attempt to tap what appears to be an enormous untapped reservoir of experience and insight ... in an effort to establish a greater comprehension of the processes at work on and off the reservation and ultimately to relate facts to policy ... (Ralph Nader to Sol Tax, 8/28/58: NAA MS 4802, Box 10)

Nader understood that in order to mobilize the various experts and expert knowledges on Indian affairs it was necessary to organize those knowledges in some way, and that he needed the advice of someone with experience in doing just that. At the end of the 1950s, he probably couldn't have done much better in his choice of advisors than Sol Tax.

Tax came of age, anthropologically speaking, during a period of crisis for anthropology. After spending the late 1930s and the war years in Central America, he returned to a regular position at the University of Chicago just as the American Anthropological Association (AAA) was struggling to contain the different needs of amateur and professional anthropologists. As chair of the Chicago local arrangements committee for the 1946 AAA meetings, Tax experienced the reorganization of the AAA from a logistical, as well as ideological, perspective (Stocking 1976). Tax would repeatedly apply his logistical experience and expertise to the service of anthropological research over the next two decades. Although he was not entirely alone in this endeavor – figures such as Clyde Kluckhohn, Julian Steward, and others also played important roles in the development of anthropological institutions over the same time period – Tax, as much as or more than anyone else of his generation, was responsible for organizing anthropology to address the changing needs for anthropological knowledge during the early decades of the Cold War.

A HERITAGE OF CONFERENCES

The years immediately following the end of World War II saw an unprecedented growth in the field of anthropology (and of academia in general). Tax estimated the number of anthropologists at the end of the 1950s at about 4000, up from about 600 at the end of World War II. A combination of several factors led to this increase: (1) the effects of GI Bill subsidization of university education for veterans returning from the war, (2) post-war prosperity allowing students for whom an advanced education would have been an unattainable luxury two decades earlier, to pursue college and graduate educations, and (3) the increased investment by government and foundation sources in developing sources of knowledge on overseas territories which, as new allies or Cold War enemies, it was necessary to incorporate into America's foreign policy.

From the time of his return to Chicago forward, Tax's career was shaped by the contingencies of this growth of anthropology as a discipline. The very terms of his appointment at the University of Chicago explicitly charged him with overseeing the development of a Masters-level core curriculum to accommodate the expected influx of students taking advantage of GI Bill educational provisions. Tax's organizational drive led him to organize conference after conference, including the Darwin Centennial in 1959 and the Ninth Congress of the International Union of Anthropological and Ethnological Sciences in 1973, as well as coordinating countless publications, promoting the establishment of a Museum of Man at the Smithsonian, and advising the US government on Indian affairs – all while remaining active at the University of Chicago and in the American Anthropological Association. Here, I will focus on two key events during the early Cold War period, one at the very beginning and the other a decade later, as the Cold War gestated into the significantly hotter years of the Kennedy administration.

Soon after returning to Chicago, Tax was invited to join the National Research Council's Committee on Latin American Anthropology, formed in response to what was perceived as a critical lack of American specialists in Latin American society and culture. In this the Committee reflected the general concern which would, over the next decade, give rise to the area studies approach. In the Social Science Research Council's 1943 report on the status of "World Regions in the Social Sciences," the need for social sciences with specialized knowledge of the various world regions was placed second only to the need for competent military officers familiar with potential combat zones (Wallerstein 1997).

When the Committee failed to endorse an Office of Naval Relations' proposal for a comprehensive program of investigation of Latin American culture, and then failed to endorse Tax's alternative proposal, Tax decided to pursue a more organized approach to Latin American studies independent of the Committee (Stocking 2000). Together with co-Committee member Paul Fejos, research director of the Viking Fund (the precursor to the Wenner-Gren Foundation for Anthropological Research), Tax began to organize a seminar of anthropologists working in Central America, in order to "put our special information into the perspective of the whole" (Tax 1968 [1952]: 8).

The seminar, "Heritage of Conquest," was held in New York in 1949, just before the 29th International Congress of Americanists held in the same city. The week-long meeting was attended by the eleven anthropologists who had contributed papers for discussion, along with 20 others who were invited as discussants. The structure of the seminar was to become Tax's trademark organizational style: a committee set out the major topics they felt should be treated; papers were written, copied, and distributed to all the other contributors and attendees; participants met in person to discuss what they had read beforehand; the authors rewrote their contributions in light of the seminar discussion; and finally a book was compiled and published. The published volume, *Heritage of Conquest: The Ethnology of Middle America* (1968 [1952]), contains each of the eleven papers as well as apparently complete transcripts of the discussions that ensued. In addition, two sessions on acculturation in general terms, and a discussion summarizing the events of the seminar for attendees of the Americanist Association meeting immediately following, are transcribed.

Heritage of Conquest lays out its field as an almost textbook example of the area studies approach. A somewhat earlier paper by Paul Kirchhoff, initially published in 1943 and entitled "Mesoamerica: Its Geographic Limits, Ethnic Composition and Cultural Composition," defines the boundaries of the geographical/cultural area under examination and delineates the cultural traits common to that area as well as those notable by their absence. The rest of the papers attempt to sum up the current state of knowledge on each major area of Mesoamerican life, and suggest avenues of inquiry for further examination. Thus, we have essays on "Economy and Technology" (Sol Tax), "Ethnic and Communal Relations" (Julio de la Fuente), "Social Organization" (Calixta Guiteras Holmes), "The Supernatural World and Curing" (Charles Wisdom), "Religious and Political Organization" (Fernando Cámara), "The Life Cycle" (Benjamin D.

Paul and Lois Paul), and "Ethos and Cultural Aspects of Personality" (John Gillin), as well as two essays on acculturation (Ralph Beals, Gertrude P. Kurath) and Tax's and Redfield's exemplary community study of an unnamed, generic "village ... group of hamlets or ... rural region" (Tax 1968 [1952]: 31). Over the course of the week-long meeting, an area was defined, its central features described, and the pressing research problems of that area delineated (perhaps not coincidentally providing the seminar's funders, Viking Fund – as well as other funders of anthropology – with a set of criteria with which to evaluate future research proposals).

BECOMING A *CA* STAR

Over the next several years, Tax would apply a similar format to dozens of conferences and seminars, experience that would profoundly shape his role in the launch of *Current Anthropology (CA)*. In addition to editing volumes like *Heritage of Conquest* and *Appraising Anthropology Today*, by the mid-1950s Tax had also served three years as the editor of *American Anthropologist*, which he had taken over in 1954 promising to increase the size, frequency, and quality of the near-moribund AAA house organ (Stocking 2000). While Tax was at *American Anthropologist*, the Wenner-Gren Foundation began what was intended as an annual series of anthropology "yearbooks," collecting the latest research in the discipline. After the first issue was published in 1955, Wenner-Gren was somewhat dissatisfied with both the expense and the quality of the finished product, and asked Tax to take over and reshape the project. Tax tentatively envisioned a yearly or twice-yearly publication examining the latest trends in various areas of the discipline, oriented towards the publication, after ten years, of a single "encyclopedia" of anthropology. As one of the conditions of his taking the position, though, Tax asked that he be allowed to organize a series of conferences and meetings around the world to find out what sort of publication would be of the greatest use to the greatest number of anthropologists.

After resigning his post at *American Anthropologist*, having accomplished everything he had hoped to do with the journal, Tax embarked on a series of meetings throughout the US and Europe, during which a consensus emerged that what was really desired was a published instrument that would allow anthropologists in every sub- and affiliated discipline, and in far-flung corners of the earth, to learn rapidly of the most recent advances in anthropological thought and practice. While it was decided that the material form of the new publication would be a bi-monthly journal, what Tax and his collaborators were really envisioning was a community of international scholars. In 1959, Tax traveled through Europe, Asia,

Central and South America, and Africa presenting this new vision for comment and approval, which with little modification was generally received positively. In September 1959, Tax sent out a "pre-issue" of the new journal to a list of about 3000 anthropologists worldwide, now christened "Associates" of the new, experimental publication/community (Stocking 2000; Tax 1965).

Stocking (2000) and Tax himself have described Tax's role in the launching of *Current Anthropology* as a direct outgrowth of the action anthropology approach Tax and his students had developed in the Fox Project, a field school-turned-experiment in social change that had been overseen by Tax from 1948 until just before the publication of the *CA* pre-issue in 1959. Working with the Meskwaki Indians of Central Iowa, Tax's students had developed a process of working with local Indians (and their white neighbors) to identify social problems in their community, generate acceptable programs to address those problems, and put those programs into effect under local control. Although the ultimate success of this approach in improving Meskwaki lives is debatable, Tax applied the lessons he and his students learned in the field to his editorship of *CA*. The exploratory meetings around the world, for instance, are a perfect example of the action anthropology approach at work, attempting to elicit local perceptions of the problems faced by professional anthropologists and local assessments of the measures needed to address those problems rather than imposing "solutions" from afar.

This approach was carried into the active life of the journal as well. Rather than simply producing a journal to which anthropologists around the world could subscribe, Tax produced a worldwide community of Associates whom he urged to think of the journal as secondary to their active involvement in that community. As such, each Associate was charged with several responsibilities:

1. To keep up to date the list of Associates and to nominate new Associates;
2. To pay a minimal fee (initially set at US $2.00 or its equivalent in local currency) as a token of interest and to help defray publication costs;
3. To review each issue of *CA* as it arrived, and to respond to each issue as requested;
4. To suggest new topics they would like to see covered in *CA* and new features they would find useful; and
5. To respond to requests for articles, comments on articles, news, and other materials.

Tax produced a number of innovations to encourage participation in the *CA* project, including soliciting and publishing peers' comments on articles along with the author's response to those comments (the

"*CA*-star treatment"), and a questionnaire included with each issue to allow voting on proposed changes and additions to *CA* as well as providing a space for general comments. Tax also wrote a "Letter to Associates," included as an insert to each issue, outlining the current issues facing the *CA* community and the concerns raised by Associates.

Tax's "Letter to Associates," included with each issue, was indicative of his whole approach to his editorship. During the Fox Project, Tax and his students had continually concerned themselves with avoiding any concentration of power – or even the *appearance* of such a concentration – in the hands of the anthropologists themselves. As editor of *CA*, Tax saw himself as a facilitator of exchange, rather than as a gatekeeper, and worked hard to make the functioning of the journal and its community as transparent as possible. Issues regularly included eight, ten, or more pages of letters, from Associates as well as other subscribers, including negative assessments of the journal or of Tax's work as its editor. Almost every major decision, ranging from the language of publication to the introduction of new "departments," was discussed at length in the "Letter to Associates," often over the course of several issues, and was put to a vote – the results of which were typically published, even when, for one reason or another, the action taken differed from that endorsed by the vote (see below).

By maintaining the transparency of the editorial process, Tax hoped to construct a position for himself as a sort of disinterested conduit for information – a neutral force giving a nudge here and a tug there but for the most part keeping out of the way. Such an orientation, however, met with some resistance from the *CA* community. On one hand, Tax was criticized for being too "democratic" – as one Associate wrote, "You waste far too much time in discussing your reaction to other people's remarks about your publication" (Tax 1965: 249). On the other hand, early "Letters" are filled with exhortations to Associates to carry out their duties by, minimally, returning their reply forms, even if they did not feel they had anything to say (blank forms communicating at least that the journal was received and read). For the most part, though, Tax seemed to have elicited a decent response to his questions, whether about *CA* policy or about wider issues in the anthropological community. Over the first few years, numerous new "departments" were introduced at the suggestion of associates, the *CA*-star treatment was refined to better meet Associates demands, and concerns over distribution, fee payment, and terminology were addressed.

Ultimately, though, for all its transparency and fair-mindedness, Tax's position was still a position of power. Throughout his editorship of *Current Anthropology*, Tax's own vision of an international cooperative of scholars remained the most crucial force in the journal's editorial and institutional development. It was Tax who decided what proposals to put to a vote. And it was Tax who made the decision, in a few, admittedly minor, instances, to override the majority. For instance, Tax's proposal to eliminate the category of "Institutional Associates" was approved by a majority, yet Tax decided to retain the category in deference to a minority of persons who responded that institutional memberships were the only way to enjoy the benefits of *CA* in their countries.

Taken together, the projects initiated in the pages of *CA* in its early years functioned to increase the visibility and legibility of the anthropological community. From the beginning, a list of Associates, with contact information and specialties, was published; soon, lists of institutions dealing with anthropology, tables of contents from anthropological journals, research proposals, titles of recently completed PhD dissertations, job, grant, and fellowship offers, and announcements of their recipients, and attempts at standardizing the usage of anthropological terminology began appearing regularly in *CA*'s pages. Over the course of a few issues, a reasonably complete "snapshot" of anthropology as a discipline at any given moment could be compiled. The natural culmination of this project was the 1962 publication of a new fourth edition of the *International Directory of Anthropologists*, last published in 1950, and the publication of a new *Directory of Anthropological Institutions* in 1964, updating the edition previously published in 1953.

In essence, then, while providing a forum for useful communication between anthropologists, *CA* also functioned to organize and delineate the field of endeavor it represented. Area specialists could more easily contact each other, and non-area specialists could more easily find such specialists. But professional anthropologists were not the only persons to whom this kind of thorough, centralized information could be useful. David Price (2003) has described the lengths to which the Central Intelligence Agency (CIA) had gone, ten years earlier, to conceal their collaboration with the AAA to compile a roster of anthropologists along with their specializations and research; now all this information could be easily tracked with a simple subscription to *CA*.

TOWARDS AN ORGANIZED ANTHROPOLOGY

James Scott uses the term "legibility" to describe the arrangement of a population "in ways that simplified the classic state functions of taxation, conscription, and prevention of rebellion" (1998: 2), a definition we might alter somewhat in this instance to include instead "the classic disciplinary functions of publication, recruitment, and peer review." In this light, the editorial position – and the position

Tax adopted in his conferences and other endeavors – can be seen as an elevated vantage point from which the entirety (or a large part, anyway) of the discipline and its practitioners were visible. As a central point overlooking the field as a whole, and through which all the channels of communication passed, Tax's editorial chair provided a clear view of the structure of the discipline as well as a leverage point from which to alter and reshape it.

The structure that Tax envisioned and effected through his editorship of *CA* was his central vision for anthropology as a whole. On a smaller scale, the "Heritage of Conquest" conference did the same thing for the field of Mesoamerican Studies (although without the long-term development that *CA* allowed). On a larger scale, Tax would later bend his directorate of the Smithsonian's Center for the Study of Man towards the same structure, envisioning the Smithsonian as a central clearing-house for anthropological research around the world, coordinating anthropologists and other social scientists in the study of the world's peoples and the application of anthropological knowledge. Comparing the possibilities to Fermi's wartime nuclear bomb research at the University of Chicago, Tax wrote:

... the opportunity for Smithsonian world leadership in the organization of anthropological research is real and very great.... [T]he organization of research on the broadest scale is a major necessity for any real breakthrough. The Smithsonian Institution, with its information exchange, the counterpart currencies, its reputation, and long tradition, is the best bet to make the breakthrough in our lifetimes. (Sol Tax to Richard Woodbury, 2/9/66: personal collection)

Thus Tax conceived America's role in the Cold War world, using its vast resources to organize anthropological knowledge and practice and place them in the service of humankind.

Tax's efforts in this regard meshed neatly with American Cold War interests overseas. In developing a transparent, open community of world scholars, Tax's work was rife with propaganda value directed at an ostensibly less-free community of Soviet-dominated scholars and laypersons. That Tax appreciated the public relations value of his anthropological vision is apparent in the series of lectures he organized in 1959 for the overseas radio propaganda network, Voice of America, collected as *Horizons of Anthropology* (1964). Although the political positions of the series' contributors were not necessarily "pro-American"– many, such as Eric Wolf, Laura Nader, and Steven Polgar, were later known for their radical views – this in itself served an important propagandistic purpose, showing the US as a country in which freedom of expression and scientific freedom were respected. This was an important message for the programs' intended audience, described by Tax in his instructions to the young contributors: "[I]magine that you are talking to a general audience at the University of Moscow ... " (Tax 1964: 6). In this fashion, the lectures functioned similarly to the traveling exhibitions of abstract expressionist art sent to the Soviet Union and the CIA-backed literary journals published in the 1950s and 1960s, holding up as eminently "American" and emblematic of American freedom works that, back home, were considered "subversive," even "Communist" (Saunders 1999).

Tax's theoretical legacy is often overlooked today. His work is rarely cited and his influence is hardly acknowledged, even by those who considered themselves indebted to him two decades ago (Stanley 1996; Stocking 2000). It is my contention, however, that attention must be paid to the impact of institutions on the production and development of anthropological knowledge, and in this arena I assert that Tax is second only to Franz Boas for sheer contribution to the field. Despite the relative absence of Tax's name from the bibliographies of today's dissertations, Tax's institutional work lent to post-World War II anthropology a structure and direction that continues to shape anthropological practice today. Given the realities of the Cold War and the necessity for anthropologists to work in a political, financial, and academic milieu oriented at every turn towards US interests, it is perhaps not shocking that Tax's vision, too, took on a shape and function that also furthered those interests. Although it may well be that Tax's theoretical work deserves reassessment, as Stocking (2000) advocates, it is likely that Tax's intellectual importance will always be overshadowed by his much more significant – if more subtle and equally unheralded – contribution to anthropology's institutional base.

ARCHIVAL SOURCES

This paper has drawn on research performed at the National Anthropological Archive during the summer of 2002, particularly the "Fox Field Notes and University of Chicago Fox Project Records" (MS 4802). I have also drawn on materials given me from the personal papers of Smithsonian staff, particularly Dr Robert Laughlin's material regarding the early years of the Center for the Study of Man, for which he and the rest of the Smithsonian's anthropology staff deserve my gratitude.

REFERENCES

Price, David. 2003. Anthropology Sub Rosa: The CIA, AAA, and the Ethical Problems Inherent in Secret Research. In *Ethics and the Profession of Anthropology: Dialogue for Ethically Conscious Practice*, 2nd edn, pp. 29–49. Carolyn Fluehr-Lobban, ed. Walnut Creek, CA: AltaMira Press.

Saunders, Frances Stonor. 1999. *Who Paid the Piper? The CIA and the Cultural Cold War*. London: Granta Books.

Scott, James C. 1998. *Seeing Like a State: How Certain Schemes to Improve the Human Condition Have Failed.* New Haven, CT: Yale University Press.

Stanley, Sam. 1996. Community, Action, and Continuity: A Narrative Vita of Sol Tax. *Current Anthropology* 37 (Suppl.): S131–S137.

Stocking, George W. Jr. 1976. Ideas and Institutions in American Anthropology: Thoughts toward a History of the Interwar Years. In *Selected Papers from the American Anthropologist, 1921–1945*, pp. 1–50. G. Stocking, ed. Washington, DC: American Anthropological Association.

—— 2000. "Do Good, Young Man": Sol Tax and the World Mission of Liberal Democratic Anthropology. In *Excluded Ancestors, Inventible Traditions: Essays Toward a more Inclusive History of Anthropology. History of Anthropology*, vol. 9, pp. 171–264. R. Handler, ed. Madison: University of Wisconsin Press.

Tax, Sol, ed. 1964. *Horizons of Anthropology.* Chicago: Aldine Publishing.

—— 1965. The History and Philosophy of Current Anthropology. *Current Anthropology* 6(3): 238, 242–69.

—— 1968 [1952]. *Heritage of Conquest: The Ethnology of Middle America.* New York: Cooper Square Publishers.

Wallerstein, Immanuel. 1997. The Unintended Consequences of Cold War Area Studies. In *The Cold War & The University: Toward and Intellectual History of the Postwar Years*, pp. 195–231. New York: New Press.

All Marxism, once you shed the theology, is a set of priorities and a set of questions. The answers come from fieldwork and study just like they always do, from experience. But questions are tricky, and good ones are few. So Marxism helps you, when you are confronted with pre-Capitalist societies, with what to look to first. (John Murra to Jyette Thorndal, January 5, 1976)

In 1946 Julian Steward was hired by Columbia University. His friend William Duncan Strong was chair of the department and instrumental in convincing Columbia to hire Steward. Upon hearing Columbia had hired Steward, Alfred Kroeber wrote that they would make an "unbeatable team." As a full professor Steward would earn $7500 a year, but he worried about the teaching load and the inevitable problems associated with departmental politics.[1] In contrast, Steward's wife was delighted; Steward wrote that she danced "up and down and clicked her heels together assuring me that this is the best damn thing that has ever happened to us" (Steward to Strong, March 16, 1946). Strong was delighted Columbia had hired Steward because he was not well suited to run the department. Strong had little interest in or patience with the polemical battles cultural anthropologists engaged in on the fourth floor of Schermerhorn Hall (Willey 1988: 75–96). Strong was also fed up with Ralph Linton, who was leaving Columbia for Yale University (Linton had been chairman since Franz Boas died in 1942).

According to Robert Murphy, it was understood that once Steward established himself on campus he would take over the department – an event that never took place (Murphy 1977: 10–11).[2] Steward's tenure at Columbia, 1946 to 1953, was short but critically important to him and the students he taught. Steward, it seemed, was ideally suited for the Anthropology Department at Columbia. The department was relatively small and Steward was at or near the peak of his influence. In contrast to the small faculty, the student population was large – during the 1946–47 academic year there were 120 graduate students (Manners

1973: 893; Shimkin 1964: 6). The student body at Columbia was unique for two reasons: first, the department had historically accepted women, and when Steward arrived there were a number of advanced and gifted female graduate students. Second, during the years that followed World War II, Columbia and virtually every university across the country was flooded with men who utilized the GI Bill.

Steward was a Boasian by intellectual upbringing. According to Robert Murphy, when Steward arrived at Columbia he did not have to found a school of thought – one was waiting for him.[3] Murphy maintained that "the student temper combined with Steward's theories and persuasiveness as a teacher" produced an "almost instant following" (Murphy 1981: 178). An unintended consequence of Steward's tenure at Columbia was that it also created a divide between male and female students: males were drawn to Steward while women were drawn to Ruth Benedict. This gender gap was further complicated by the theoretical animosity between Steward and Benedict. I do not mean to imply that Steward was disrespectful of Benedict – he was well aware her career did not reach its potential because she was a woman. Rather, he supported Benedict but did not have a high opinion of the culture and personality studies she spearheaded. The gulf between Steward and Benedict and their students was well known, and the chasm was as deep as it was unfortunate. Another factor involved was the growing tensions of the Cold War and the rampant McCarthyism that dominated much of the 1950s. All of these factors led to the creation of the Mundial Upheaval Society (hereafter the MUS) – a group that would become well known on the Columbia campus and within the folklore of the discipline. The MUS is particularly important for several reasons: first, no scholar has analyzed the significance of the MUS and other similar groups, illustrating that there is "a longstanding gap in publication possibilities for the history of anthropology as a critical theoretical enterprise engaging the very center of disciplinary practice" (Darnell and Murray 2001: xiii). Second, the creation of the MUS highlighted that the Department of Anthropology at Columbia was polarized between Benedict and Steward and between male and female graduate students. Third, the MUS had a profound and long-lasting affect on the careers of important scholars such as Morton Fried, Sidney Mintz, Elman Service, Eric Wolf, and others. Fourth, the MUS also mirrored the larger socio-political tensions that dominated academic discourse before and after the McCarthy era.

THE MUS AND DEPARTMENTAL DIVIDES

Steward fit well within the larger Columbia milieu. Steward's reliance on facts and empirical data had been inculcated in him by Kroeber and formed a natural link with the department's Boasian history and positivist tradition. Steward's materialistic approach to anthropology may have appeared to be a departure from the Boasian School but this was not the case. Murphy recalled that Steward's favorite aphorism was that "there are no theories unless based upon fact, but facts exist only within the context of a theory" (Murphy 1977: 8). Like Boas, Steward was drawn to politics, but this aspect of his scholarship was subsumed. It did not, however, stop him from making what were, in retrospect, radical comments in class. For example, several of Steward's former students and colleagues recalled that, when lecturing, he was blunt about the political implications of his theories and used the Chinese Revolution as an instance of independent evolutionary change. Comments such as these drew intense interest from students who were radically inclined, even if the man making them was not. Steward was well attuned to students' interests. He was sensitive to this and to their professional ambitions. To this end, when hired by Columbia one of the first things he wanted to create was graduate student seminars specifically designed to meet student interest and enhance career opportunities. Steward wrote he wanted to:

> ... cover anthropological studies of contemporary communities.... This would be to examine the objectives, methods, and conclusions of these studies; to show how anthropology does or doesn't differ from sociology; to ascertain what new field methods anthropologists needed in dealing with more complex cultures and more numerous populations; to see which cultural processes were the same and which different in these different societies. I suggest this because so many jobs for anthropologists in the future are going to involve such studies because the question is always asked, "What is the difference between sociology and anthropology?" I think it would be a way of equipping students with the answers; that is, of showing how anthropology projects its studies against a comparative and historical background instead of accepting our own culture as the yardstick for sociological analysis. Such a course, too, would inevitably give an opportunity for me to throw in my own pet slants on this and that. (Steward to Strong, April 10, 1946)

Those students drawn to Steward and, more generally, materialism, included Pedro Carrasco, Stanley Diamond, Clifford Evans, Louis Faron, Morton Fried, Anthony Leeds, Robert Manners, Rufus Mathewson, Daniel McCall, Betty Meggers, Sidney Mintz, Robert F. Murphy, John Murra, Elena Padilla, Charles Rosario, Henry Rosenfeld, Vera Rubin, Edwin Seda, Elman Service, Elliott Skinner, Eric Wolf, and others. As a group, these students would go on to produce remarkably diverse theoretical contributions. It was not simply Steward and materialism that they were attracted to, but rather the place that contemporary society figured in anthropological scholarship. In this sense, it was not Steward but the commitment to anthropology that he, Leslie A. White, Karl Wittfogel, V. Gordon Childe, and other materialistically oriented anthropologists and archaeologists were dedicated to that attracted them. Collectively they believed that White, Steward, and Childe were not antagonists but a highly influential triumvirate. Some students were drawn to one man; for example, Robert Murphy was theoretically close to Steward and acknowledged this in print and throughout his career.[4] In addition, it must be noted that between 1946 and 1948 Kroeber, Lowie, and White were exchanging their sharpest barbs regarding the value of evolutionary theory in a host of journals. Eric Wolf recalled that this was "something we all talked about very much. Evolutionism was in the air, and then Steward came with his multilineal-evolution story and the discussion became firmly institutionalized" (Wolf in Friedman 1987: 109). Robert Murphy recalled the aforementioned students:

... pursued their own courses, their own interests, and their own ideas. What unites them, however, is a basic assumption, a premise, that social thought emanates from social action and that the imperatives of work, power, and sex are prior to the symbolic forms that encapsulate them. It is this very elemental and general kind of materialism that prevails to this day at Columbia, and not one or another particular theory ... its faculty and students display a variety of talents and inclinations that range the gamut of current anthropological theory. But beneath this diversity there exists a community of understanding and a common language that was inspired by Franz Boas and crystallized by Julian Steward. (Murphy 1981: 181–82)

The spirit that Murphy described was best evidenced by the MUS. While the group did not exist for a long period of time – roughly between 1946 and 1953 – it secured a place in the folklore of the discipline.[5] As for the Columbia students who preceded them, and the many that followed, access to over-burdened full-time faculty members was difficult. In response, Columbia graduate students had created a tradition of forming independent study groups. None of these study groups except the MUS ever amounted to much. The MUS was different in that it was not only taken seriously by its members but was, and remains, the most successful group ever created by graduate students at Columbia. No doubt this is in large part due to the fact that a disproportionate number of its members attained professional prominence in anthropology. The people who formed the MUS did so because of their displeasure at what was being taught at Columbia – specifically, dissatisfaction with what Benedict was teaching. Post-war graduate students were not opposed to Benedict's poetic and humanistic approach. They were aware of its importance and respected her work. Rather, some students, mostly men, found her teaching style awkward (Model 1983: 158). Eric Wolf stated that when he arrived at Columbia the department "was really in shambles. As I look back on that education, I think it was one of the worst educational experiences, in terms of teaching, that I ever heard about" (Wolf 1999: 8). Morton Fried called the situation at Columbia after World War II "muddled." Referring to the departure of Service for Michigan and the firing of Gene Weltfish in 1953, he wrote he was "sorry to see them go, because it means another gaping hole in the inactive remnants of the MUS, more's the pity. Columbia must now think of filling two spots" (Fried to Eric Wolf, April 25, 1953).[6]

The Department of Anthropology at Columbia after World War II and well into the 1950s was entirely committed to graduate studies. Limited resources were available for undergraduate courses in anthropology. Only one year-long class, Introduction to General Anthropology, was consistently offered. This class was part of Columbia's School of General Education, akin to an extension course. It was taught by Gene Weltfish until she was fired during the McCarthy era (Murphy 1977: 8). Members of the MUS all recall that the saving grace of Columbia was the student body. In the years after World War II the department was still reeling from the death of Franz Boas. Steward wrote to Kroeber that Boas's "ghost haunts our halls, and I haven't determined whether he is helping or hurting our morale. He is something to live up to, and to live down" (Steward to Kroeber, December 22, 1947). This uneasiness was compounded by the fact the department was fractured into two groups – those associated with culture and personality, and those drawn to a materialist philosophy. Service recalled this dichotomy was:

> ... related to the sudden rise in significance of the materialistic theory of cultural evolution which we [MUS] could relate as a positivistic science to the major social and political problems of the day. Our differences with the P-and-C [Personality and Culture] students [were] largely that, while they (and all other anthropologists) shared those aspects of Boasianism that were antiracist, they seemed to conceive of cultural anthropology as part of the humanities rather than a positivistic science. Ruth Benedict was the foremost contemporary proponent of this humanistic view. Steward, on the other hand, spoke for scientific evolutionism, and a kind of materialism he called cultural ecology. (Service 1988: 149)

The division Service described was further complicated by its proponents, Benedict and Steward, and by gender inequality (Kerns 2003: 235–62; Model 1983: 161–66; Young 2005: 156–62). While Benedict was a force to be reckoned with because of her fame and the enormous grants she was able to bring into the department, she did not hold a significant place in Columbia's academic hierarchy (when Steward was hired she was still an associate professor). To make matters worse, Steward and Benedict "were known to scorn one another's views, and they were in a position of rivalry for students. During the year, the students came to be aligned with one or the other star professor, and the alignment turned out to be one of gender as well" (Young 2005: 158).[7] In this diverse stew "full of rivalries and impatient drive, there was still a holdover of the spirit of equality that Boas had established in recognition of the need for ethnographic knowledge to be gathered by both women and men" (Young 2005: 159).[8] One cannot dispute the profound gender-based inequities that female students and faculty faced, nor can one ignore the materialist history of the department – a point that struck me in a visceral way when writing this chapter. I had never noticed the lintel above the entrance to Columbia's Schermerhorn Hall, where the Anthropology Department has been housed since its inception. The inscription is: "Speak to the earth and it shall teach thee" – a constant reminder of the department's Boasian roots.

The members of the MUS came of age during the Depression, two had fought in the Spanish Civil War (John Murra and Elman Service), and every man had been in the military during World War II. Given their lower middle-class backgrounds, none of the men could have dreamed of entering Columbia University had it not been for the GI Bill. Wolf recalled that: "We were all veterans, we had all come out of whatever number of years in the army, all of our energies were organized for us" (Wolf 1999). Mintz echoed Wolf's characterization, writing: "Most of us were veterans and, as it happened, we were all males. Having to readjust to civilian life caused strain, and I think that there were feelings of dissatisfaction with the kind of anthropology we were learning. Isn't there always?" (Mintz 1994: 19). Elman Service also wrote about this time noting that "ex-GIs were extremely earnest and anxious to make up for lost time" (Service 1988: 149). Stanley Diamond recalled that many veterans at Columbia were "on a male bonding trip in the aftermath of the war" (1993: 111).

As a group, they all believed they learned more from one another than they did from classroom lectures. All the men did fieldwork and a number of them worked on Steward's Puerto Rico Project. At some point during the late 1940s and early 1950s, Mort Fried went to China; Elman Service, Sidney Mintz, and Eric Wolf worked in Puerto Rico; and Robert Manners and Stanley Diamond went to the Caribbean. In looking back on his career Wolf has noted that his experience in Puerto Rico contained elements that dominated the rest of his career:

... concerns of history, which I certainly got out of my Central European experience, a concern for class, an interest in peasantry. It began to crystallize a number of significant issues for me, in an area where I learned Spanish for the first time; I still have a Caribbean accent when speaking Spanish. (Wolf 1999: n.p.)

Elman Service wrote that members of the MUS thought Ruth Benedict's class on social organization, dominated by female students drawn to her work and teaching, was a waste of time. Benedict was not a gifted teacher. Her male students returning from the war did not appreciate the fact she failed to consider the practical applications of fieldwork. The students who took classes with Benedict and Steward began to socialize more and the dichotomy between their respective professors was perceived to be stark. In many ways Steward was the antithesis of Benedict. Eric Wolf noted that he and many others admired Benedict's "ability to pick up culturally phrased behavior or texts and use them as diagnostic metonyms of general cultural configurations" but the "cultures and personalities seemed to exist in some timeless no-man's-land" (Wolf 2001: 4). In contrast, Steward had served as editor of the six-volume *Handbook of South American Indians* (1946–50) and his research was solidly grounded in empirical data. Steward's cultural ecological approach transformed the culture-area concept and students were drawn to his idea of successive transformations in the form of bands, tribes, chiefdoms, and civilization (Patterson and Lauria-Perricelli 1999).

During the 1946–47 academic year members of the MUS became more frustrated with what was being taught. As their exams drew closer, they met on a regular basis. Depending upon a particular person's recollection, the MUS met once a week or once a month. These meetings were taken seriously, topics were assigned, presentations made, and papers were circulated in a round-robin fashion. Service described these meetings:

We met nearly every week during the school year, Thursdays from 8:00 p.m. until eternity. We scheduled different topics each week, featuring a paper or lecture by a volunteer. Most of these efforts were valuable even in subsequent years; some became the basis of publications. We worked hard in preparing our individual stints, but also listened and argued so usefully that is was difficult to break off and go home to sleep. (Service 1988: 149)

While it may seem unusual that members of the MUS met weekly, in part this can be explained by the fact they all lived within a few blocks of one another. They were on campus every day and Service wrote: "it was simple to meet more often and we were thoroughly imbued with the necessity for learning; learning as fast as we could" (Service n.d.: 41). Given what they experienced during the war, members of the MUS realized they had a rare opportunity to discuss their views and bond in a way that was unique and extraordinary.

In those days we had an apartment only one block from the anthropology department building, and Mort Fried was also about one block away in another direction, and I believe our first meetings were mostly held either at my apartment or at Morton Fried's apartment. Later on, when Fried and I were teaching and sharing an office at Columbia, we held the meetings in our office about once a month. But in those early days when we were just students, we were gradually organizing ourselves more firmly into a more structured group. Because we were so serious most of us attended every meeting. (Service n.d.: 41)

While no faculty acknowledged the existence of the MUS, the group was perceived as a powerful clique. Some of those in the broader Columbia community were not impressed. Likewise, several people within the Department of Anthropology – such as Alta and Joe Jablow, Helen Codere, Eleanor Leacock, and Marion Smith – resented the MUS.[9] The name itself, Mundial Upheaval Society, was an inside joke – derived from a cartoon drawn by Morton Fried. Fried liked art and, for one of the first MUS meetings, created an old-fashioned mock radical pamphlet. On the cover Fried had drawn a capitalist, a fat man with a cigar, riding on the shoulders of a peasant and flicking ashes on his head. At the bottom of the drawing was a small caption that stated "published by the Mundial Upheaval Society". Largely at the behest of Elman Service, who thought the acronym MUS and cartoon was funny, the name stuck.[10] Those who were not members or part of the core group, mostly women, were not amused. Eleanor Leacock in particular thought the MUS purposely excluded women and considered the group an exclusive "all boys club."

What began as a small group of graduate students concerned about what was being taught would become well known. In part, this was due to the fact that MUS members began publishing articles and books in which they acknowledged the MUS. The MUS was thus gossiped about and even subject to a futile FBI investigation. While it may seem incredible that a group of graduate students could come to the attention of the FBI one must keep in mind how oppressive the socio-political climate was. All the members of the MUS had leftist tendencies. Eric Wolf recalled:

All of us were some variant of red. Some of us had actively been members of "the Party" at some point. Others were Fourth Internationalists, or Three and Three-quarterth Internationalist. I think that was one of the strong bonds to us ... a Marxian stew but not necessarily with any commitment to a particular party line. Sid Mintz and I used to march in the May Day parades. Eleanor Leacock would show up wheeling all her babies. FBI men were busy taking pictures all the time. (Friedman 1987: 109)

It should be emphasized that just because members of the MUS had leftist tendencies, this did not mean they were united politically. During the 1950s the left was fractured into distinct, incompatible, and hostile groups. Service maintained that the profound differences between communist and socialist groups had something to do with the MUS's inability to embrace any one political party or particular scholar's work. In this instance, the work of Leslie A. White and the degree to which he did or did not influence MUS members is particularly interesting, because his work was read and discussed by the MUS. One can readily imagine ways in which White's work could be embraced by the MUS. When this is combined with the fact White taught at Columbia in the summer of 1948, it is logical to assume some members of the MUS embraced White's work. This was not the case in large part because of the animosity that existed between communist and socialist groups. As I have discussed elsewhere White was member of the Socialist Labor Party (SLP), an affiliation that was an anathema to those interested in or associated with the Communist Party (Peace 2004).

White's influence on the MUS was subject to debate in a series of letters exchanged between Robert Carneiro and Elman Service.[11] Each scholar debated the merits of White's work and the impact White had on their respective careers. Service wrote to Carneiro that there were several reasons why he did not think White directly affected the MUS or other graduate students at Columbia. Service argued that White was not of sufficient stature to influence students because the *Science of Culture* had not been published. Service also noted that, in 1948, "the jury was still out" as to who was getting the better of the debate between White and Lowie that was being waged in the *American Anthropologist*. Service remembered that, in the summer of 1948 when White was teaching, no members of the MUS, aside from Stanley Diamond who took a class with White, were in New York. According to Service, Diamond "argued [with White] all the time about it (as being 'deviationist' – or something like that)" (Service to Carneiro, January 3, 1978). When asked by Carneiro about the influence White's explicitly political work had on students at Columbia, Service replied that the SLP:

... was very purist Marx and was also anti-Communist Party. I don't know whether you want to consider saying this, but this kind of Marxism was "non-activist", and I believe this was the original source of White's emphasis on determinism and anti-free will attitudes. (This is why Diamond was against him.) Mechanical, non-dialectical, because he did not actively champion the current party line causes, propagandize them, march on May Day, etc. I had many long discussions with Diamond, Eleanor Leacock, Gene Weltfish and other communist type Marxists about this. Many of the Boasians at Columbia in my days there hated LAW's [White's] culturology because it did not help wake up the masses etc. (Service to Carneiro, January 26, 1979)

MUS members were profoundly affected by their experiences at Columbia and their initial fieldwork experiences. For example, Elman Service dedicated *The Origins of the State and Civilization* "To Morton H. Fried and the Fellows of the M.U.S." Service also wrote that John Murra was his best critic. Of those who acknowledged the MUS, Service was the most explicit in his characterization of how the group influenced his work. This may be due to the fact that Service was also older than other graduate students and was highly respected by them. Eric Wolf recalled that Service:

... was something of a hero: he hailed from Tecumseh, Michigan, certainly an improbable place to come from for most New Yorkers; he had boxed in the Golden Gloves tournament; he had fought in Spain; and he had done fieldwork among the Havasupai. More than that, he had actually taken courses with Leslie White, who was then carrying on a lively debate on evolutionary explanations with Robert Lowie in the pages of the *American Anthropologist* and in the new and innovative *Southwestern Journal of Anthropology*. To our discussions and group seminars Elman brought his substantive knowledge of kinship studies and his evolutionary perspectives on the transformations of social organization. Many of his insights have since been incorporated into the ongoing stream of the discipline, but in the theoretical doldrums of post-Boasian anthropology, they were new and exciting. (Wolf 2001: 370–71)

BROADER VIEW OF THE MUS

There is no doubt that members of the MUS were driven to succeed. They had a particular view of the world and the role that anthropology figured in it. As a group, they were not satisfied with the state of the discipline and intended to not only have productive careers but to change the direction of the field. These were lofty goals – ones met at an individual and disciplinary level. The most explicit evidence that the MUS had aspirations well beyond the Columbia milieu was written in 1952. In a letter begun by Eric Wolf and sent to Fried, Mathewson, Mintz, Murra, and Service, Wolf wrote that he wanted members of the MUS to think about a particular idea – specifically, publishing an anthropological journal in Mexico. Wolf wrote that the expense of producing 500 copies of a 90-page journal appearing twice a year based in Mexico was negligible ($300). Wolf wrote that a publishing house was already interested and had the means to print and distribute the proposed journal. Wolf discussed this idea with Pedro Armillas, Angel Palerm of the Social Science Office of the Panamerican Union, Molins (editor of *Mexico City Daily* and part-time anthropologist), and Julio de la Fuenta (Wolf to Dear Friends, February 4, 1952). The men agreed the idea was worth exploring and that they would lend their support. According to Wolf:

All agree that the journal should be "sectarian", in the sense that we would try to build up in it a body of theory and practice in anthropology which would bring our point of view to the attention of other anthropologists. Armillas suggested some title such as "Economy and Society". The primary focus would be on problems of the clan, disintegration of the clan, formation of the state, characteristics of early or primitive states, etc. If we could keep the journal alive for more than 4 years, we would have a substantial body of material. The following have offered material: Armillas is very interested in working out a correlation of economic and religious types in the Valley of

Mexico; Molina has an excellent article on the Aztec tribute structure; Palerm could re-write his first-rate article on Spanish history and could also offer a semi-book review on the structure of the Aztec clan. (Wolf to Dear Friends, February 4, 1952)

In response to Wolf's suggestion Mintz, Service, and Murra met and had a long discussion. In an unsigned reply, one that was likely written by Mintz, Murra, and Service, they pointed out that one of the reasons they were drawn to American anthropology was because it was not dominated by a single theoretical position. They also noted that anthropology was the only discipline that had not as yet been fractured by the Cold War. Members of the MUS were able to publish their work in respected peer-reviewed journals – though they acknowledged they did have to "sugar coat" explicitly Marxist terminology. Regardless, their work was not being rejected on theoretical grounds alone. The letter explained that they were treated fairly and that our:

... understanding of the moment when one starts a publication devoted to presenting only a single point of view – is the moment when one can no longer get a hearing within the profession. When that moment is reached – and it may well come one of these days – then by all means let us be heard, but until then communication with other anthropologists is best served by publishing where these others are sure to see it and thus be exposed to it, en masse. (Fried, Mintz, Murra to Wolf, February 9, 1952)

Aside from the concern with self-isolation expressed above, the most serious weakness with regard to Wolf's suggestion was the nationalistic nature of anthropological scholarship. American anthropologists rarely published or read the work of foreign anthropologists – even when language was not a barrier. A better idea in their estimation was not to start a new journal but rather influence editors to publish the work of foreign writers in American anthropological journals. Mintz, Murra, and Service were drawn to Wolf's notion of the "elaboration of a body of theory and practice." This was the most important idea contained in Wolf's letter of February 4.

Publication or no publication, what we need is more contacts, more seminars like the [MUS] last year ... more preparation for the various meetings, conferences, round tables etc. With only a little care one can find out well in advance what meetings are going to take place and thus volunteer for the program committee, or suggest certain symposia or sessions devoted to topics likely to further the development of anthropology. We and our friends write too little, we rarely attend meetings and if we do we are not always prepared to give papers, serve on committees etc. (Mintz, Murra, and Service to Wolf, February 9, 1952)

Before Wolf could respond, Mintz, Murra, and Service wrote to Wolf again stating that his letter had inspired them to organize anew the members of the MUS not in the field (Mintz, Murra, and Service to Wolf, February 27, 1952). In an undated letter – but one clearly composed as a response to the two letters written by Mintz, Murra, and Service – Wolf stated that he had shown it to a number of people. Based on numerous conversations, Wolf wrote that he thought a round-robin letter should be sent to Mintz at Yale, Murra in New York, Service – who would be responsible for "distribution among the inhabitants of the Morningside District" – and Angel Palerm. Wolf noted that he thought a few conclusions had emerged from their letters and discussions. Wolf believed that the objection to creating a journal from a "sectarian point of view" was accurate. He and Palerm agreed it could isolate the MUS, who were already publishing in established journals. However, this did not preclude the use of "existing channels of communication as far as possible" and "trying to find supplementary means and ways of making communication easier among ourselves and trying to find new ways of communication which does not isolate us" (Wolf to Friends, undated). The bulk of Wolf's letter was devoted to ideas others had presented so that the MUS, referred to as "our group," could become more effective. To this end, Wolf pointed out four avenues of approach, beginning with the translation and circulation of papers from various languages, specifically English, Spanish, and German. Palerm suggested translating Steward's article "Cultural Causality and Law" into Spanish, and Palerm's article on types of cultivation in Middle America into English. Second, all agreed that the articles written by MUS members and those with a similar point of view were "scattered to the four winds." This was a significant issue as it was impossible for a broad readership to appreciate the fact that a coherent theory and practice existed. Citing Palerm's work, Wolf pointed out he had published work in *Runa* in Argentina, *Antiquity* in England, and a third article in Mexico. To correct this problem, Wolf suggested circulating the bibliographies of scholars such as Pedro Armillas, V. Gordon Childe, Kalervo Oberg, Leslie White, and Karl Wittfogel. In addition, Wolf wrote, "a list should be made of all articles available by members of the MUS or people working in Mexico on similar pathways: Morty Fried, Elman Service, Sid Mintz, John Murra, Angel Palerm etc." (Wolf to Friends, n.d.). Wolf also wanted to create a list of references for works known and unknown or buried in archives. He proposed that the MUS should write abstracts and annotate bibliographies on topics of interest to be agreed upon.

Wolf thought two types of seminars – those centered around a topic or an individual theorist – should be held. Murra pointed out that previous successful MUS meetings had discussed feudalism or a particular North American Indian culture or problem. Wolf suggested a future topic seminar could be about the Urban Revolution in Middle America or Patterns of Warfare. As to seminars about a theorist, Palerm suggested Oberg's work could be discussed and a bibliography of his publications circulated before the seminar took place – a bibliography that would be annotated afterward with appropriate comments. Wolf maintained that minutes should be taken at all seminars, that these should be circulated, opinions sought out, and criticism discussed. Finally, Wolf wanted the MUS to be more visible – papers needed to be given at the AAA meetings and networks of communication with sympathetic scholars developed. Wolf knew the ideas put forth were ambitious.

I am aware that all of this taken in conjunction sounds like a lot. Perhaps some things are more immediately feasible than others. Perhaps careful division of labor can be of help. Perhaps we can get some secretarial help somewhere. Perhaps, some of us could be organized into a committee, others into another, etc. Perhaps, there should be some sort of rotating chairmanship at some place where secretarial help and mimeograph apparatus can be found. I am of the opinion that all this could be done, if worked out carefully enough. Please write and discuss these various points, and means of implementing them. The time is ripe. (Wolf to Friends, n.d.)

The ideas set forth by Wolf were never acted upon by the MUS. No journal was created, nor were bibliographies circulated. Seminars were not held. This does not mean, however, that the ideas set forth failed. The ideas may not have been acted upon by the MUS, but individual members of the MUS certainly did follow through on parts of what Wolf proposed. While this may not have had the MUS imprimatur stamped on it, these actions were taken by individuals who were part of the group. For instance, at the 1954 AAA meeting virtually every member of the MUS gave a paper that, at some point, been subject to discussion at an earlier MUS meeting. And some members of the MUS set aside time to "lecture to the last drunk standing." When the *American Anthropologist* published a special issue on Latin America, members of the MUS published their work and were able to reach a wide audience. This was accomplished much to the chagrin of Sol Tax and Robert Redfield, who strenuously objected to elements of their work. When viewed less broadly, what Wolf's letter inspired in the short term was to rally the "NY MUS," who held a series of meetings *circa* 1952–53. According to Murra, people who stepped forward included himself on his thesis topic, Fried on his fieldwork in China, and Mintz on Puerto Rico.

MUS COOPERATION, CONTROVERSY, AND THE MAINSTREAM

An integral part of the MUS was the decision to share material in round-robin style. Not only was this intellectually stimulating but it forced members to hone arguments, disagree with established theoretical constructs, and prepare them for professional careers.

One specific example in this regard is enlightening. In a letter to John Murra, Robert Manners wrote that he was pleased as "reports from mundial stations throughout the nation are most encouraging. I saw Eric's [Wolf] article in ms but haven't seen the SWJ for a re-reading yet. At the time I thought it was a splendid and revealing job" (Manners to Murra, March 3, 1952). Seeing Wolf's article in print inspired Manners to bring up a short communication he had written, one already discussed by MUS members the previous year. In discussing this communication with Fried and Service, Manners felt it could benefit from another reading providing:

... the extra advantage of having been worked over by a number of interesting people. To this end, I'm enclosing a letter I wrote to Herskovits.... As you will note, old no-space rejected it at the time, but when I saw him in Chicago he suggested I send it on to him for re-consideration. I would like to get your reaction and comments. Of course, this is not the full answer to Goldschmidt or to anyone else. But if Herskovits will use it I think it should appear. (Manners to Murra, March 3, 1952)

The communication that Manners is referring to here concerned the publication of Laura Thompson's *Culture in Crisis: A Study of Hopi Indians*. Thompson's book was part of a series of papers and monographs produced as a result of investigations carried out by members of the Indian Personality and Administration Research Program. Some reports that appeared during its ten year existence were jointly sponsored by the US Office of Indian Affairs and the University of Chicago's Committee on Human Rights – later succeeded by the Society for Applied Anthropology. Well received when published, Thompson's book took a holistic approach that sought to provide a living portrait of the Hopi people. The aim of Thompson's research and of the investigators involved was:

... to study the Indians both as individual personalities and as tribal societies in order to discover by scientific inquiry, how the effectiveness of Indian Service long-range policy and programs might be increased from the standpoint of improving Indian welfare and developing responsible local autonomy. (Thompson 1950: xvi)

Manners thought Thompson's work had serious methodological implications – ones that he discussed with the MUS after her book was published. Manners discussed his concerns in both written and oral form with the MUS and this formed the body of what he was able to publish – here I refer to Manners' "Brief Communications: Anthropology and Culture in Crisis" (Manners 1952). According to Manners, there was much more involved in Thompson's work than policy and programs managed by government agencies. Manners wrote that "broader theoretical implications for cultural analyses" were evident because Thompson's work created a field of theory of culture and cross-disciplinary methodology that utilized anthropology, psychology, public administration, and ecology. Manners was led to comment:

It is not the argument of this paper that anthropology must depend upon a "traditional approach" – whatever that may be; nor that experimentation with new methods and techniques for arriving at better understandings of culture origin and process is to be shunned simply because they are new. Each of the sciences must, of course, be continually critical of its methods and assumptions, continually searching for improved ways of working and understanding the subject of its concern if it is to remain viable and productive. We need not be bound by tradition in anthropology any more than any other discipline need be so bound. But the work of many of the "popular" anthropologists violates tradition less than it violates careful scholarship and scientific method. This is the complaint of many of the "non-popular" anthropologists today. (Manners 1952: 134).

If the ending of Manners' "Brief Communication" appears cryptic it is because Herskovits deleted three pages from the original text. In a letter to Murra, Manners wrote that Herskovits believed the way in which he ended his essay was not appropriate and would not under any circumstances publish them. Herskovits believed Manners' words were nothing short of reckless and "would only get me attacked for being a brash young man while they added nothing to my argument" (Manners to Murra, March 3, 1952). Herskovits had a point; for example, the following passage by Manners was one he deleted:

Apart from the indisputable fact that the Hopi's balance as an individual depends first upon his ability to acquire the raw materials of survival – food, shelter, clothing – and only afterwards upon the security elements stressed by the author, what is the deeper significance of her interpretations and conclusions? It would be patently unfair to accuse either Dr. Thompson or any of her co-workers of biologism or racist leanings. Yet, no other inference from the foregoing conclusions is tenable. (Manners, unpublished draft, National Anthropology Archives, John Murra Papers)

After reading passages such as those above, Murra was blunt in his estimation of Herskovits and wrote that:

... the cut pages from the Thompson communication sure would have made a difference, particularly in so far as clarifying that cryptic remark about popular anthropologists. Herskovits is an idiot. Curious, how one frequently can get more from a nonpolitical editor than from a so-called progressive. The latter is too damn scared, feels guilt in advance and has no pulse-taking experience with public opinion in the profession. In this case I agree that he cut the most important part of the communication. (Murra to Manners, March 17, 1952)

Murra went on to bemoan the lack of controversy, debate, and hard discussion that characterized Herskovits' editorship – an opinion that was shared by other anthropologists such as Lesser and Radin.

Herskovits was correct in that, had he published the excised pages, Manners would have been attacked. While acknowledging that the Hopi Project of the Indian Personality and Administration Research Program involved many gifted and well-known social scientists and anthropologists, the findings had alarming implications. As originally worded Manners wrote:

The staff of the Hopi Project of the Indian Personality and Administration Research Program reads like a partial Who's Who of the social sciences and psychiatry, with special emphasis on anthropology. This is both significant and alarming. It is significant that so many highly esteemed professionals in their respective fields should be involved – directly or otherwise – in the production of a single work of this or any other kind. And it is alarming that the book to which they appear at least inferentially (some of the staff died before final publication) to have given their blessings should be so questionable from a methodological standpoint, so boldly pretentious in its aims and concepts, and so given to unwarranted conclusions from inadequate data or to partial neglect of the data in the formulation of conclusions. (Manners, unpublished draft)

Echoing the sentiments of the MUS, Manners went on to conclude "the whole of anthropology finds itself in crisis, forced to defend itself against the accusations of other scientists for the sins of a minority of overly-eager, intuitive writers who, in the guise of anthropologists, repeatedly betray scientific anthropological procedures" (Manners, unpublished draft).

Murra wrote to Manners that, in some ways, he was pleased that Herskovits deleted the above words, because it inspired him to send them to Lesser and were a way in which he could "blast Lesser for his isolation and lack of publication" (Murra to Manners, March 17, 1952). Murra's actions prompted Lesser to publish "Evolution in Social Anthropology" (1952). As is well known, Lesser's article was presented at the 1939 AAA meetings but not published until 13 years later, in the *Southwestern Journal of Anthropology*, with the following comment:

The text was lost for a good many years. It is offered now, as given in 1939, because of the greatly increased interest in the subject that has developed during the intervening years, and because a good many personal inquiries about the paper have led the author to believe that its publication, even unchanged, may still be useful in 1952.

It is not known if Murra was primarily responsible for inspiring Lesser to publish his essay, but it is likely. Murra was at the 1939 meetings where not only was Lesser's paper delivered, but also Leslie White's first assault on Boasian anthropology. Thus, taken together, White and Lesser made a definite theoretical break with Boasian anthropology – a viewpoint that was often mentioned (Malinowski 1944: 17). It gave Manners great pleasure to read Lesser's article for the first time.

However, he noted that it gave him an "uncomfortable feeling that here was a thirteen year old article that was most unfortunately just as timely and as necessary as it had been when it first came out. It's a splendidly lucid exposition" (Manners to Murra, October 21, 1952).

THE MUS AND ITS PLACE IN THE CAREERS OF ITS MEMBERS AND IN THE HISTORY OF ANTHROPOLOGY

The MUS declined at Columbia because the reason it existed – to exchange ideas and navigate the divide between Benedict and Steward – was no longer relevant. With advanced degrees in hand, Diamond, Fried, Leacock, Manners, Mintz, Padilla, Rubin, Service, and others left Columbia (as did Steward in 1953). The departure of the aforementioned scholars led to the second phase of the MUS's existence. That is, MUS members' work began to reach a much wider audience through the development of ideas that were fostered when they had been graduate students. This development took the form of papers presented at various meetings, lectures given on a multitude of campuses, and publications in prominent publications.[12] For example, Service gave a paper on the Paraguyan *encomienda* that was published in the *Hispanic American Historical Review*. Wolf and Mintz presented a paper on godparenthood, or *compadrazgo*, that was rejected by the *American Anthropologist* (Herskovits was the editor) but was later published in the *Southwestern Journal of Anthropology*.

What the members of the MUS shared was a vision of anthropology that was fostered at Columbia and came to florescence in their respective careers and in those they influenced. As a group, I believe the MUS considered anthropology to be a cumulative enterprise that could only be undertaken with a thorough knowledge and appreciation of the past. From this perspective, the MUS reflected several dynamic tensions within the department at Columbia and well beyond its confines. As George Stocking noted:

... there are clearly points at which the organizational history of the discipline becomes the focus for significant historical change – the place where divergent threads of intellectual and institutional development, embodied in the interaction of particualar individuals, responding to the impact of broader forces from outside the discipline, can all be grasped at once. (1976: i)

Given this, the existence of the MUS highlighted the difference between first- and second-generation American anthropologists. The first generation – scholars taught by Boas or his students such as Goldenweiser, Lesser, and Radin – were satisfied to create a scientific basis upon which a critique of civilization could rest. In contrast, the second generation, as characterized by the work of the MUS, adopted an evolutionary outlook that considered directly observed

social change, along with global and cross-cultural transformations. Members of the MUS did not necessarily remain evolutionists
throughout their careers; indeed some diverged sharply from this
paradigm. However, what remained constant was a philosophical
approach to the discipline. Although directly written about Wolf,
the following quote aptly characterizes the work of those involved
in the MUS:

> From the 1950s on, Wolf approached anthropology as a form of humanistic
> understanding that combined theory and interpretation within a historical
> and comparative perspective markedly influenced by Marx and Marxist writers.
> In developing this bridge, Wolf saw the problem of culture as a historical
> and processual emergent in which class and power relations are critical for
> understanding what culture means as a local expression and as a concept
> paramount to American anthropology. (Yengoyan 2001: vii)

It is simply not possible here to review all the works produced by
members of the MUS as they scattered and moved across the country.
In fact, it is hard to even give a cursory summary of the work carried
out by MUS members as such an undertaking would be a daunting
and exhaustive task. However, I will provide one specific example
of how the MUS created a social network of scholars.[13] Here I refer
to what Robert Murphy and others characterized as the Columbia–
Michigan Axis. The first indication that a link between Columbia and
Michigan existed was in 1953, when Service was hired by Michigan.
Shortly after hiring Service, Fried was also hired by Michigan but he
stayed in Ann Arbor for just one year (he was subsequently hired
by Columbia where he remained for his entire academic career).[14]
By the late 1950s to early 1960s there was a regular exchange of
people between the two institutions, graduate students and young
faculty members from Michigan who went to Columbia and from
Michigan to Columbia. This regular exchange was never formally
acknowledged but, within the folklore of the discipline, a Columbia–
Michigan Axis certainly existed. The cross-fertilization of students and
faculty members between Columbia and Michigan was based on the
unwritten underlying philosophy of and approach to anthropology
that was fostered by members of the MUS and was intellectually
compatible with that of other scholars hired at the time.[15]

In looking back at the MUS over 50 years later, it is sad to note
that only one member is still alive – Sidney Mintz who recently
celebrated his 80th birthday. In 1991, sensing his own mortality,
Mintz wrote to John Murra that Rufus Mathewson, Morton Fried,
and Stanley Diamond had all died in quick succession. Mintz told
Murra that there was "less time than we think to reconnect with
old friends and intellectual peers" (Mintz to Murra, May 10, 1991).
Mintz's effort to reach Murra was not the first such attempt made by
the aging members of the MUS. The most serious attempt was made

in 1977. In a letter to Service, Manners, Mintz, and Wolf, Morton Fried, at the urging of Diamond, tried to get the members of the MUS together at an upcoming meeting of the AAA in Houston. According to Fried, Diamond was "getting somewhat mushy in his old age" and felt it "appropriate to get all the MUS members together one last time before it is too late" (Fried to Wolf et al., January 20, 1977). The original idea had been for the MUS to meet informally, but Diamond contacted the AAA program editor who was enthusiastic about the idea. If a formal session was established, money for travel could be awarded to participants. Based on the exchange of letters between Diamond, Fried, Manners, Mintz, and Murra, it was clear that not only did the men feel a bond, but that they also had warm memories of the MUS. Wolf noted that life-long friendships were formed and that an informal gathering was a good idea. However, Wolf was opposed to an:

... official program: (a) because I don't feel much charity towards official *anthropoliteia*, and (b) because it would look much too much like a waving of flags and accoutrements, begging for History to Notice US, a sort of "poor-Schindler" substitute for the Festschrifts that celebrated older ancestors. (Wolf to Fried, February 3, 1977)

Wolf's reservations about an official program were well founded for two reasons. First, at various points in their careers, former members of the MUS clashed and there was some dispute about who was and was not a member. Fried wrote that, even though there were "estrangements in the past," it may be time to "bury the hatchet for a day or two to have a reunion" (Fried to Wolf, January 20, 1977). Fried went on to note that he was in the fortunate position of feeling close to all members of the MUS and that a gathering could give members the opportunity to say something about what the discipline was like 30 years ago. Unfortunately, such a reunion never took place, in spite of the common bond many members shared. While I understand the inherent difficulties such a reunion would have posed, as a historian of anthropology I cannot help but mourn a meeting that never took place. Second, historians of anthropology have not been reflexive. Too often the history of the discipline is written in a formula that reminds me of Lewis Henry Morgan's unilinear *Ancient Society*. Some have identified this as a "whiggish" approach – a characterization I find inadequate because, while accurate, it fails to offer an alternative. The way the history of anthropology has been written in the last decade has undergone a great deal of change. Darnell has noted that "presentism in this reflexive sense, choosing issues for historical attention because they matter today, is fully commensurable with historicism" (2001: 1). Darnell is not alone in her efforts to provide a more nuanced history of anthropology, an approach that is reflected in the series of books she and Stephen Murray have edited, *Critical Studies in the History of Anthropology*, as well as in the work of David Price (Price 2004). This approach to the history of anthropology would have delighted members of the MUS because there is a sense of urgency and historical continuity that considers not just the factual data of the past but the role of individual scholars in their time. In linking the past and present, anthropology and politics, I for one look forward to the study of overlooked anthropologists such as Bernhard Stern, Melville Jacobs, Alexander Lesser, and others.

NOTES

1. Steward had good reason to be worried. While a gifted teacher, Steward preferred research and writing. Steward was expected to teach nine hours a week and Benedict told him that there were a large number of PhD students who would demand much of his time. Two letters from Steward to Strong (April 4 and 10, 1946) give an excellent summary of the problems Steward encountered upon his arrival in New York.

2. When Steward was hired, there were only six faculty members: Ruth Benedict, George Herzog, Harry Shapiro, Marion Smith, Charles Wagely, and Gene Weltfish. By the time Steward left Columbia University his friendship with Strong had been fractured. According to Kerns, their relationship was doomed after Strong introduced Steward to a colleague as his "right-hand man" (Kerns 2003: 243).

3. My views about the history of Columbia anthropology and Steward were profoundly influenced by Robert Murphy (I knew him as a graduate student). Like Murphy, I think Steward's years at Columbia were his most productive intellectually. While at Columbia, Steward's work on what he characterized as multilinear evolution and cultural ecology were on the cutting edge of anthropological theory. These years also witnessed the publication of the full gamut of Steward's research, ranging from cultural evolution, prehistory, archaeology, area studies, acculturation, and the study of contemporary society, to the examination of how nationalist systems dominate and affect local indigenous populations.

4. In contrast to Murphy, Wolf felt he was too closely aligned with Steward. He wrote to Murra that:

   > Steward has offered me a job as his research associate for the coming year, if I don't land something else. I suppose that wouldn't be the worst thing, but I do hope to find some other locality for a change and to get away from this patriarcholocal residence which seems to turn me into a sort of appendage to Steward. (Wolf to Murra, February 9, 1954)

5. Discussions of the MUS are not detailed and are restricted to the recollections of its members. There are minor inconsistencies in the details of exactly who was a member and how often they met. Another rich source of information was the obituaries of its members written by colleagues and friends.

6. Fried's characterization of the department as "muddled" was apt. The department rarely worked together during Steward's tenure. That is, the

department was considered to be an independent fortuitous entity where one pursued individual goals rather than working towards a common departmental philosophy. Steward knew this when he arrived and hoped that he and Strong could change the department (Strong to Steward, April 10, 1946).

7. Aside from overt sexism, Young implies that two black men, Julius Okala and William Willis, were also purposely excluded from the MUS. These two men were the only male students "who remained outside the Mundial Upheaval Society" (Young 2005: 159).

8. It is beyond the scope of this chapter to deal with the issue of gender inequality that was prevalent during the 1940s. Hard feelings existed among faculty and students in terms of gender inequality. For example, Caffrey wrote: "there was a definite anti-female bias" and that Benedict considered some returning veterans from lower middle-class backgrounds to be "barbarians" (Caffrey 1989: 340). None of the members of the MUS recall purposely excluding women such as Elaine Padilla or Eleanor Leacock. However, this did not mean women were included. Mintz wrote: "we didn't deny anybody admission," but acknowledged: "we were pushing young women out of the way without even knowing we were doing it" (Diamond 1993: 19). Leacock wrote that the MUS was like a "street-corner gang" that brought honor to itself by excluding women. There is no doubt that the exclusion of women had something to do with what Stanley Diamond characterized as "male bonding" within their "cadre of radical young men" (Diamond 1993).

9. Service bristles when recalling what Leacock said about the exclusion of women. He wrote that there were not many women around in those early days who were congenial to us and "our more or less anti-Benedictian origins." Service maintained:

> Eleanor Leacock was not included because she wasn't there. We didn't know her that first year. I got acquainted with her a year or so later through other contacts. But she was not a student at the time. She had been a student before the war and somehow she thought that we were nothing but a sort of skull and bones type honorary society or something that excluded her and other women. Well, there weren't any other women, except Elena Padilla.... We had invited her to our meetings, so we had nothing against females. (Service n.d.: 42)

Leacock's recollections differ significantly from Service's. Leacock wrote that there was an overwhelming anti-female bias at Columbia and throughout academia. Her views with regard to the Anthropology Department before and after the war are sobering and thought-provoking (Leacock 1993: 1–31). They also are in agreement with the views of Marian Smith, who did not like Murra, Steward, and, by extension, Wolf. Smith's views had as much to do with the way the Puerto Rico Project was supervised by Steward and Murra as they did with the MUS. Letters Padilla exchanged with Murra in 1948 are heated and indicate that there were not just hard feelings but intense divisions between men and women.

10. When I was a graduate student at Columbia I asked Robert Murphy and Mort Fried about the MUS. Murphy did not have much to add, except that the group was important. Fried recalled the group and its members with great fondness. Much to my regret, I do not recall anything of substance

he spoke about. I do recall that when I saw Fried the following week he showed me the original drawing he made. According to Elman Service, Fried was an accomplished painter and cartoonist (Service 1988: 149).

11. Robert Carneiro was generous enough to share these letters with me.

12. It is also represented in the dissertations written by members of the MUS, such as Manners and Service in 1950; Diamond, Fried, Mintz, and Padilla in 1951, Leacock in 1952; and Faron and Sahlins in 1954.

13. Here I am building upon the work of Regna Darnell and her discussion of the *Invisible Genealogies* in American anthropology (Darnell 2001). Like, Darnell I see continuities in the development of American anthropology that are tied to theoretical practices and informal as well as formal scholarly associations.

14. For information about the history of the Anthropology Department at the University of Michigan see Peace (2001: 1–32).

15. White did his best to prevent a school of thought from forming at Michigan. He believed that schools of thought fostered a cloistered hermetic quality, inhibiting intellectual growth and new ideas. White was not opposed to the cross-fertilization of ideas between Columbia and Michigan – he considered this a healthy intellectual exchange. However, he was not the person primarily responsible for this cross-fertilization. This distinction is reserved for Fred Thieme. Thieme received his PhD from Columbia in 1950 and was the first Columbia graduate hired by Michigan. Thieme was a gifted administrator and was influential in the rapid expansion of the Anthropology Department at Michigan.

ARCHIVAL SOURCES

Bentley Historical Library:
Leslie A. White papers
Eric Wolf papers
National Anthropology Archives:
William Duncan Strong papers
John Murra papers

REFERENCES

Caffrey, Margaret. 1989. *Ruth Benedict: Stranger in this Land*. Austin: University of Texas Press.

Darnell, Regna. 2001. *Invisible Genealogies: A History of American Anthropology*. Lincoln: University of Nebraska Press.

Darnell, Regna and Stephen O. Murray. 2001. Series Editor's Introduction. In *Invisible Genealogies: A History of American Anthropology*, pp. xiii–xv. By Regna Darnell. Lincoln: University of Nebraska Press.

Diamond, Stanley. 1993. Eleanor Leacock's Political Vision. In *From Labrador to Samoa*, pp. 111–14. Constance Sutton, ed. Arlington, VA: Association for Feminist Anthropology/American Anthropological Association.

Friedman, Jonathan. 1987. An Interview with Eric Wolf. *Current Anthropology* 28(1): 107–17.

Kerns, Virginia. 2003. *Scenes from the High Desert: Julian Steward's Life and Theory*. Urbana: University of Illinois Press.

Lesser, Alexander. 1952. Evolution in Social Anthropology. *Southwestern Journal of Anthropology* 17: 40–48.

Malinowski, Bronislaw. 1944. *A Scientific Theory of Culture*. Chapel Hill: University of North Carolina Press.

Manners, Robert. 1952. Brief Communications: Snthopology and Culture in Crisis. *American Anthropologist* 54: 127–34.

—— 1973. Julian Haynes Steward, 1902–1972. *American Anthropologist* 75: 886–903.

Mintz, Sidney. 1994. An Impartial History of the Mundial Upheaval Society. *AnthroWatch* 2(3): 19.

Model, Judith. 1983. *Ruth Benedict: Patterns of a Life*. Philadelphia: University of Pennsylvania Press.

Murphy, Robert. 1977. Introduction: The Anthropological Theories of Julian Steward. In *Evolution and Ecology: Essays on Social Transformation*, pp. 1–39. Jane C. Steward and Robert F. Murphy, eds. Urbana: University of Illinois Press.

—— 1981. Julian Steward. In *Totems and Teachers*, pp. 171–208. Sydel Silverman, ed. New York: Columbia University Press.

Patterson, Thomas C. and Antonio Lauria-Perricelli. 1999. Julian Steward and the Construction of Area Studies Research in the United States. In *Julian Steward and the Great Basin*, pp. 219–40. Richard O. Clemmer et al., eds. Salt Lake City: University of Utah Press.

Peace, William J. 2001. Introduction: The University of Michigan's Department of Anthropology. In *Retrospectives: Works and Lives of Michigan Anthropologists, Michigan Discussions in Anthropology* 16: 1–32.

—— 2004. *Leslie A. White: Evolution and Revolution in American Anthropology*. Lincoln: University of Nebraska Press.

Price, David H. 2004. *Threatening Anthropology*. Durham, NC: Duke University Press.

Service, Elman. n.d. Segments of Oral History and Cultural Anthropology with Special Emphasis on the Formation of Schools of Thought. Unpublished manuscript.

—— 1975. *Origins of the State and Civilization*. New York: W.W. Norton.

—— 1988. Morton Herbert Fried. *American Anthropologist* 90: 148–52.

Shimkin, Demitri B. 1964. Julian H. Steward: A Contribution to Fact and Theory in Cultural Anthropology. In *Process and Pattern in Culture: Essays in Honor of Julian Steward*, pp. 1–17. Robert Manners, ed. Chicago: Aldine Publishing Co.

Stocking, George. 1976. Ideas and Institutions in American Anthropology. In *Selected Papers from the American Anthropologist, 1921–1945*. Washington, DC: American Anthropological Association.

Thompson, Laura. 1950. *Culture in Crisis: A Study of the Hopi Indians*. New York: Harper and Bros.

White, Leslie A. 1949. *Science of Culture*. New York: Farrar and Straus.

Willey, Gordon R. 1988. *Portraits in American Archaeology*. Albuquerque: University of New Mexico Press.

Wolf, Eric. 1999. Eric Wolf: Talk at Yale, 1984. Transcript from Re-Recording of 5/27/99. Bentley Historical Library, Eric Wolf Papers.

—— 2001. *Pathways to Power*. Berkeley: University of California Press.

Yengoyan, Aram. 2001. Foreword: Culture and Power in the Writings of E.R. Wolf. In *Pathways of Power*, pp. vii–xvii. By Eric Wolf. Berkeley: University of California Press.

Young, Virginia Heyer. 2005. *Ruth Benedict: Beyond Relativity, Beyond Pattern*. Lincoln: University of Nebraska Press.

8 AFTERWORD: RECONCEPTUALIZING ANTHROPOLOGY'S HISTORIOGRAPHY

Robert L.A. Hancock

In their April 1967 *Newsletter*, the Fellows of the American Anthropological Association (AAA) read that collectively they had approved the proposed "Statement of Problems of Anthropological Research and Ethics" in a referendum with a resounding 92.5 percent in favor (AAA 1967b: 1). Though the results were not binding on the AAA or any of its members, Eric Wakin asserts that "it was an indication that the Association was concerned enough about such activities [as Project Camelot] to instigate a formal investigation and put forth a consensual public statement on the results" (1992: 32). In retrospect, it also appears symptomatic of a wider shift both in the profession and in North American society more generally.

The ethics proposal had been mailed to the members with a simple ballot several weeks previously,[1] and the January issue of the *Fellows Newsletter* had included a 12-page "Background Information on Problems of Anthropological Research and Ethics" (AAA 1967a). Asserting that "[c]onstraint, deception and secrecy have no place in science" (AAA 1967c: 1), the "Statement" outlined three main areas of concern: freedom of research, support and sponsorship of research, and anthropologists in United States government service. Reiterating in full the Association's 1948 resolution on the freedom of anthropologists to publish their research (AAA 1949), the first section asserted that the government should not interfere in anthropological research, especially in terms of scrutinizing requests to conduct research outside of the country, or by demanding extreme levels of security clearance for researchers working under contract and imposing classified status on the work they produce (AAA 1967c: 1–2). The second section, on support and sponsorship, began by acknowledging the value of federal funding for anthropological research before asserting that researchers must be conscious of how their funding sources may be perceived by subjects in the field, must be open and forthcoming about their projects and sources of support, and must not use anthropological research as a cover for the gathering of intelligence or other covert actions (1967c: 2). The third and final section stated that "[i]t is desirable that social science advice be made more readily available to the Executive Office of the President," and advocated for the inclusion of anthropologists in the planning of projects and recruitment of staff, while ensuring that researchers remained connected to the discipline and its ideals (1967c: 2).

In a paper he had delivered to the Southwestern Anthropological Association (SWAA) the previous spring, Ralph Beals, the author of the "Background," outlined the process by which he came to make the recommendations he put forward in the Statement. Alarmed by the US military's use of anthropological research and fieldworkers, scholars unaffiliated with such undertakings were concerned that they would lose access to "their" fieldwork sites should all anthropological field research be associated with American military intervention, particularly in light of the revelation of Project Camelot (e.g. Horowitz 1967). With these worries in mind, the Fellows of the AAA passed a motion at the Denver meetings of November 1965 directing "the Executive Board and the Secretariat … to explore during the coming months the widely ramified issues involving the relationship between anthropologists and the agencies, both governmental and private, that sponsor their research" (Beals 1966: 1). In response, the Board asked Beals and the Executive Secretary, Stephen Boggs, to form a committee to fulfill the demands of the motion; financial support was soon forthcoming from the Wenner-Gren foundation. To aid his research and ensure wide geographic coverage, Beals enlisted a group of anthropologists to gather information on the situation in the areas of the world which fit with their own expertise. Beals wrote that he hoped that "the committee may ultimately produce some guidelines which will be presented primarily to aid individuals in reaching decisions concerning their own ethical problems" (1966: 3).

But that is not the whole story. A month before his SWAA presentation, Beals had written a letter to Peter Kunstadter, where he outlined the approach he was taking to the central issue under debate, anthropological research performed on behalf of, or utilized by, the American government:

My personal viewpoint, let us assure you that this is shared by a good many people, is that in the reality world [*sic*] in which we live not only is government going to make use of anthropologists and anthropological research, often in ways which cannot be predicted in advance, but that on the one hand there is an obligation of government to utilize such information and to support research, and that the profession should welcome this in principle. If this is to be granted, then it seems to me our problem is to discover ways in which the relations between government and the profession can be improved as well as the manner in which government uses anthropologists and anthropological research.

In taking my present assignment I have made it clear that I will not suggest a code of ethics although a set of guidelines treated sufficiently broadly to meet a variety of situations may be desirable.

Thus far no one taking extreme points of view has presented specific evidence for their position and I do not propose to take seriously general accusations and suspicions. Most of the people I have talked to so far and most of the written material I have received suggest that your fears of Association criticism of your research are unfounded. Even people who have stated that they would under no circumstances accept funds from the Department of Defense have also stated explicitly that they would not condemn anyone who did, although there are some exceptions. (RLBP, Box 75, 1 March 1966; cf. Beals 1966: 3)

My analysis of Beals's process and proposals is that they were designed to protect government-sponsored research from criticism on ethical grounds. Beals saw great value for the profession in providing research to the various departments of the American government and sought to ensure that this practice was protected by the AAA, even if it was unlikely to be endorsed by the majority of its members. Given his own work on behalf of the American government, both internally as an expert witness in Indian Claims Commission (ICC) cases (Beals 1985), and externally, as Director of the Social Science Research Council (SSRC) for six years in the early post-war period (Beals 1982: 13–14; Patterson and Lauria-Perricelli 1999), Beals himself had extremely close ties with government research and was hardly a disinterested observer in the debates (e.g. Trencher 2002).

These activities, along with his role as a "consultant" in the reorganization of the AAA in 1947, brought Beals quite closely into Julian Steward's sphere of influence. In fact, the Beals report, including its published form (Beals 1969), can be read as the ultimate justification of the sort of social science Steward envisioned, offering a defense of anthropological engagement with, and its potential supporting role in, the ongoing American colonial project. The "Statement" appears to say that anthropologists could feel fine about participating in military and governmental adventures as long as they did not do it in a clandestine fashion; in fact, the report almost goes so far as to say that anthropologists have an obligation to share their knowledge with the government. This support is particularly telling in the context of the discipline's continuing neglect of its role in the colonial projects on the North American continent (but see Pinkoski and Asch 2004); as Pinkoski (2006) has demonstrated, it was the American materialist tradition promoted by Steward and his students and those who, like Beals, worked on behalf of the American government in the ICC cases, that was truly the handmaiden of colonialism. It was even a particularly devoted one – so dedicated to the colonial project that it is still unable, or more probably refuses, to recognize, let alone examine, its role in the ongoing attempts to subjugate indigenous nations "at home," or even to acknowledge the situation as colonialist.

The status of Steward's method and theory as a colonial science developed in support of the expansion of American hegemony both at home and abroad is beyond dispute. Pinkoski's analysis (2006; see also Pinkoski in this volume) of archival and published materials – covering both Steward's work for the Bureau of Indian Affairs and the Department of Justice against American Indian groups at the ICC, and his work for the SSRC in the development of area studies research internationally – demonstrates the extent to which Steward shaped his approach to fit the demands of American colonialist policy. For example, in his early research on the Shoshone, Steward (1936) acknowledged their political autonomy and landholding patterns, stating that all peoples live in groups that are at least this developed. However, in his testimony in the Paiute cases at the ICC in the 1950s, Steward asserted that the Shoshone occupy a unique evolutionary level, acephalous and atomistic, with no social organization that could hold property – and therefore had no right to prevent American expansion into their territory (Pinkoski 2006: 147–68; Steward 1955). In a way, this shift makes sense in the context of his faith in manifest destiny, and his assertion, in his area studies handbook, that the social sciences only have value if they are of use to the American government in its attempts to expand its sovereignty and at times of war (Steward 1950: 155, xii; cf. Kerns 1999, 2003). Beals's work served to give a patina of ethical behavior to the theoretical approaches developed by Steward.

Compared to the later ethics crises, which rocked the discipline in the next few years, the work of Beals has received little attention from historians (but see Berreman 2003; Nader 1997; Trencher 2002; Wakin 1992).[2] However, this relative lack of attention does not reflect the true importance of the Beals reports, as I see it. At a basic level, his work set the parameters of debate, between supporters of an "objective, scientific" anthropology – a conservative old guard, with its involvement in government research – and the opponents of this approach – a radical vanguard. These parameters have held since the beginning of the debate. More immediately, Beals's work laid the groundwork and provided the contemporary context for the later controversy around the use of anthropological research in government-sponsored counter-insurgency research in Thailand. Beals reflected the perspective of the conservatives, seeking to define and defend a position for government research in the discipline. Those advocating a staunchly ethical position, seeking a radical rejection of government involvement in anthropological research, represented the vanguard. Anthropologists could no longer pretend they were participating in and contributing to an objective science; they were forced explicitly to reckon with the political aspects of their research, and the ethics of the political positions they assumed.

ETHICS, POLITICS, AND THE HISTORIOGRAPHY OF ANTHROPOLOGY

The Beals report and the reactions and responses it provoked represent a pivotal shift in the self-perception of anthropologists working in North America. The chapters in this volume represent a similar shift in the historiography of the discipline. If we accept that that current historiography has its roots in the work of George W. Stocking – without forgetting the work of A.I. Hallowell (1965) and Dell Hymes (1962) – this shift becomes readily apparent.

Stocking's work was the first comprehensive attempt to craft a systematic historiography of anthropology, one which emerged in the context of a nascent American intellectual history (Higham 1954; cf. Seidman 1983). His path-breaking essay, "On the Limits of 'Presentism' and 'Historicism' in the Historiography of the Human Sciences" (1968 [1965]), first published in the *Journal of the History of the Behavioral Sciences*, lays out in relatively stark terms what he saw as the two options for describing and analyzing a discipline's history. The first is a "presentist" or "Whiggish" mode, one where the historian:

... reduces the mediating processes by which the totality of an historical past produces the totality of its consequent future to a search for the origins of certain present phenomena. He [*sic*] seeks out in the past phenomena which seem to resemble those of concern in the present, and then moves forward in time by tracing lineages up to the present in simple sequential movement.... Because it wrenches the individual historical phenomenon from the complex network of its contemporary context in order to see it in abstracted relationship to analogues in the present, it is prone to anachronistic misinterpretation. Because it assumes in advance the progressive character of historical change, it is less interested in the complex processes by which change emerges than in agencies which direct it, whether they be great men, specific deterministic forces, or the "logic" of historical development itself. (Stocking 1968 [1965]: 3–4)

The second is an "historicist" mode, one with "the essential quality of the commitment to the understanding of the past for its own sake" (Stocking 1968 [1965]: 4). Counterposing these positions explicitly, he writes that he:

... would suggest – in a frankly provocative, but open-minded spirit – that each of these orientations will tend to find its natural adherents among the historiographers of the behavioral sciences, and that each orientation carries with it a characteristic motivational posture. The orientation of the historian approaching the history of the behavioral sciences will tend to be "historicist" and his motivational posture "affective." Presentism is by no means a dead issue in the historical fraternity, and historians are undeniably conditioned in a thousand subtle ways by the present in which they write. But in general the historian approaches the past rather in the spirit of the mountain climber attacking Everest – "because it is there." He [*sic*] demands no more of it than the emotional satisfaction which flows from understanding a manifestation of the changing human self in time. The approach of the professional behavioral scientist, on the other hand, is more likely to be whiggish or, more broadly, "presentist," and his motivational posture "utilitarian." He may share the historian's emotional satisfaction, but he tends to demand of the past something more: that it be related to and even useful for furthering his professional activities in the ongoing present. (Stocking 1968 [1965]: 5–6)

Clearly, having created a space for his work in the explication of these positions, Stocking placed himself firmly on the side of the historicists (Stocking 1992: 5).

In his subsequent work, Stocking has continued to work in the mode of the ostensibly disinterested outsider, maintaining that his position as a participant-observer, simultaneously inside and outside of the discipline, offers a privileged vantage point from which to assess anthropology's past. In particular, he represents the elision of theoretical contributions to current debates in the discipline as something of a strength of his analyses, placing them beyond the postmodernist presentism ascendant in the discipline during the 1980s and 1990s (Stocking 1992: 7–9). At the same time, though, this leads to a strangely denuded history of anthropology, one that examines and discusses anthropologists without linking their theories to later developments in the discipline.

At a gross level, Stocking's history of anthropology seems written from what intellectual historians have identified as an external approach, where the analyses of ideas "lead outward to an external context of events and behavior" and in which "[i]ntellectual history becomes an investigation of the connections between thought and deed" (Higham 1954: 341). This external perspective can be contrasted with an internal perspective, which:

… has insisted principally on establishing the internal relationships between what some men [*sic*] write or say and what other men write or say. This kind of intellectual history directs attention away from the context of events in order to enlarge and systematize the context of ideas. It seeks the connections between thought and thought. (Higham 1954: 341)

Scholars interested in the historiography of anthropology inevitably need to come to terms with Stocking's work, and perhaps equally inevitably their work comes into dialogue with his. The opening for such dialogue – debate, dissension, disagreement – are numerous: scholars can privilege presentism over historicism, or an internal analysis over his external one. Or, as in the case of Regna Darnell, the most important of Stocking's interlocutors for the historiography of the discipline, there is the option of subtly refashioning the categories to offer another narrative understanding of the discipline's history. Engaging explicitly with Stocking's approach, which offers the history of the discipline while eschewing an explicit consideration of its theory, as well as with the postmodernists, who offer an ostensibly innovative theoretical approach largely devoid of an understanding of the discipline's past, Darnell's goal is:

... to reclaim the history of anthropology so that it can serve anthropologists as a means of constructing contemporary professional identities upon continuity with the past. Presentism in this reflexive sense, choosing issues for historical attention because they still matter today, is fully commensurable with historicism. It is only when we fail to distinguish the contexts of our own theoretical positions from those of the past that presentism becomes a methodological millstone. (Darnell 2001: 1)

She goes on to offer a proudly internalist account of Americanist anthropological theory, tracing its development, through the connections between anthropologists, and its continuing influence and salience. It is impossible – and somewhat pointless – to try to say whether her analysis is a presentist-influenced historicism or an historicist-influenced presentism.

Taken together as a group, the chapters in this present volume similarly blur the distinction between internal and external readings of anthropology's history. While Stocking offered the history of anthropology without theory, and Darnell offers the history of theory, the chapters here examine the influence of politics on the actions of anthropologists. They represent facets of an emergent approach which is simultaneously a presentist genealogical project, seeking to identify forebears of a particular intellectual approach and political commitment, and a historicist attempt to recover streams of thought and scholarly careers which, for a variety of reasons – often political – have fallen from the collective disciplinary memory. At the same time, it is important to stress that this historiographical analysis of shifts in emphases and approaches is neither a narrative of evolutionary development nor one of dialectical synthesis. It is also not strictly paradigmatic, in that these different approaches to the depiction of the history of anthropology represent parallel processes rather than successive replacements, mirroring in some ways the process of theoretical thinking in anthropology more generally (cf. Barrett 1984: 53–62). It reads less as a totally new approach than as an attempt to build on and expand the earlier ones, to answer questions that they did not ask or answered only partially.

In drawing a connection between politics, theory, and practice I should note that I am using an expansive and perhaps heterodox notion of politics. In my formulation, the concept of *politics* and *political thought and actions* speaks to a person's notion of the kind of world she or he wants to live in or seeks to create. This definition goes beyond simple reference to the state, the nation, or other societal structures, to encompass all thought and action aimed at remaking or changing the world beyond the bounds of the individual. These visions, these politics, and the activities that seek to enact them, are necessarily tied to an ethics, which represents and demarcates the bounds of actions acceptable in the work of bringing these worlds into existence. That is, it is an ethical framework that allows us to decide whether any means necessary to bring about a particular political vision are reasonable, or if there are limits on the methods we use to try to change the world.

I will return to the question of ethics in a moment, but it is important to stress at this point the important contributions the chapters in this book make to the explicit recognition and coherent explication of the political positions assumed by a number of anthropologists in the early post-war/Cold War era. In a period where the Soviet allies of the US quickly became its communist enemies both at home and abroad, and given the utter and excessive virulence of the anti-communist movement commonly known in the US by the shorthand "McCarthyism," it is hardly a surprise that anthropology would be riven by the same competing political visions in contestation in wider North American society.

Some work has already been done in this direction. Price's (2004) magisterial analysis of the efforts of the US government to undermine the careers of "activist anthropologists" provides a framework for understanding what was at stake in this era, and points the way to an understanding of the implications of the Cold War for anthropology as a discipline and as a profession. Also, perhaps as part of the process of coming to terms with his own engagement with communism (cf. Yelvington 2003: 368) and his personal intellectual history, George Stocking has recently published a major biographical piece on Robert Armstrong, an anthropologist trained at Chicago whose career was derailed by an FBI investigation into his communist sympathies (Stocking 2006).

The authors collected here offer a number of innovative analyses for an historical understanding of the effects of political developments on particular anthropologists and the discipline more generally. Peace's work on the Mundial Upheaval Society, and its members, many of whom achieved great prominence and made significant contributions to the discipline and its theory, points to crucial questions of influence: not only in terms of the intellectual influence of their mentor, Steward, and which aspects of his approach they took from him, what they rejected, and what they changed and adapted in their own work, but also in terms of the influence of Marxism and the left more generally on their outlook both beyond and within anthropology. This raises a question central to several chapters in this book: what does it mean to refer to an anthropologist or anthropologists as "Marxist," or when they call themselves that? In many ways such an appellation opens up more questions than it answers, raising as it does issues of internecine splits, debates, and battles such as those between socialists and communists, Trotskyites and Stalinists. In this context, Wax's work to reclaim Tax as an ancestor and alternative to both the Marxists and the more conservative faction shows that Marxism was – and remains – neither the only alternative to the dominant theory, nor the most radical critique of it.

Other chapters, such as those by Sperling, Salamone, Price, and Pinkoski, make important contributions by demonstrating that the "politicization" of anthropology was not solely the preserve of the "radicals," and that the conservative faction was as influenced by politicized perspectives as the radicals they were so quick to condemn. The questions of anthropological participation in US government research projects – unproblematic during World War II and the battle against fascism, but more contentious after McCarthyism and particularly during the Vietnam era – raised by Salamone and Ross offer specific, contextualized examples of this politicization, and begin to raise questions of who benefited from a willingness to collaborate with government interests by betraying colleagues or accepting funding for questionable research. Ross's discussion of Murdock and, particularly, Price's examination of Wittfogel's career, begin to answer these questions about the identities of those conservative or reactionary researchers who sought to advance their careers at the expense of more "radical" scholars.

While the works in this collection make an extremely important move in a direction which explicitly recognizes the impact of politics, both personal and societal, on anthropological thought, there is still room to expand the historiography of anthropology. In particular, what these chapters underplay, in spite of their attention to the links between political standpoints and anthropological research, is the explicit and intense connection between personal political visions and the theoretical analyses offered by anthropologists. Linked to this is a still outstanding need to examine the ethics of anthropological theory; it is not enough to discuss the politics of research and researchers without simultaneously assessing their ethics in terms of the implications not only for the people who are ostensibly the "subjects" of anthropology but also for the world as a whole. In this way, the chapters in this volume contribute to a growing literature in a field marked out by such contributions as Pinkoski's dissertation on Steward (2006), which links his theory and his work for the US government in numerous, explicit ways, and Susan Trencher's work on post-war American anthropology, which is shaped by her conviction that anthropological work is "an anthropological subject for study which simultaneously acts as a heuristic device for the investigation of American experience and culture" (Trencher 2000: 1).

The point I want to make is that, as engaged anthropologists, we must examine anthropological theory with the same ethical interest that we examine research methods and practice. For example, the eminent political philosopher James Tully sets out a simple yet powerful formula for assessing the ethics of works in his discipline, by asking:

How does political theory hinder or help the liberation of indigenous peoples? That is, in what ways can political theory help or hinder the struggles of indigenous peoples *for* and *of* freedom? (2000: 36, emphases in original)

These questions are seemingly simple but extremely powerful markers for assessing the impact of a theoretical approach, as applicable to anthropology or any other discipline as they are to political philosophy, and they set a benchmark for recognizing that the theories we craft and apply to describing and understanding the world simultaneously have significant and lasting impacts on that world. They call for an intense, meaningful collaboration with others in our research, and reject emphatically the notion of detached, "objective" observers who exist independently of the subjects of their study.

To close, I would like to mention an exchange of letters in the prestigious journal *Science* in 1968, in which Julian Steward and Stanley Diamond outlined the basic parameters of the anthropological debate about theory, politics, and ethics. Responding to a review by Wolf (1967), of a three-volume collection of papers he edited, Steward asserted that science is the opposite of politics, and that scientists should not be held responsible for subsequent applications of their research discoveries (Steward 1968). Countering this, Diamond, also a former student of Steward's, explicitly rejected the notion of a value-free approach to research and asserted that, "[i]f anthropology is a science, it is a moral one" (Diamond 1968: 1050). This is still the fundamental question today: is anthropology a "pure, objective" science, unconcerned with the impact of its research and theoretical pronouncements and unwilling to acknowledge the political and ethical choices that undergird them, or is it a moral one, concerned, as Diamond contended, with applying its knowledge to the betterment of humankind? If the answer is the first option, then we are back to the position advocated by Beals in favour of government-sponsored research. If the answer is the second option, then we are laying the foundation for a truly ethical anthropology, one that requires a historiography of its own.

NOTES

An earlier version of portions of this chapter was presented in the session "Ethical Anthropology: Past, Present, and Future" at the 105th Annual Meeting of the American Anthropological Association in San José, CA, 18 November 2006. I am grateful to Leslie Sponsel for inviting me to participate in the session, and to Gerald Berreman, David Price, Carolyn Fluehr-Lobban and Regna Darnell for their helpful comments and suggestions in that setting. I also appreciate the patient, astute editorial interventions of Dustin Wax.

This chapter represents a small component of a much larger, multi-year research project examining the relationship between anthropology and colonialism in the US and Canada (Pinkoski and Asch 2004; Asch forthcoming). I am indebted to the other members of this group – Michael Asch, Marc Pinkoski, and Tony Fisher – for the insights they have shared and the support they have offered over the past several years.

Part of the research for this chapter was supported by a Social Sciences and Humanities Research Council of Canada Doctoral Fellowship (Award No. 752-2003-1298).

1. The ballot asked only if members approved or disapproved of the "Statement," and instructed them to return their ballot in a signed envelope by March 20, 1967 (AAAR, Box 106).
2. Beals's work on the "Statement" (AAA 1967c) and the "Background Information" (AAA 1967a), and the debates these fostered both amongst the Executive Board and amongst the Fellows generally were, of course, only one part of a series of interconnected events, beginning in 1966 with an attempt to pass a resolution condemning American actions in Vietnam (Trencher 2002: 456–57), which brought to the fore questions of ethics and politics and the role of the AAA in national and international affairs (cf. e.g. Berreman 2001; Wakin 1992).

ARCHIVAL SOURCES

AAAR (American Anthropological Association Records), National Anthropological Archives, Smithsonian Institution, Suitland, MD.
RBLP (Ralph L. Beals Papers), National Anthropological Archives, Smithsonian Institution, Suitland, MD.

REFERENCES

American Anthropological Association (AAA). 1949. Resolution on Freedom of Publication. *American Anthropologist* 51(2): 370.
—— 1967a. Background Information on Problems of Anthropological Research and Ethics. *Fellow Newsletter* 8(1): 1–13.
—— 1967b. Referendum Approved. *Fellows Newsletter* 8(4): 1.
—— 1967c. Statement on Problems of Anthropological Research and Ethics. AAAR Box 106.
Asch, Michael. Forthcoming. Colonial Governmentality. *Anthropologica*.
Barrett, Stanley R. 1984. *The Rebirth of Anthropological Theory*. Toronto: University of Toronto Press.

Beals, Ralph L. 1966. Committee on Research Problems and Ethics. Paper presented at the Southwestern Anthropological Association, Davis, CA, April 7, 1966. AAAR Box 82.

—— 1969. *The Politics of Social Research*. Chicago: Aldine.

—— 1982. Fifty Years in Anthropology. *Annual Review of Anthropology* 11: 1–23.

—— 1985. The Anthropologist as Expert Witness: Illustrations from the California Indian Land Claims Case. In *Irredeemable America: The Indians' Estate and Land Claims*, pp. 139–55. Imre Sutton, ed. Albuquerque: University of New Mexico Press.

Berreman, Gerald D. 2003. Ethics versus "Realism" in Anthropology: Redux. In *Ethics and the Profession of Anthropology: Dialogue for Ethically Conscious Practice*, 2nd edn, pp. 51–83. Carolyn Fluehr-Lobban, ed. Walnut Creek, CA: AltaMira.

Darnell, Regna. 2001. *Invisible Genealogies: A History of Americanist Anthropology*. Lincoln: University of Nebraska Press.

Diamond, Stanley. 1968. Moral Engagement of the Scientist. *Science* 159(3819): 1049–51.

Hallowell, A. Irving. 1965. The History of Anthropology as an Anthropological Problem. *Journal of the History of the Behavioral Sciences* 1(1): 24–38.

Higham, John. 1954. Intellectual History and its Neighbors. *Journal of the History of Ideas* 15(3): 339–47.

Horowitz, Irving L., ed. 1967. *The Rise and Fall of Project Camelot: Studies in the Relationship between Social Science and Practical Politics*. Cambridge, MA: MIT Press.

Hymes, Dell H. 1962. On Studying the History of Anthropology. *Kroeber Anthropological Society Papers* 11(2): 81–86.

Kerns, Virginia. 1999. Learning the Land. In *Julian Steward and the Great Basin: The Making of an Anthropologist*, pp. 1–18. Richard O. Clemmer, L. Daniel Myers, and Mary Elizabeth Rudden, eds. Salt Lake City: University of Utah Press.

—— 2003. *Scenes from the High Desert: Julian Steward's Life and Theory*. Urbana: University of Illinois Press.

Nader, Laura. 1997. The Phantom Factor: Impact of the Cold War on Anthropology. In *The Cold War and the University: Toward an Intellectual History of the Postwar Years*, pp. 107–46. André Schiffrin, ed. New York: New Press.

Patterson, Thomas C. and Antonio Lauria-Perricelli. 1999. Julian Steward and the Construction of Area-Studies Research in the United States. In *Julian Steward and the Great Basin: The Making of an Anthropologist*, pp. 219–40. Richard O. Clemmer, L. Daniel Myers, and Mary Elizabeth Rudden, eds. Salt Lake City: University of Utah Press.

Pinkoski, Marc. 2006. Julian Steward and American Anthropology: The Science of Colonialism. PhD Dissertation, University of Victoria, BC.

Pinkoski, Marc and Michael Asch. 2004. Anthropology and Indigenous Rights in Canada and the United States: Implications in Steward's Theoretical Project. In *Hunter-Gatherers in History, Archaeology and Anthropology*, pp. 187–200. Alan Barnard, ed. Oxford: Berg.

Price, David H. 2004. *Threatening Anthropology: McCarthyism and the FBI's Surveillance of Activist Anthropologists*. Durham, NC: Duke University Press.

Seidman, Steven. 1983. Beyond Presentism and Historicism: Understanding the History of Social Science. *Sociological Inquiry* 53(1): 79–94.

Steward, Julian H. 1936. The Economic and Social Basis of Primitive Bands. In *Essays on Anthropology in Honor of Alfred Louis Kroeber*, pp. 311–50. Robert Lowie, ed. Berkeley: University of California Press.

—— 1950. *Area Research: Theory and Practice.* New York: Social Science Research Council.

—— 1955. *Theory of Culture Change: The Methodology of Multilinear Evolution.* Urbana: University of Illinois Press.

—— 1968. Scientific Responsibility in Modern Life. *Science* 159(3811): 147–48.

Stocking, George W. Jr. 1968 [1965]. On the Limits of "Presentism" and "Historicism" in the Historiography of the Human Sciences. In *Race, Culture, and Evolution: Essays in the History of Anthropology*, pp. 1–12. New York: Free Press.

—— 1992. *The Ethnographer's Magic and Other Essays in the History of Anthropology.* Madison: University of Wisconsin Press.

—— 2006. Unfinished Business: Robert Gelston Armstrong, the Federal Bureau of Investigation, and the History of Anthropology at Chicago and in Nigeria. In *Central Sites, Peripheral Visions: Cultural and Institutional Crossings in the History of Anthropology. History of Anthropology*, vol. 11, pp. 99–247. Richard Handler, ed. Madison: University of Wisconsin Press.

Trencher, Susan R. 2000. *Mirrored Images: American Anthropology and American Culture, 1960–1980.* Westport, CT: Bergin and Garvey.

—— 2002. The American Anthropological Association and the Values of Science, 1935–70. *American Anthropologist* 104(2): 450–62.

Tully, James. 2000. The Stuggles of Indigenous Peoples for and of Freedom. In *Political Theory and the Rights of Indigenous Peoples*, pp. 36–59. Duncan Ivison, Paul Patton, and Will Sanders, eds. Cambridge: Cambridge University Press.

Wakin, Eric. 1992. *Anthropology Goes to War: Professional Ethics and Counterinsurgency in Thailand.* Monograph No. 7. Madison: Center for Southeast Asian Studies, University of Wisconsin.

Wolf, Eric R. 1967. Heritage and Modernity. *Science* 158(3802): 759–62.

Yelvington, Kevin A. 2003. A Historian among the Anthropologists. *American Anthropologist* 105(2): 367–71.

CONTRIBUTORS

Robert L.A. Hancock is an interdisciplinary PhD candidate in anthropology and history at the University of Victoria in British Columbia, Canada. His dissertation research focuses on anthropological representations of Indigenous economies and land use in Canadian courts and tribunals during the 1970s.

William J. Peace is an independent scholar. He is author of *Leslie A. White: Evolution and Revolution in American Anthropology*. He earned his PhD at Columbia University. His areas of interest include the history of anthropology, disability studies, and body art and modification.

Marc Pinkoski is a post-doctoral Research Fellow in the Department of Anthropology at the University of Victoria, British Columbia. He is currently doing research on the representations of Indigenous peoples in anthropological theory, focusing on the implications of such representations in bolstering the doctrine of *terra nullius* in current Aboriginal rights claims in Canada.

David Price is Associate Professor at St Martin's University where he teaches courses in anthropology and social justice. He has conducted cultural anthropological and archaeological fieldwork and research in the United States and Palestine, Egypt and Yemen. He is writing a three-volume series examining American anthropologists' interactions with intelligence agencies: *Threatening Anthropology* (2004, Duke University Press) examines McCarthyism's effects on anthropologists; *Anthropological Intelligence: The Deployment and Neglect of American Anthropology in the Second World War* (forthcoming, Duke University Press) documents anthropological contributions to World War II, and a third volume will explore anthropologists' interactions with the CIA and Pentagon during the Cold War.

Eric B. Ross received his BA in anthropology in 1968 from the University of Pennsylvania and his PhD in anthropology in 1976 from Columbia University. His doctoral research focused on the ecology of diet and warfare among the previously unstudied Peruvian

Achuara, a sub-group of the so-called Jivaro Indians of the Upper Amazon. Much of his subsequent work has concentrated on the political, economic, and ecological conditions that shape dietary patterns, but with increasing concern with complex social systems, the dietary consequences of colonialism, and the nature of food systems within the framework of contemporary globalization. Major works include *Death, Sex and Fertility: Population Regulation in Preindustrial and Developing Societies* (with the late Marvin Harris; 1987), the landmark collection, *Beyond the Myths of Culture: Essays in Cultural Materialism* (1980), and *The Malthus Factor: Poverty, Politics and Population in Capitalist Development* (1998). He currently teaches at the Institute of Social Studies in The Hague, where, until recently, he directed the MA program in Development Studies. He is also the founder and editor of the online political magazine, *The Porcupine.*

Frank A. Salamone is the immediate past Chair of the Sociology and Anthropology Department at Iona College. He is also a facilitator at the University of Phoenix. He has written a number of books, including *Gods and Goods in Africa, Who Speaks for the Yanomami?* (1974), and *The Italians of Rochester: 1900–1940* (2000). He has written over 100 articles. Fieldwork and ethics are two of his major research interests. He has carried out fieldwork in Nigeria, the United States, England, and Venezuela. He has recently been awarded an National Endowment for the Humanities Summer Fellowship at the Virginia Foundation for the Humanities to be one of 15 people attending Joseph Miller's seminar on "Roots: The Atlantic Connection."

Susan Sperling is a writer and teacher in the San Francisco Bay Area. After surviving various Hot Wars in the Berkeley anthropology doctoral program, she worked as a post-doctoral researcher in medical anthropology at the University of California San Francisco, wrote about why sociobiology and other forms of neo-social Darwinism misrepresent Darwin, and pursued other iconoclastic heresies. She teaches anthropology in a working-class immigrant community near, but not at, Berkeley and is writing a biography of the late Ashley Montagu for Oxford University Press.

Dustin M. Wax is a PhD candidate in cultural anthropology at the New School for Social Research in New York City, where he is completing a dissertation on action anthropology and the development of an engaged anthropological practice. He currently teaches anthropology at the Community College of Southern Nevada and Women's Studies at University of Nevada, Las Vegas. His research interests include the history of anthropology, Cold War history, Native American cultures, anthropology and education, gender roles and sexual identity, and the representation of culture and identity in scientific literature, museums, and the mass media. He has also been active in attempts to use the Internet to improve and broaden research, education, and academics' involvement with their society, and is a founding contributor of the anthropology site Savage Minds (www.savageminds.org).

INDEX